THE SHIP
THAT NEVER WAS

THE SHIP THAT NEVER WAS

A Story of U.S. Armed Guard
and the Merchant Ships of World War II

B.J. Bryan

Copyright © 2011 by B.J. BRYAN.

Library of Congress Control Number:		2011903195
ISBN:	Hardcover	978-1-4568-7767-5
	Softcover	978-1-4568-7766-8
	Ebook	978-1-4568-7768-2

All rights reserved. No part of this book may be reproduced or transmitted in any form or by any means, electronic or mechanical, including photocopying, recording, or by any information storage and retrieval system, without permission in writing from the copyright owner.

This book was printed in the United States of America.

To order additional copies of this book, contact:
Xlibris Corporation
1-888-795-4274
www.Xlibris.com
Orders@Xlibris.com

Major-general James William McAndrew, Chief of Staff, A. E. F., May 5, 1918, to May 26, 1919.

IN MEMORY OF

Pvt. Bryan Turner, Jr.
1922-1945

Oris LeRoy "Roy" Bryan, Sr.
1935-2001 and

To all the men who served and came home
All the men who served and died

FOREWORD

During World War II a merchant ship was a lot like a sample of a civilized country at war. The function of a tanker, a freighter or a troop transport in wartime is different from its function in peacetime, but only to a degree.

The United States at war was devoting part of its national purpose to defeating the enemy; but people still lived in homes, did their jobs at work and sent their children to school—just as they did before the second world war began. Life on a freighter, a tanker or a troop transport was largely the same in World War II as it was in peacetime. The sea watches was the same; the discipline was the same, except for the blackout provisions at night; living conditions were the same; the air was the same; the water was the same, and the horizon was the same distance away.

The crew of an American merchant ship was composed mostly of civilians, mostly union men, who were doing a war job which nobody else could do so well. They were doing the job by the use of their peacetime skills and training. And yet every man on board knew that each minute at sea for a six-month voyage might have been his last one alive. Ships were torpedoed without warning. Ships collided without warning. Ships hit mines without warning.

In some ways a six-month trip in wartime, broken only by shore leaves, could be likened to enduring a six-month continuous air raid or being under fire in a slit trench for six straight months.

But there was a difference, too. In the case of the hypothetical air raid or ordeal in a trench you would know what the danger was with at least, one of your five senses: you could hear it, or see it, or smell it, or do all at once.

During the major part of the voyage at sea, there was sensual inducement by every sense to forget danger from the enemy; he was nowhere evident. But you could never get him out of your mind. And that constant awareness of hidden danger generated a mounting tension that did unusual things to all the members of the crew.

Add to this, the danger of collision with another ship, perhaps larger and with more armor, and faster moving. You can then better visualize the dangers that overtook the crew, gunners, and troops aboard the McAndrew, which is so aptly described by B.J. or Bon to close friends.

This book needed to be written and she has written it. It very well describes the disruption and the end to so many lives. You have to read this book.

Tom Bowerman
Anniston, Alabama

INTRODUCTION

A question the reader might ask is "How did a woman happen to become interested in this kind of history?

The way this book came about is and of itself, a story out of fiction. It goes thusly:

My brother-in-law was in the Army, a tank battalion unit, during World War II and kept journals whenever he could from the time his unit arrived in England until the war was over in Germany. He sent them to me several years ago and commissioned me to write a book. He was one of those men who did not talk about his war experiences.

As it happened, probably from self-defense, he then suffered a stroke along with some dementia. I thought it was because he knew I would be asking a lot of questions about things I felt needed explanation. Of course, I say this "tongue in cheek."

Ernest Humphries, my brother-in-law, passed on to his "greater glory" 2 February 2000, at 11:15 a.m. central standard time ("CST"). Two of the men who served with him came to his funeral; that greatly pleased my sister and her family. But I digress.

An entry in one of his journals noted that a Pvt. Bryan was shot and killed in France, near Angville-Ay-Sur, on 13 July 1944. I sent for his individual deceased personnel file ("IDPF") and received the wrong one. As I began reading the file the thought occurred to me: "What an interesting story this would make."

I wrote to several agencies and received correspondence stating they "had no information in their files" on the ship John W. McAndrew. Actually, it was the U.S.A.T. *James W. McAndrew* (see footnote 1, page 70) but I didn't discover this until much later. I wrote additional letters correcting the name and again, "they had no information." It was then that I said to my husband, "Hot Damn! Now I know there's a story here." The rest, as is said, is history.

A friend (ex-Navy) put a notice on the Internet in a military chat room for me, asking any survivors of the U.S.A.T. *James W. McAndrew* to contact me at my e-mail address.

About two days later, I had my first contact from an ex-Armed Guardsman ("AG"), Thomas Roy Bowerman, in Alabama; we quickly became e-mail buddies. I have reserved a special section of this book for him. Mr. Bowerman referred me to others who, in turn, referred me to more, and the list kept growing.

I e-mailed, corresponded with or received occasional telephone calls from ex-AGs. This also includes other Army personnel or relatives of the deceased young men who are located all over the continental United States. There are prior members of His Majesty's Royal Navy ("HMRN") still residing in the United Kingdom, and another individual in Wales, all of who have proven to have an interest and who have provided assistance in this undertaking, whether it is information or just encouragement and support.

Occasionally I received telephone calls from World War II servicemen, whom my husband always referred to them as my "senior sweeties." The name stuck. From that day forward, I continued to call them by that special name. They have proven to be my "senior sweeties"; that they are trusting of a complete stranger, providing photographs, stories, countless other kindnesses, helpfulness, and have a genuine feeling of excitement that their story is finally going to be told. Once I have their stories on my computer, each correspondent is sent his own history in order that it is verified; corrections, additions and comments can be made.

I wrote many letters and post cards to which I hoped would be surviving relatives of the men who drowned. Either they decided not to respond, were not close relatives, did not inform me, or for the better part of valor, did not wish to "become involved or renew old heartaches." Whatever their reasons, I decided to respect that decision.

The letters and e-mails that you will read are as I received them. An exception would be that in order to make the sentences more understandable, I have inserted words in brackets. Remember that some of these young men never graduated from high school and one was as young as 14, a farm boy, who joined to help out his family. This is not intended as an insult; I respect the fact that most of them were young farm boys and gave up their youth to fight a war. One must remember that they were just those—boys—with many others only slightly older.

So few people knew or have heard about the Armed Guard, including many of those enlisting unless the families were directly involved with the Navy. Even today, fewer people than ever know about or understand exactly what an Armed Guard was or what they did in World War II, much less what they accomplished. In many instances, people today have never even heard of the Armed Guard.

The best way to explain it is: A lot of allied merchant ships were sunk during the 1940-41 period. Congress could not or would not authorize the placement of guns aboard the cargo ships due to the 1939 Neutrality Act. It was not until 7 November 1940-41, when Section 2 of the Act was repealed that steps were taken to arm vessels and even then, five more merchant ships were sunk before Pearl Harbor was bombed on 7 December 1941.

But this story is not just about a ship and its crew, but also the young fresh replacement troops headed to Europe to relieve the tired, the wounded, the dying, and the deceased. Instead, their lives were cut short by dying in what was termed "a non-battle death," i.e., an accidental collision.

It is also a story about many ships, many men, many crossings across the sea to deliver war supplies to several nations that were considered friendly toward the United States and needed our help to fight and supply them with much needed materials.

While some might not be able to empathize with the suffering these young men must have undergone at the time of the collision or what they endured during their last moments. No matter what branch of the military they represented, we must and should claim them as the best we were and the best we had to give.

I am hoping that those men about whom I have been unable to locate information for whatever reason, that the relatives contact me with photographs, newspaper articles, and such, to carry on with their stories of lives cut short.

THE SHIP THAT NEVER WAS

**A Story of U.S. Armed Guard
and the Merchant Ships of World War II**

U.S. ARMED GUARD, U.S. ARMY AIR CORPS, U.S. NAVY, U.S. MERCHANT MARINE PERSONNEL ABOARD THE USAT J. W. McANDREW

MARCH 15, 1945
IN THE MEDITERRANEAN

COLLISION BETWEEN THE McANDREW AND THE BEARN WHILE IN CONVOY

Major John S. Hobb, Troop Transport Commander
George Kuipers, Naval Gunnery Officer

Sgt. Kazimir Adamowicz
Pvt. Gerald O. Beers
Pfc. Walter L. Blanchard
AG Robert Bowman
Pvt. Walter A. Buckles, Jr.
Cpl. Archie E. Buckowitz
Pfc. Louis J. Burgo
Pvt. Joseph M. Canalichio
Cpl. Douglas L. Casteel
Pfc. Lawrence T. Charboneau
Pvt. Robert M. Clark
T/3 Jacob E. Cook
Pfc. B. M. Cranford
Pfc. William I. Deacon
Pvt. Melvin E. Dingman
Pfc. Randolph C. Doty
Pvt. Danny S. Dunn
Pvt. Robert E. Ebbitt
Cpl. Jacob NMI Estey
Pvt. Howard D. Floyd
M/Sgt. Homer L. Freeman
Pfc. Nathan NMI Gurwitz
AG Orell S. Harris
Pvt. Leon M. Hennessey
Pvt. Eugene C. Holly
T/3 Joseph C. Hurtuk
AG Carlos A. Inman

Pfc. Clarence J. Beer
T/4 Walter P. Behr
T/5 Stanley P. Boudreaux, Jr.
AG Paul R. Brosius
Pvt. Charles F. Bucko
Pvt. Johnny D. Bullard
Pvt. Oscar M. Butler
Pfc. Richard E. Carroll
Pfc. Harold E. Caveney
Pvt. Peter J. Clark
Pvt. James E. Coleman
Sgt. James E. Cox
Cpl. Aubrey R. Dailey
AG Arthur Delledonne
Pfc. Geral R. Dopkin
AG George Dragovich, Sr.
Cpl. Edwin L. Dyrness
Pvt. Robert J. Egan
Pfc. Edgar Finsmith
Cpl. Harvey E. Freeman
AG John R. Gable
Pvt. William E. Hagerty
Pfc. Charles F. Haupt
Pvt. Alf W. Hirsch
Pvt. John F. Hunsucker, Sr.
Cpl. Lionel T. Hymel
Cpl. Waldo C. Jackman, Jr.

Cpl. Werner R. Kelm
AG George Kuipers
Pfc. Clarence E. Lemen
Pvt. George E. McFall
Pfc. Donald E. Nelson
Pvt. Clifford NMI Nowak
AG Leonard S. Patricio
Pvt. Harry A. Pierce, Jr.
AG William H. Rowley, Jr.
Sgt. John C. Schneider
Cpl. Dixie NMI Skipper
Pfc. Paul J. Staybrook
Pfc. Roy W. Thorpe
Pvt. Bryan Turner, Jr.
AG James A. Tyler
Pvt. Carl S. Wanamaker
Pfc. John NMI Wiechers
AG David H. Wilson
OS William A. Young, Sr.

Sgt. Harold R. Kerr
Pfc. Laurier N. Lavoie
Pfc. Walter A. Lewis
Cpl. James R. Mitchell
Pfc. Joseph J. Nohlechek
Pvt. Jesse L. Parker
Pvt. Russell A. Peace
Pfc. Arthur E. Rourke
Pfc. Leonard NMI Savitz
Pfc. Earl Sinnett, Jr.
Pvt. Howard F. Smith
Pfc. Harold E. Tatro
Pfc. Joseph C. Tuohey
Pvt. Thomas B. Twilley
Pfc. Robert C. VanRavenswaay
Pvt. Edward W. Weckman
AG John Wilde
Pfc. Herman J. Wilhelm

PERSONNEL LOST ON THE FRENCH AIRCRAFT CARRIER BEARN

Q.M. 1C1 Jean Lorrain, Machinist
MOT Albert Egault, Crew
S/Spte Georges Derrien
S/Spte Didace Rivas

Photo Courtesy of Walter Adamowicz

SGT. KAZIMIR "CHARLIE" ADAMOWICZ
BORN: 11 April 1923, Connecticut
Enlisted: 10 December 1941
Died: 13 March 1945

According to his IDPF (Individual Deceased Personnel File)

Cause of Death: Result of sinking of U.S. Army Transport

Sgt. Adamowicz was 5 feet 8-1/4 inches tall, weighed 163 pounds, had hazel eyes, brown hair. Fort George G. Meade, Maryland was where he had been assigned to Headquarters Battalion, Anti-Aircraft Corps Training Center ("AAATC"), leaving there by ship for Europe aboard the "Mac." The military bases where he had been stationed are listed as Camp Edwards, Massachusetts where he took basic training, Fort Eustis, Virginia, and from there he was sent to Camp Pendleton, Virginia, and Camp Smith, the last one not having the state listed for its location.

The address of his family is given in the IDPF; that was where I wrote to see if any surviving relatives could be located.

Shortly thereafter, I received a letter from the wife of the 8*th* child, Henry, a brother of the above. Mrs. Sandra Adamowicz states that her husband served in the Navy during the Korean Conflict.

Later, on 14 July, I received a letter from another brother of Charlie. She relates the following history:

"Ref. Charlie Adamowicz.

It sounds like you're working very hard and diligently on the project [writing the book]. I'll try to answer all the questions to the best of our recollection.

Enclosed is a letter we received from his Sgt. Bolinsky. It does give a very descriptive story of the night of March 13, 1945. He [Adamowicz] was inducted on December 10, 1941. I am writing for his brother, Walter, who is not sure if he had basic training in Massachusetts or New Jersey. Walter recalls he was with the anti-aircraft (AAC). Charlie was a perfectionist and in control of every thing he did, even in his younger years. The Army made him Sgt. in three months after entering the service. He wanted to go overseas but they needed him to train here in the States. After leaving the country no one knew where he was going in Europe.

I'm not sure of just how much information you would like about Kazimir "Charles" Adamowicz. There were eight boys and three girls in the family, listed as follows:

Kazimir Adamowicz, Cromwell, CT., World War II—killed in the service
Stanley Adamowicz, Cromwell, CT., World War II—deceased
Edward Adamowicz, Cromwell, CT., World War II—deceased
Joseph Adamowicz, Cromwell, CT., World War II—deceased
Walter Adamowicz, Cromwell, Connecticut, World War II
Lucy A. Johnson, Ohio, World War II—nurse
Francis Adamowicz, Winterhaven, Florida, Korean Conflict (Army)
Henry Adamowicz, Auburndale, Florida, Korean Conflict (Navy)
Raymond Adamowicz, Middletown, CT., Korean Conflict (Army)
Genevieve Adamowicz, Cromwell, CT., deceased
Florence A. deMauro, Berlin, CT.
The first six of the family served in the military at the same time, including Lucy.

Sincerely yours,
Lori Adamowicz, wife of Walter"

"It was I that had the picture reprinted for you but another sister-in-law of Henry, (Sandra) mailed it out for me from Auburndale, Florida.

Would appreciate if you do need any more information, Walter and I will be glad to help you at our address in Cromwell.

We certainly would like to purchase the book someday.

Yes! You do have our permission and authorization to put into your book any of this information." (Signed and dated).

Letter attached:

"Podldorf, Germany
May 20, 1945

Hello Ruth & Wally,

In this letter I'll try to give you the story on Adamowicz. His family received word that he was missing at sea & I can't say he was killed because I didn't see his body. On March 13 at 3:40 a.m. we were about half way across the Atlantic when the accident took place. Along side of the boat we were in, there was a French aircraft carrier that was one of the many boats in the convoy. The electrical power went kaput and it was very foggy and dark that night. The carrier turned left and hit our boat head-on making a hole in our boat about the size of a small house. Adamowicz & I were in Lower One, which is the first hole at the front end of the ship. The roughest sea of the entire voyage was on that day and the day before. The waves rushing in through the hole had terrific force and knocked the beams and bunks loose. We were all in bed at that time but we moved fast and very few men got panicky. The iron stairway was washed away so we had to use the small cargo ladder along side the stairway. Adamowicz was hit in the head and too weak to reach from the ladder to the broken stairs at the opening of the hole. He dropped to the bottom. I climbed out safely uninjured but I was completely soaked and cold. I came out through my own stupidity and loss of time. Water was rushing in and I, like a dope, stopped to put my shoes on. I got one on and the other one washed away but another one came floating by so I put that one on. While I was putting my shoes on, the steel stairway was knocked out. If I didn't stop to put my shoes on I would have to go under the stairway to get to the bottom of the stairway & of course I would be crushed under them or I'd be on top of them when they came down. That was the first time I ever came so close to death. I didn't have time to say any prayers & all my faults of the past didn't come before me. I just said so long to Jo & the family & then I decided that there might be a chance to get out so I made a beeline for the exit. I don't think I could tell you how many men were killed but I had a fifty percent (50%) chance of coming out alive, possibly injured. After things calmed down we traveled at a very slow rate of speed & reached the Azores in 5 days. We stayed at the Azores for a week living on the boat. It was a neutral port so we could not stay on land. Nearly everybody got a two-hour pass to see the town. An English boat picked us up & took us to England.

Sgt. Ed. Bolinsky
Co. G 38 7th Inf. APO 445
C/o P.M. New York, NY"

Another letter was received from Lori Adamson:

"Sorry it took so long to reply to your interesting letter but part of it was vacation time.

To answer some of your questions about Charles Adamowicz—the family recalls that Charlie did train in Camp Edwards, Massachusetts. And yes, his parents did receive a flag and some compensation.

Your letters always sound so interesting and working diligently for such a good cause. May God bless you!

Sincerely,"

Photo Courtesy of Walter Adamowicz

I have continued to receive an occasional note and/or Christmas card from Florence (Charlie's sister) and Harold DeMauro.

I also wrote letters to different historical societies, newspapers, etc. and although letters were received from them, the excitement of receiving correspondence from the deceased soldier's family more than compensated for lack of information from the historical societies, newspapers, etc.

PFC. CLARENCE J. BEER
BORN: 25 March 1919, Wisconsin
Drafted: 8 August 1942
Died: 13 March 1945

Pfc. Beer was 5'9-1/2", weighed 160 pounds, brown hair and eyes. From October 1942 through February 1945 he was stationed at Carlsbad, New Mexico in Company B, Infantry, 1*st* Platoon. On 23 February 1945 he was transferred to Fort George G. Meade, Maryland where he had been assigned to Company B, 1*st* Replacement Regiment, Detachment 18, 853*rd* Ordinance Service Company and then boarded the "Mac" for overseas duty. His IDPF gave his last known address in Stillwater, Minnesota.

Photo Courtesy of Florence and Harold Beer.
Clarence Beer

My first contact was with the Chamber of Commerce, Stillwater, giving me the name and address of the local newspaper. Ms. Lorraine Weber, Volunteer at the Chamber of Commerce also included the names and telephone numbers of all the Beers listed within the surrounding area.

My second contact was with the brother of Clarence, Harold Beer. The news article stated that I was looking for relatives and it was noted their hometown is just across the river from Minnesota in Houlton, Wisconsin. When Harold's mother passed away all the information regarding Clarence's death was thrown away although he thought a relative in Washington might have some information. I wrote Terry and Mr. Beer called her to no avail.

The letters follow:

"In regard to your letter sent to the Stillwater Chamber of Commerce, Clarence Beer was my brother. Our family lived in Houlton, Wisconsin, a small town across the river from Stillwater. At that time we received our mail and our address was Stillwater. St. Joseph is our township and our county is St. Croix, Wisconsin.

We only have two newspapers and two historical societies that might have records.

My mother and older sister lived together and now both are gone. A niece took care of them. We don't know of any pictures, death notice and etc., was left when she cleaned things out.

There were eight children in the family; seven out of the eight were in the Service.

Hope this answers some of your questions."

Article from the Stillwater Gazette dated March 27, 1945:

"The Houlton soldier reported missing in the Mediterranean is Pfc. Clarence J. Beer, son of Mr. and Mrs. Ernest Beer of that village. He is reported missing since March 13. He has been in the service three years and has a brother, Harold, in the Army, and a sister Bernice, in the WAVES. Two 17-year-old twin brothers are expecting to be called to the colors any day, both having passed their physicals. Another brother, Herbert, recently was honorably discharged from the Merchant Marine."

"Bonnie,

Found this picture in a family tree Aunt Erma put together for her family on Christmas. Cannot ask where the picture same from—she died of cancer.

I called Terry and left a message on her phone—have not heard from her at all. I know there was a wedding in the family in June, when they came to the twin cities. I thought she might call and tell me she had the pictures.

But hope this picture is OK. Sorry it took me so long before writing.

God bless you and all this work.

Florence and Harold"

PVT. GERALD O. BEERS
Rescued—See TESTIMONIES

T/4 WALTER P. BEHR
BORN: 27 February 1918, Pennsylvania
Enlisted: 17 February 1941
Died: 13 March 1945

Memorialized at the North-African
Cemetery & Memorial, Carthage, Tunisia

Although I wrote to all the Behrs listed in and around Pittsburgh, Pennsylvania, none were returned and no response received. According to his IDPF, Technician/4 (T/4) received the Good Conduct Medal, World War II Victory Medal, and the Honorable Lapel Button.

He was 5'9-1/2", weighed 174 pounds, brown eyes and hair. He began basic training at Ft. George G. Meade, Maryland from February 1941 until he was transferred to Fort Myer, Virginia in February 1943. He then was sent to Camp Stewart, Georgia in February 1944, then to Camp Gruber, Oklahoma in December 1944. At some point in late 1944 or early 1945, he was transferred back to Fort George G. Meade, Maryland when he was assigned to Company B Infantry, Group 155(A), boarding the "Mac" for Europe.

I do find in his IDPF that his father received a flag of the United States furnished by the Veteran's Administration.

PFC WALTER L. BLANCHARD
BORN: 27 February 1918, Pennsylvania
Drafted: 1 January 1943
Died: 13 March 1945

What little information I have been able to locate on Pfc. Blanchard is that he was a member of Company B, 1st Platoon, Replacement Infantry out of Fort George G. Meade, Maryland where he boarded the "Mac" for overseas duty and his final resting place.

T/5 STANLEY P. BOUDREAUX, JR.
Enlisted: 29 May 1942
Died: 13 March 1945

This is all of the information I have received from his IDPF. It should be mentioned here that there was a fire at the National Archives in 1973 and a lot of records were destroyed. Even my own DD214 has a burned border all around it although it is still readable.

I did write a letter to Senator Diane Feinstein to see if she could assist; however, one of her assistants called me without much hope of her doing so.

PVT. WALTER A. BUCKLES, JR.
BORN: Not listed, Tennessee
Drafted: 21 June 1944
Died: 13 March 1945

Memorial at the U.S. East Coast Memorial,
Battery Park, New York City, New York

Pvt. Buckles was awarded the Good Conduct Medal, World War II Victory Medal, Honorable Service Lapel Button, and Purple Heart. His last known address while Stateside was on Maryland Avenue, Bristol, Tennessee.

I wrote several letters to the Buckles in Bristol, Tennessee. None were returned and none were answered.

PVT. CHARLES F. BUCKO
Drafted: 3 June 1944
Died: 13 March 1945

This is all of the information I have been able to locate on Pvt. Bucko.

CPL. ARCHIE E. BUCKOWITZ
BORN: 29 April 1913, New York
Enlisted: 12 June 1942
Died: 13 March 1945

Memorialized at the Brittany American
Cemetery and Memorial at
St. James, France

I wrote to the Brooklyn Historical Society and located an address for a Mr. F. Buckowitz in Brooklyn. Cpl. Buckowitz's last known address in 1942 was on 16th Street, Brooklyn; however, both letters were returned. The first stated as "not deliverable" and the second (to Mr. Buckowitz) "forwarding order expired."

PVT. JOHNNY D. BULLARD
BORN: 19 November 1922, Georgia
Enlisted: 19 January 1943
Died: 13 March 1945

Memorialized at the Brittany American
Cemetery and Memorial,
St. James, France

Columbus Ledger, 29 March 1945, pg. 15:

"MISSING IN ACTION

Pfc. (notice difference in rank between IDPF and the newspaper) Johnny D. Bullard (infantry) has been reported missing in action in the Mediterranean area since March 13, in a telegram received from the War Department by his parents, Mr. and Mrs. J. W. Bullard, this week.

Pvt. Bullard was employed at Fort Benning and later by the Eagle Phenix Manufacturing Company before entering the service in 1943. He went overseas early in February of this year.

The private has a brother, Pfc. Willie Lee Bullard, serving with the Second Army Tank Battalion, somewhere in Italy. He went overseas in 1941."

In correspondence with the Simon Schwob Memorial Library connected to Columbia State University, the widow of Willie Lee, Lucille is still alive and sent me her address. The widow did not respond to my correspondence, as have none of the other Bullards.

PFC. LOUIS J. BURGO
BORN: No date given, no place of birth
Drafted: 8 November 1943
Died: 13 March 1945

I have been unable to locate any additional information.

PVT. OSCAR M. BUTLER
Located

It was initially thought that Pvt. Butler had washed out to sea and drowned but was later found at the third roll call.

PVT. JOSEPH M. CANALICHIO
BORN: No date given, no place of birth
Drafted: 6 January 1944
Died: 13 March 1945

I have been unable to locate any additional information.

PFC. RICHARD E. CARROLL
BORN: No date given, no place of birth
No date given for draft or enlistment
Died: 13 March 1945

I have been unable to locate any additional information.

CPL. DOUGLAS L. CASTEEL
BORN: 5 October 1920, Alabama
Enlisted: 22 August 1942
Died: 13 March 1945

Memorialized at Brittany American
Cemetery & Memorial
St. James, France

I have received enough information to determine that Cpl. Casteel was 5'9-3/4", weighed 143 pounds, had gray eyes, brown hair, and wore a 9E shoe. He had been stationed, presumably for basic training with the HQ (Headquarters) Reconnaissance Company at Camp McClellan, Alabama on 22 August 1942. He then transferred to the Company Reconnaissance Center at Fort McPherson, Georgia on 12 September 1943. From there he transferred to HQ AAF in Gulfport, Mississippi December 1944. At the time of his death, Cpl. Casteel had been assigned to Company A, 1st Platoon, HQ Company aboard the "Mac." He left a young widow, Thelma Mae as well as a young daughter, Shirley Ann. His mother, Ethel was still living at that time.

He received the following medals: European-African Middle Eastern Campaign Medal, Good Conduct Medal, and the World War II Victory Medal. I found the form letter where Mrs. Casteel could request a flag, but do not find the form requesting such a flag was sent to her by the Veteran's Administration.

PFC. HAROLD E. CAVENEY
BORN: No date given, no place of birth
Drafted: 27 December 1943
Died: 13 March 1945

I have been unable to locate any additional information.

PFC. LAWRENCE T. CHARBONEAU
BORN: No date given, no place of birth
Drafted: 19 March 1943
Died: 13 March 1945

I have been unable to locate any additional information.

PVT. PETER J. CLARK
BORN: No date given, New York
Enlisted: 22 January 1943
Died: 13 March 1945

An IDPF Form state Pvt. Clark was buried at sea, as were basically all those lost at sea. Only one actual burial at sea was accomplished as noted later.

Pvt. Clark was awarded the Gold Star Lapel Button. I have been unable to locate any additional information.

PVT. ROBERT M. CLARK
BORN: 15 July 1923, Michigan
Drafted: 22 January 1943
Died: 13 March 1945

Memorialized at the Brittany American
Cemetery and Memorial
St. James, France

Pvt. Clark's last known address was on East Euclid, Detroit. I wrote to the Detroit Public Library and was advised by letter that there had been a severe thunderstorm, water seeped into the basement level storage areas and much material destroyed. They are trying to reclaim everything but as of late, they are still in the process of trying.

Pvt. Clark received the Purple Heart.

PVT. JAMES E. COLEMAN
BORN: No date given, no place of birth
Died: 13 March 1945

The form received from the National Archives state "We regret that our sources do not contain the information on next of kin." Therefore, without any clue as to where to begin my research, there is no additional information available.

T/3 JACOB E. COOK
Rescued—See Testimonies

SGT. JAMES E. COX
BORN: No date given, no place of birth
Drafted: 3 February 1943
Died: 13 March 1945

I have been unable to locate any further information.

PFC. B. M. CRANFORD
BORN: 16 January 1921, Mississippi
Drafted: 29 August 1942
Died: 13 March 1945

I first corresponded to all Cranfords listed in a small community in Mississippi. All were returned. I then wrote to the post office listing the names and addresses of the Cranfords still purportedly living there. The post card was returned to me with the present appropriate addresses of each person that was given as the routes now had street names.

Pfc. Cranford was 5'8", weighed 133 pounds, had blue eyes, blonde hair, and wore 9-1/2C shoes. He was an unassigned infantryman. His IDPF does not list where he received basic training and for that matter, no other base is mentioned. It can only be presumed that his last base would have been Fort George G. Meade, Maryland when he boarded the "Mac" for overseas duty.

A letter I received from one of the Cranfords is as follows:

"This letter is in response to your letter dated August 25, 2000. At the request of my brother, Frank Cranford, I am sharing the following information with you.

B. M. Cranford, known as "B" to his family and friends, was born in Clarke County, Mississippi on January 16, 1921. He grew up on a farm and attended country schools. At the age of 18 he joined the

Civilian Conservation Corps ("CCC"). Upon completion of one year with the CCC, he then worked as a sheet metal specialist in shipbuilding before he was drafted into the Army Air Corps. He was trained as a medic and later transferred into the infantry. At the time of B's death, his destination overseas was unknown to his family.

B's personality was very quiet and easy going, never in trouble or caused trouble. He well understood the hard times of the depression of the 1930s.

I give you permission to use this letter and photograph in your book. Please let me know how I can obtain a copy.

Sincerely"

PFC B. M. CRANFORD

Photo courtesy of Frank Cranford

CPL. AUBREY R. DAILEY
Located

Cpl. Dailey had been presumed to have washed overboard, but was later located at the time of the third roll call. His date of service was from 13 January 1943 to 12 February 1946. He received an honorable discharge with the rank of Technician Fifth Grade at Camp Beale, California where he was with the 387th Infantry. His decorations and awards included the American Campaign Medal, Asiatic Pacific Campaign Medal, European African Middle Eastern Campaign Medal, World War II Medal, the Good Conduct Medal, and the Honorable Service Lapel Button.

PFC. WILLIAM I. DEACON
BORN: 19 April 1921, New York
Drafted: 21 January 1943
Died: 13 March 1945

Memorialized Brittany American Cemetery and Memorial
St. James, France

Pfc. Deacon's last known address was on Milburn Avenue, Baldwin, New York. He earned the Purple Heart and was with the United States Infantry.

I wrote first to the New York Genealogical and Biographical Society. I was forwarded the address of the New York Public Library and never received a response.

PVT. MELVIN E. DINGMAN
BORN: 10 July 1923, Michigan
Drafted: 1 May 1944
Died: 13 March 1945

Memorialized Brittany American Cemetery and Memorial
St. James, France

Pvt. Dingman's last known address was on Vino, St. Clair, Michigan. He earned the Purple Heart and was a member of the Infantry.

I wrote to the area library as well as the Dingman addresses in the surrounding communities. One was returned as "undeliverable" whereas there were no responses from the others.

PFC. GERALD R. DOPKIN
BORN: No date given, New Jersey
Drafted: 5 March 1943
Died: 13 March 1945

Memorialized at Brittany American Cemetery and Memorial
St. James, France

Pfc. Dopkin was assigned to the Infantry, location not available. As of March 1945, his last known residence was listed as New Jersey. On the form received from National Archives, the notation is given: "No record located. It may have been destroyed in a fire on July 12, 1973."

PFC. RANDOLPH C. DOTY
Died: 13 March 1945

I was unable to obtain any information, not even a form from the National Archives.

PVT. DANNY S. DUNN
BORN: No date given, no place of birth
Drafted: 24 June 1943
Died: 13 March 1945

I received the National Archives form stating, "the file may have been lent to the Department of Veteran Affairs (VA)."

CPL. EDWIN L. DYRNESS
BORN: No date given, no place of birth
Drafted: 10 March 1943
Died: 13 March 1945

I received the National Archives form stating "The military record needed to answer this inquiry is not in our files. If the record were here on July 12, 1973, it would have been in the area that suffered the most damage on that date and may have been destroyed."

PVT. ROBERT E. EBBITT
BORN: No date given, no place of birth
Drafted: 23 May 1944
Died: 13 March 1945

The same information as given above for Cpl. Dyrness is the same information for Pvt. Ebbitt.

PVT. ROBERT J. EGAN
BORN: No date given, no birthplace given.
Drafted: 12 May 1944
Died: 13 March 1945

Again, the same information as given above for Pvt. Ebbitt is the same for Pvt. Egan.

PFC. JACOB ESTEY
BORN: No date given, no birthplace
Drafted: 9 April 1943
Died: 13 March 1945

The same information as given above for Pvt. Egan is the same for Pfc. Estey.

PFC. EDGAR FINSMITH
Rescued—See Testimonies

PVT. HOWARD D. FLOYD
BORN: No date given, no birthplace
Drafted: 27 June 1944
Died: 13 March 1945

Again, the same information as given above for Pfc. Estey is the same for Pvt. Floyd.

CPL. HARVEY E. FREEMAN
BORN: 19 January 1911, Alabama
Enlisted: 19 October 1942
Died: 13 March 1945

Cpl. Freeman was 5'10" tall, weighed 146 pounds, had blonde hair and blue eyes. He, as far as I can tell, was one of the oldest soldiers aboard the "Mac." Cpl. Freeman was with Company B, 155th Infantry Regiment, 31st Infantry Division and assigned to the "Mac" with no other bases listed with the notation, "Not of Record."

Cpl. Freeman was awarded the Good Conduct Medal, Purple Heart, World War II Victory Medal, Combat Infantryman Badge, Bronze Star, and the EAME Campaign Medal. His widow, who was residing in West Virginia at the time, ordered the American Flag; I have been unable to locate her.

I sent several letters and received back this response to one:

"I know nothing about Harvey E. Freeman and have never heard the name mentioned. Sorry I can't be of help to you. Empire is just a "wide place in the road" as the old saying goes—post office and that's about it. I live in Dilworth on Empire route (rural mail carrier comes and delivers mail). Fine place to live, I must say. Empire is located about 40 miles north of Birmingham. Highway 78 is close to my house. Thanks."

Other correspondence was mailed, none returned and no additional responses were received.

In November 2004 I received two additional responses and have forwarded letters requesting additional information. The first letter read as follows:

"Last Monday evening of the 4th at the Wyoming County General Society meeting, your query re: Cpl. Harvey Freeman came to my attention. While his was not, the name of his widow was familiar. It took a day to evoke an image of a middle-aged lady encountered

40 years ago. Instead of knowing her, I knew people that did. It has taken three days to contact one of them and learn that Ruby Cook Freeman died several years ago. The recommended source of further information was a clerk at the local Pineville Furniture Store, name not recalled, but she was thought to be a close relative of the late Mrs. Freeman. If you desire further inquiries please advise by email (which I did). As of late November I have yet to receive a response to said email.

The second letter says: "In regards to your letter in the Independent Herald of 11/03/04 about Harvey Freeman. He was married to my aunt, Ruby Cook. She died a few years ago. I remember Harvey as being a very nice person—I was 11 years old when he got killed. I don't know any information about it. I have an uncle living in Arizona—he might know more than I do. I have an Aunt Ernestine Duty living in Rockview, West Virginia 24880." She included the name and address of her uncle. I have written to both people as of the date as given above, 11/03/04, I have not had a response.

PVT. HOMER L. FREEMAN
BORN: No date given, no birthplace given.
Died: 13 March 1945

I have been unable to obtain additional information.

PFC. NATHAN GURWITZ
BORN: No date given, no birthplace given.
Died: 13 March 1945

I sent two separate requests for information from the National Archives. They did not respond to either.

PVT. WILLIAM F. HAGERTY
BORN: No date given, no birthplace given.
Died: 13 March 1944

I did not receive any information from the National Archives, as they did not respond.

PFC. CHARLES F. HAUPT
BORN: 15 June 1923, Long Island
Enlisted: 28 November 1942
Died: 13 March 1945

Pfc. Haupt's last known address was on 114 Road, Queens, Long Island, although he entered the service on Lexington Avenue, New York City. He was awarded the Purple Heart. Prior to boarding the "Mac", he was with the Infantry, Company B, 1st Platoon that leaves me to believe he left from Fort George G. Meade, Maryland, to board the "Mac".

His information form states he was lost at sea "northwest of the Azores Islands due to a ship collision." It also states that he had four years of high school with eight years of elementary education. Information also included was that he "left U.S. for Foreign Service on March 7, 1945, as a casual on shipment No. GP155(a) aboard the U.S. Army Transport J. W. McAndrew."

I wrote to several residents in the surrounding communities. None were returned nor any responses received.

PVT. LEON M. HENNESSEY
BORN: No date given, no birthplace given.
Died: 13 March 1945

No response was ever received from National Archives regarding Pvt. Hennessey.

PVT. AFT W. HIRSCH
BORN: No date given, no birthplace given.
Died: 13 March 1945

No response was ever received from National Archives regarding Pvt. Hirsch.

TEC/3 JOSEPH C. HURTUK
BORN: No date given, no birthplace given.
Died: 13 March 1945

No response was ever received from National Archives regarding Tec/3 Hurtuk.

CPL. LIONEL T. HYMEL
BORN: 12 April 1920, Louisiana
Enlisted: 11 October 1941
Died: 13 March 1945

Cpl. Hymel's last known address was LaPlace, Louisiana. I located several residents by the last name of Hymel and wrote to each of them. The letters were not returned nor did I receive any responses. The Louisiana Genealogical and Historical Society was also contacted by mail but was returned as "not known."

MEMORIAL HEADSTONE LOCATED IN SCOTLAND, INDIANA OF CARLOS A. INMAN, THE ONLY ARMED GUARDSMAN KILLED AT TIME OF COLLISION BETWEEN THE U.S.A.T. J. W. McANDREW AND THE FRENCH AIRCRAFT CARRIER, BEARN.

U.S. NAVY ARMED GUARD

SEAMAN 1ST CLASS CARLOS A. INMAN
BORN: 23 March 1925, Indiana
Died: 13 March 1945

Memorialized by headstone in cemetery at Scotland, Indiana

Seaman 1/C Inman was the only Armed Guard killed at the time of the collision. He was in his gun turret at the Bearn's and the "Mac's" points of impact ("POI"). He fell to his death, dying instantly.

"Burial at sea of Carlos Inman"
photo courtesy of Orell Harris

"Burial at sea of Carlos Inman"
photo courtesy of Orell Harris

"Burial at sea of Carlos Inman" photo courtesy of Orell Harris

After contacting several residents in Indiana, the following letter was received:

"Re: Carlos A. Inman, DOB 3-3-25 (note difference in date of birth) at Burns City, Indiana. I have this information on Carlos A. Inman that might help you.

He was the son of Cleveland Inman and lived in Bloomfield, Indiana and is buried in the Scotland Cemetery.

My nephew, Frank Trester, who is the son of my sister, Helen Inman Trester, has been studying the Inman family and can tell you exactly what you need to know about Carlos's father. She provided it, including his e-mail address and telephone number.

Later I received the following letter from Mr. Trester:

U.S. NAVAL ARMED GUARD CENTER
First Avenue and Fifty-Second Street
Brooklyn, N. Y.

CITATION

In accordance with General Order No. 194

<u>Inman, Charles A.   S1c</u>
  (Name)   (Service No.) (Rate)

is authorized to wear the following campaign ribbon(s) by virtue of having served as a member of an Armed Guard gun crew in each of the designated areas for a period of at least thirty (30) days:

[X] American Area

[X] European-African Middle Eastern Area

[-] Asiatic-Pacific Area

No stars or numerals are authorized unless an endorsement to this citation is made by the Commanding Officer, U. S. Naval Armed Guard Center, Brooklyn, N. Y.

WM. J. COAKLEY,
Commanding

John T. Kennedy
Ensign, D-V(S)

OFFICER IN CHARGE,
Armed Guard Crew

Date 8 May, 1944

Burial at sea of Carlos Inman" photo courtesy of Orell Harris

"I am the family historian if you can call it that. My mother and Thelma were sisters. My mother has passed away. I stumbled onto a history of the Inman family one night while searching the Internet. The history of the Inmans just stopped at my grandfather, Dawson Inman, who was Thelma and my mother's father.

A couple of weeks ago I went to the cemetery in the little town of Scotland, Indiana where my grandparents are buried and was looking for information on the tombstones of all the Inmans buried there. I found the grave of Cleveland Inman who was Carlos's father. Cleve, his wife, and daughter are all buried there. On the plot was a memorial marker for Carlos stating that he had been killed in World War II and was buried at sea. That is how I found out about him.

I was four years old in 1945 so I do not remember him (Carlos) at all. I do remember his father very well. He ran a little repair/blacksmith shop in a building behind his house in Bloomfield, Indiana. He repaired lawn mowers, did welding, etc. I was in the shop many times with my grandfather and he always referred to Cleve as Cousin Cleve. I assume that is our correct relationship but I have not had time to prove that as yet.

INFORMATION RELEASABLE UNDER THE FREEDOM OF INFORMATION ACT

WE ARE PROVIDING THE RELEASABLE MILITARY SERVICE INFORMATION BELOW, BASED ON RESTRICTIONS IMPOSED BY THE MILITARY SERVICES CONSISTENT WITH DEPARTMENT OF DEFENSE REGULATIONS AND THE PROVISIONS OF THE FREEDOM OF INFORMATION ACT AND THE PRIVACY ACT OF 1974. ANY ITEM MARKED "NA" DENOTES THAT THE INFORMATION IS NOT AVAILABLE IN THE RECORDS HELD BY THIS CENTER. RELEASABLE INFORMATION WILL BE TRANSCRIBED, PHOTOCOPIED, OR A COMBINATION OF BOTH, IN ORDER TO COMPLY WITH YOUR REQUEST.

Name: INMAN, CARLOS A
Serial/Service Number(s): _____
Date of birth: 3-23-25
Dates of service: 7-14-43 TO 3-13-45
City/state of residence, date of address: BLOOMFIELD, IN 3-13-45
Dependents: NA
Duty status: KIA
Marital Status: SINGLE
Rank/grade: S1/C
Salary: _____
Assignments & geographical locations: SEE ATTACHED
Education level: Military: NA
Education level: Civilian: 9TH
Decorations & awards: SEE ATTACHED

Transcript of court martial/trial: NA
Photograph: NA
Place of: Entry: EVANSVILLE
Place of: Separation: NA

IF THE PERSON NAMED ABOVE IS DECEASED, THE FOLLOWING ITEMS ALSO MAY BE RELEASED.
Place of birth: BURNS CITY, IN
Last known street address: _____
Date and location of death: _____
Place of burial: AT SEA

☐ The record needed to answer your inquiry is not in our files. If the record were here on July 12, 1973, it would have been in the area which suffered the most damage in the fire and may have been destroyed. The information listed above was obtained from alternate record sources.

All of these Inman relatives lived in and around the Scotland/Bloomfield area. At one time there was a high school in Scotland but that has been gone since the early 1950s. If Carlos attended Bloomfield High School, they might be able to give you some information on his educational background, athletics, etc.

From the research that I have done I have not found any living relatives who might have any insight as to his life before the war. As I continue my research I will be happy to keep you informed if I uncover anything. Any information that you could give me on the Inman family would be appreciated. You might want to check the web site.

That site I located and am updating. If I can be of any other assistance, please feel free to contact me and I will gladly lend any assistance that I can. In the meantime, I will also check with my two living aunts to see if they can shed any light on Carlos."

Mr. Trester and I have continued to send e-mails back and forth over the years. To my surprise, he was a pilot during the Cold War and has asked me to write a book about him and his crew. He's in the process of gathering the information in order that this commission is accomplished. I have also been invited to one of their reunions but was unable to attend. They are held approximately every two years, have located and purchased their aircraft that the crew has repainted it in the Navy colors, rudders have been recovered and a new sound system installed to be used during tours. The crew works on it during different times with the hopes of turning it into a museum after renovation. I hope to make the next reunion.

SUMMARY OF SERVICE

Vessel or Station	From—	To—	Rate
NSNRS, Evansville, Ind.	7/14/43	7/21/43	AS
USNTS, Great Lakes, Ill.	7/22/43	10/7/43	S2c
AGS, Gulfport, Miss.	10/8/43	11/4/43	S2c
AGC, New Orleans, La.	11/7/43	7/11/44	S1c
AGC, Brooklyn, New York	7/10/44	3/13/45	S1c

Final average in all marks upon discharge 3.68

R. C. MOUREAU, Commander USN

State Summary of War Casualties

[INDIANA]

U. S. NAVY

1946

INDIANA — DEAD

HOFFMEIER, Victor William, Motor Machinist's Mate 1c, USNR. Parents, Mr. and Mrs. Jacob Hoffmeier, Guilford.
HOFMANN, James Lohrmann, Aviation Ordnanceman 2c, USNR. Parents, Mr. and Mrs. John Peter Hofmann, 1349 Kappes St., Indianapolis.
HOLLAND, Linus Noal, Pfc., USMC. Mother, Mrs. Hester V. Fancher, Rt. 1, Rising Sun.
HOLLINGSWORTH, John William, Fireman 1c, USN. Parents, Mr. and Mrs. Mark Edward Hollingsworth, 5110 W. Washington St., Indianapolis.
HOLTZLIDER, William M., Pfc., USMCR. Parents, Mr. and Mrs. Clyde Holtzlider, 511 W. Washington St., Greensburg.
HOLZBAUR, Robert Walter, Ship's Cook 3c, USNR. Wife, Mrs. Lois B. Holzbaur, Flint Lake Rd., Valparaiso.
HOMCO, Joseph Walter, Seaman 1c, USNR. Parents, Mr. and Mrs. Michael Andrew Homco, 4813 Homerlee Ave., East Chicago.
HOOD, Charles Angus, Seaman 1c, USN. Mother, Mrs. Pearl Wise, 927 Boyer St., Richwood.
HOPE, Garrett G., Jr., Sgt., USMCR. Mother, Mrs. Mollie Hope, 306 Jackson St., Renselaer.
HOPPER, Albert R., Pfc., USMCR. Parents, Mr. and Mrs. Jodie Hopper, Lynnville.
HOPPER, Prentice William, Seaman 1c, USNR. Mother, Mrs. Audie Belle Hopper, Rt. 1, Winslow.
HOPPER, Roy Lee, Aviation Machinist's Mate 1c, USNR. Wife, Mrs. Dora Jane Hopper, 112 Monroe St., Decatur.
HORNE, Robert David, Lieutenant (jg), USNR. Mother, Mrs. Gladys Roberts Salt, 621 E. State Blvd., Ft. Wayne.
HORNE, Robert Henry, Ship's Cook 3c, USNR. Mother, Mrs. Lula M. Campbell, 1047 Baldwin Ave., Anderson.
HOSTETLER, Joseph O., Pfc., USMC. Mother, Mrs. Wilma Hostetler, 1130 Willowdale Ave., Elkhart.
HOUCHIN, Simon V., Pfc., USMCR. Mother, Mrs. Pearl Houchin, Patoka.
HOUGH, Paul Glenn, Fireman 1c, USNR. Parents, Mr. and Mrs. William A. Hough, Portland.
HOUSEMAN, Harry L., Pfc., USMCR. Wife, Mrs. Harry L. Houseman, Rt. 6, Box 273, Marion.
HOVER, Edgar James, Seaman 1c, USNR. Son, Master Michael James Hover, c/o Mrs. Agnes Hover, 615 W. Center St., Warsaw.
HOWELL, Leroy, Coxswain, USN. Father, Mr. Frederick M. Howell, 107 S. F St., Gas City.
HOWELL, Marion Patrick, Sgt., USMCR. Father, Mr. Homer C. Howell, Rt. 18, Indianapolis.
HOWERTON, Ed David, Aviation Machinist's Mate 3c, USNR. Parents, Mr. and Mrs. Paul Thomas Howerton, 628 E. Maryland St., Evansville.
HOWLAND, Bernard J., Pfc., USMCR. Father, Mr. Ralph M. Howland, Sr., 109 Towle Ave., Mishawaka.

HOWSER, Walter Mahlon, Jr., Signalman 2c, USN. Parents, Mr. and Mrs. Walter Mahlon Howser, Sr., 820 N. Jefferson Ave., Indianapolis.
HUBBARD, Oliver Wayne, Lieutenant, USNR. Mother, Mrs. Jennie Hubbard, Rt. 4, Bedford.
HUFFMAN, Roger Wayne, Pfc., USMCR. Parents, Mr. and Mrs. Lee Huffman, Rt. 1, Straughn.
HUMBLE, Robert C., Sgt., USMCR. Wife, Mrs. Robert C. Humble, 109 3rd St., Aurora.
HUMPHREY, Orville F., Cpl., USMCR. Parents, Mr. and Mrs. Homer L. Humphrey, Box 44, Smithville.
HUNCKLER, Fred J., 2d Lieutenant, USMCR. Wife, Mrs. Fred J. Hunckler, 727 Meigs Ave., Jeffersonville.
HUNT, Charles William, Torpedoman's Mate 3c, USN. Mother, Mrs. Lula Ann Myers, Rt. 7, Box 273, Indianapolis.
HUNTER, John Clore, Seaman 1c, USN. Parents, Mr. and Mrs. Stanley C. Hunter, 518 Indiana Ave., Aurora.
HUNTER, Robert Thomas, Machinist's Mate 2c, USN. Father, Mr. Fred J. Hunter, Rt. 4, Warsaw.
HUNTER, Robert Wellman, Ensign, USNR. Sister, Mrs. Mary Hunter Brown, 2305 N. Meridian, Indianapolis.
HUNTZINGER, John Rolland, Electrician's Mate 2c, USNR. Wife, Mrs. Margaret Huntzinger, 1554 Monument St., Noblesville.
HURLEY, Roland L., Assistant Cook, USMCR. Parents, Mr. and Mrs. Orville Hurley, Newburgh.
HURLEY, Wendell Ray, Musician 2c, USN. Father, Mr. Raymond Hurley, 3636 S. Gallatin St., Marion.
HUNTLEY, William Walter, Seaman 2c, USN. Mother, Mrs. Jane Kabrick, 735 W. 2nd St., Anderson.
HUSTON, Walter Wayne, Gunner's Mate 3c, USN. Mother, Mrs. Mary Levina Huston, 312 S. 8th St., West Terre Haute.
HUTCHINSON, John S., Pfc., USMC. Brother, Mr. Amos Hutchinson, Gen. Del., Albion.
HUYS, Arthur Albert, Seaman 1c, USN. Mother, Mrs. Margaret Barbara DeVlieger, Box 54, Wabash.
HYLAND, John T., Cpl., USMCR. Mother, Mrs. Marie Snell, 19 N. Chester, Indianapolis.

I

ICE, Robert L., Pfc., USMC. Mother, Mrs. Mildred B. Ice, 2605 S. Nebraska St., Marion.
INGRAM, John Raymond Willard Pfc., USMCR. Parents, Mr. and Mrs. Joe Ingram, Rt. 6, Boonville.
INMAN, Carlos A., Seaman 1c, USNR. Parents, Mr. and Mrs. Cleveland Inman, Bloomfield.
IRWIN, George Edward, Electrician's Mate 2c, USN. Father, Mr. George N. Irwin, Rt. 2, Columbus.

J

JACKS, Charles Elbert, Boatswain's Mate 1c, USN. Father, Mr. Joseph F. Jacks, Rt. 1, Rockville.
JACKSON, Edward H., Sgt., USMCR. Wife, Mrs. Edward H. Jackson, 524 Dodge St., West LaFayette.

JAMES, Joseph Holman, Jr., Machinist's Mate 2c, UCNR. Parents, Mr. and Mrs. Joseph Holman James, Sr., 331 Independence St., Tipton.
JAMESON, Clarence Albert, Seaman 1c, USN. Parents, Mr. and Mrs. Louis O. Jameson, Stewart St., Rt. 1, Aurora.
JEFFERS, Wallace Mansfield, Coxswain, USNR. Father, Mr. Wallace Mac Jeffers, 1732 Division St., New Albany.
JEFFRIES, Thomas E., Pfc., USMCR. Father, Mr. Chauncey Jeffries, Rt. 1, Judson.
JENKIN, Herbert Lane, Radioman 3c, USNR. Father, Mr. Fred C. Jenkin, Rt. 4, Bloomfield.
JENKINS, Robert M., Pvt., USMCR. Mother, Mrs. Katherine Jenkins, 724 E. 48th St., Indianapolis.
JOHNSON, Delmar Joseph, Fireman 2c, USNR. Mother, Mrs. Cardes Bailey, 2129 John St., Ft. Wayne.
JOHNSON, Edwin Fay, Pvt., USMCR. Parents, Mr. and Mrs. Faber G. Johnson, 337 E. 6th St., Rushville.
JOHNSON, William Edgar, Seaman 2c, USNR. Mother, Mrs. Nina Marie Johnson, 606 E. Oak St., Boonville.
JONES, David Levi, Seaman 2c, USNR. Mother, Mrs. Effie Jones, Oak.
JONES, Edward Clayton, Pfc., USMCR. Wife, Mrs. Sadie Jones, Gen. Del., Mt. Summit.
JONES, John Norbert, Watertender 3c, USNR. Wife, Mrs. Evelyn Margaret Jones, Rt. 1, Vincennes.
JONES, Maurice Oliver, Photographer's Mate 1c, USNR. Wife, Mrs. Beulah Jones, 1312 Circle Tower, Indianapolis.
JONES, Thomas P., Cpl., USMCR. Parents, Mr. and Mrs. Elza Jones, Gen. Del., Winslow.
JORDAN, Paul Immel, Aviation Radioman 2c, USNR. Parents, Mr. and Mrs. George H. Jordan, 2125 Oakley St., Ft. Wayne.
JORDAN, Ralph Loyd, Radioman 2c, USN. Mother, Mrs. Pearl Darr, 613 S. Michigan St., Plymouth.

K

KAIL, William E., Pfc., USMCR. Parents, Mr. and Mrs. Austin E. Kail, 915 E. 7th St., Auburn.
KAISER, Robert O'Brian, Electrician's Mate 3c, USNR. Sister, Mrs. Mildred Pate, 215 Madison Ave., Anderson.
KARIE, Robert J., Pfc., USMCR. Mother, Mrs. Stasia Burkhart, 678 Fillmore St., Gary.
KAROLIK, Andrew Leo, Assistant Cook, USMCR. Wife, Mrs. Irene Karolik, 2111 New York Ave., Whiting.
KASHMER, Paul Joseph, Ensign, USNR. Parents, Mr. and Mrs. Joseph John Kashmer, 523 E. Lincoln Way, La Porte.
KASHNER, Alonzo Richard, Jr., Machinist's Mate 3c, USNR. Wife, Mrs. Hazel Puckett Kashner, 1027 Dudley Ave., Indianapolis.
KASTELIK, Chester Joseph, Seaman 2c, USN. Father, Mr. Michael Kastelik, 333 Park St., La Porte.

CPL. WALDO C. JACKMAN, JR.
BORN: No date given, Missouri
Died: 13 March 1945

Memorialized at the Brittany American
Cemetery and Memorial
St. James, France

The National Archives form states: "The record needed to answer your inquiry is not in our files. If the record were here on July 12, 1973, it would have been in the area that suffered the most damage and may have been destroyed".

CPL. WERNER R. KELM
BORN: No date given, no birthplace given.
Died: 13 March 1945

I received no response to my inquiry; therefore, no additional information is available.

SGT. HAROLD R. KERR
BORN: No date given, no birthplace given.
Died: 13 March 1945

I received no response to my inquiry from the National Archives.

PFC. LAURIER N. LAVOIE
BORN: No date given, no birthplace given.
Died: 13 March 1945

No response to my inquiry was ever received from the National Archives.

PFC. CLARENCE E. LEMEN
BORN: No date given, no birthplace given.
Died: 13 March 1945

The same applies here as to the above Pfc. Lavoie's matter.

PFC. WALTER A. LEWIS
BORN: No date given, no birthplace given.
Died: 13 March 1945

I received no response from the National Archives.

PVT. GEORGE E. McFALL
BORN: 12 March 1915, no birthplace given
Drafted: 4 October 1943
Died: 13 March 1945

Memorialized at the Brittany American
And Memorial Cemetery
St. James, France

No additional information was received from the National Archives.

CPL. JAMES R. MITCHELL
BORN: No date given, no birthplace given.
Died: 13 March 1945

There was no additional information forthcoming from the National Archives.

PFC. DONALD E. NELSON
BORN: No date given, no birthplace given.
Died: 13 March 1945

I never received a response to the inquiry from the National Archives.

PFC. JOSEPH J. NOHLECHEK
BORN: 20 February 1922, Michigan
Drafted: 9 September 1942
Died: 13 March 1945

The Menominee Area Chamber of Commerce sent a letter that they had no information, however, I was given the address to the Menominee County Historical Society, Inc.

According to Pfc. Nohlechek's IDPF, he was 70 inches tall, weighed 150 pounds, had gray eyes, and brown hair. In December 1942 he was stationed at Fort Bragg, North Carolina and then transferred to Baer Island, Indiana on 15 June 1944. He was a member of the 806th Army Air Force Battalion.

In late 2001, a roundabout way in the following research took place:

I wrote to the Postmaster of the community asking if there were any Nohlecheks residing in the area. My letter was returned with the names, addresses, and telephone numbers of two. The information included the information also that there was a Max Nohlechek but passed away several years ago. I wrote to the only male (Patrick) listed.

The Chamber of Commerce was contacted but there was no information regarding Pfc. Nohlechek.

In February 2002, I received correspondence from a relative of Patrick Nohlechek who wrote:

"My cousin's son contacted me about the letter you sent him asking for information concerning Joseph Nohlechek (I remember him as Joey). He may have been registered as born in Menominee, Michigan, but we all lived in Birch Creek a few miles north of Menominee. Our farms were about three miles apart—seemed a great distance when I was young. Joey was the youngest of three children born to Frank and Mary Nohlechek: brother Alfred, sister Rose, and Joseph.

I'm 74 but I have a vivid memory of losing relatives and dear friends in World War II.

If you had asked for information prior to 1966 we would know more. Joey's sister Rose passed away that year. We were very close and saw her often. His brother Alfred passed away many years ago. All cousins my age have passed away in the last seven years.

What I remember about Joey is his ship was hit by another and he was washed out to sea. As for his wife Elizabeth, she never lived in Menominee or Birch Creek. I don't know if the Nohlecheks ever met her. I heard she married Joey just before he left for overseas, then when he was deceased, she received the insurance. Sad because his parents were elderly and extremely poor living on their very small farm.

You asked for newspaper articles and photos. I'm sure Rose would have had some. The only one I have is one of all of us in a group school picture when he was about 11 years old. Small one-room country school grades one through eight. I feel sure he graduated from Menominee High School. I don't know if after graduation he worked on the farm, if he was drafted or enlisted. We had left the farm to move to Menominee in 1935. As poor as we all were, no car, no phone, and not much contact after that. As I said, by then seven miles from Menominee to their farm was a long way.

Sorry I don't have more information than this. Good luck with your book.

Sincerely

P.S. Let me know if I can be of any further assistance."

Later in the month I received a second letter from Joey's cousin that included the school photograph. It truly was of a one-room schoolhouse with the students posing for their picture. Lois gives the location of Rose in the back row—boy, boy, teacher, boy, Rose. On the third row from the bottom—boy, Joey (11 years old—he had approximately 12 more years to live). Mrs. Kostroski is on the bottom row—boy, Lois (6 years old). Also on the bottom row, fifth from the right is Lois's brother Ed (in black sweater). This photograph reminds me of early Americana.

I wrote to the last address Mrs. Kostroski sent me to see if I could locate the convent Rose had entered a few years after her husband's death. She became a hospital nun. It was amazing that the response was sent from the Archives in Canada. In the letter the Sister gave me Rose's only child, George's home address as well as the address of his place of employment (car dealership). Placing a telephone call to the car dealership I learned that George was no longer there and hadn't been in years. Asking the receptionist if she would confirm his home address I had, she replied that she would confirm it but if it were not correct, she would not be able to give me the correct one, which of course, I already knew. As luck would have it, she confirmed.

Writing a letter to George regarding Pfc. Nohlechek, I never received a response. The response Lois wrote is at the beginning of this. As I already knew, when one does research, one never knows which twists and turns one will go through before reaching a conclusion.

Calling Mrs. Kostroski on 30 March, I spoke with her for about 20 minutes as she still had company. She stated that once Rose entered the convent and the family went to visit her, not one of them ever talked about either Joey or Alfred.

In additional correspondence with Mrs. Kostroski she added the additional information:

"Joey's older brother Alfred never married, died as a young man. His sister, Rose Nohlechek Champeau, had one son George. Last known address of George was Madison, Wisconsin that I'm aware of." I called information and there was no listing of him.

"My cousin, Rose, joined a religious order (Sister Rose Champeau) several years after her husband passed away. We were in close contact with her from approximately 1980. We even visited her in Canada when she was on a temporary assignment. She then went to Antigo, Wisonsin and our final visits were to New London, Wisconsin. She died in 1955.

The nuns, if they are still there, may be able to give you George's last known phone number and address. When she left Menominee to become a nun, she most probably dispersed of all her possessions, but if you're able to contact her son, he may be able to help you.

You asked how Joey and I were related. He was my cousin—his father Frank was my father's oldest brother. There were seven boys and six girls in the Nohlechek family. None of the girls married and many died young or as infants.

That's the best I can do on the school picture. I only spent one year there—first grade and then my Mom sent us to Catholic School in Menominee. A high school student gave us a ride to school—better than walking two miles to the Birch Creek School, rain or shine. I can remember walking home crying because my hands were so cold and my Mom would hear me and come to meet us, and try to warm my hands. Of course, I can also remember her hanging clothes on the line that would freeze stiff in a matter of minutes—clothes she laundered on the old scrub board. Bet you don't remember the 3-holer (outhouse) on the farm or the slop jar under the bed.

Sincerely,"

NOTE: We had a 2-holer several hundred feet from the back of the house. Heated water on the stove to do laundry with a scrub board and had a "mechanical" wringer that one had to turn by hand. We never had a slop jar but I had a friend who had one in her bedroom.

Mrs. Kostroski and I continue to keep in touch with each other. She doesn't use a computer so it is done by "snail mail."

PVT*. CLIFFORD NOWAK
BORN: 30 January 1923, Wisconsin
Enlisted: 8 March 1941
Died: 13 March 1943

*In portions of the IDPF, Pvt. Nowak is also listed as a Sergeant, although in the records of the men who lost their lives, he is still listed as Pvt.

According to newspaper articles received from the Portage County Historical Society, Sgt. Nowak's mother passed away in March 1934 survived by her husband Max, daughter Dorothy, and son Clifford, age 11. His father passed away in October 1959.

Sgt. Nowak was a member of the Army Air Force and stationed as follows:

Kessler Field, Mississippi, 2 December 1941; Gulfport, Mississippi, 12 April 1943; Champaign, Illinois, 4 February 1944; Camp Crowder, Missouri, 7 November 1944; Fort George G. Meade, Maryland, February 22, 1945. His dental chart shows he had 8 teeth extracted—three on top, five on the bottom. He had graduated from St. Peter's Parochial School and Stevens Point High School.

He was 65-1/2 inches tall, weighed 135 pounds, had green eyes, and brown hair. At the time he arrived at Fort George G. Meade, Maryland, he was assigned to Company B, Group 155(a) Infantry.

At the time of his death, Sgt. Nowak was married with a small daughter residing in Biloxi, Mississippi.

Sister Dorothy was the one who signed the form to receive the American flag and later moved to San Francisco, California.

At the time of the collision, his IDPF shows it took place 41° 50° N, 36° 31° W of the Azores Islands.

It appears that an application for a government flat bronze grave marker was applied for. It also leaves no question as to his rank as the form also states: "Available records indicate the highest grade held by the decedent was Sergeant while serving with the 414th Technical School Squadron, Army Air Force. Pvt. Nowak's sister Dorothy signed the form. The marker was defective in that it had his date of birth listed as January 30, 1913 instead of January 30, 1923. There is a letter in the file stating that the new bronze marker had been corrected and would be sent as soon as the incorrect one was received and destroyed. Of course, another form had to be completed! Both forms are in the file which was finally completed 6 May 1960.

*I have changed the rank from Private to Sergeant in the text.

PVT. JESSE L. PARKER
BORN: No date given, no birthplace given.
Died: 13 March 1945

I sent two inquiries; the National Archives responded to neither.

PVT. HARRY A. PIERCE, JR.
BORN: 6 November 1923, Rhode Island
Died: 13 March 1945

I wrote to the Pawtucket Public Library and states that they have no information on Pvt. Pierce. However, included was a list of the telephone directory from 1944 and there he is: "Harry A. Pierce, Jr., USA, Marbury Av." In the 1945 telephone directory, he is again listed: "Harry A. Pierce, Jr., (Marbury Av.) USA—missing in action."

On 9 November 2001 at 9:30 a.m., I received a telephone call from Ron diMacio, postmaster for Pawtucket regarding the Pierce family.

He stated he was unable to locate the Pierce names in some of the old telephone books and talked with a retired postmaster who remembered the Pierce name but not the family. He said they had to have moved prior to 1991 as that was how far back the telephone books went.

Pvt. Pierce was 69-1/2 inches tall, weighed 151 pounds, had brown hair and eyes. He was assigned to Company B in the Infantry.

According to the IDPF this is another part of the story of the collision: "Passenger on U.S. Army transport *J. W. McAndrew* en route to Europe where northwest of the Azores Islands, ship was struck by the French Aircraft Carrier *Bearn* which had a mechanical failure and was off course. The McAndrew suffered a gaping hole in the #1 hold and washed the troops out to sea. Body not recovered. No other information on file this branch."

A second report states: "On the morning of 13 March 45, about 0400 hours, NW of the Azores Is., the ship was struck by the French aircraft carrier "*Bearn*", which was in the convoy and off course due to mechanical failure. The ship was struck where men were sleeping, and 81 of them were washed out to sea by the onrushing water. Thirteen of them were saved; he was among those who perished."

Both parents are listed as living at the residence given above.

There is a letter pertaining to the burial flag, but there is no response is in IDPF file.

PFC. ARTHUR E. ROURKE
Drafted: 31 March 1943
Died: 13 March 1945

The National Archives gave only the above information.

PFC. LEONARD SAVITZ
BORN: 7 July 1921, Pennsylvania
Enlisted: 12 September 1942
Died: 13 March 1945

**Memorialized at the Brittany American
Cemetery and Memorial
St. James, France**

I had to send twice for inquiries to the National Archives. The first inquiry form was returned marked with the following:

"1) The record needed to answer your inquiry is not in our files;

2) The enclosed information was obtained from an alternate record;

3) However, complete personnel/medical records cannot be reconstructed; and

4) However, we regret that these sources do not contain the particular type of information or document requested." I sent the inquiry form a second time.

Pfc. Savitz was in the Infantry. His last known address was on North Uber Street, Philadelphia. In checking the Internet, I located several addresses for people with the same last name. Letters were written; none were returned and no responses received.

Pfc. Savitz was 66" tall, weighed 132 pounds; he had brown hair and eyes.

In September 1942, he underwent basic training at the Aberdeen Proving Ground, Maryland, company not of record. He transferred in February 1944 to Lexington, Virginia and in November 1944 to Fort Monmouth, New Jersey. February 1945 found him assigned to Fort George G. Meade, Maryland with Company B, 155th Infantry Group, 31st Infantry Division and the "Mac".

There was a medical form in the IDPF but the writing was so light it was unreadable; however, he was hospitalized from 18 November to 13 December 1943. The dental chart shows no cavities or extractions. He was of the Jewish faith.

There is a letter in the IDPF stating that a Burial flag will be provided upon application. There is not a form in the file that a flag was requested.

His parents survived Pfc. Savitz, but were divorced.

SGT. JOHN C. SCHNEIDER
BORN: 24 September 1913, Kentucky
Enlisted: 20 August 1943
Died: 13 March 1945

I wrote to and received a list of names and addresses of Schneiders from the Henderson County Historical Society, Inc. A letter of contact had also been written to the post office and received the card back with the notation "None listed."

The remarks on one of the pages in the IDPF state: "Missing after collision of NY 534, U.S.A.T. *J.W. McAndrew* and Y.Y. 629 French aircraft carrier *Bearn* at 41 degrees at 50 minutes North Latitude and 36 degrees 31 minutes West Longitude. Enlisted man was passenger aboard the *J. W. McAndrew*, out of New York Harbor."

There is a letter in the file regarding a Burial flag and the application form signed by his mother dated January 7, 1947.

Sgt. Schneider was 5'8", weighed 144 pounds, and had brown hair and black eyes. He was assigned to Company B, 155th Infantry Group. His four wisdom teeth had been extracted.

It appears Sgt. Schneider took basic training at Camp McClellan, Alabama in September 1942. He then transferred to Miami, Florida where he was from October 1942 through March 1943. Finally, he arrived at Fort George G. Meade, Maryland in February 1945, to ship out on the "Mac" in March 1945.

NOTE: I was also stationed at what was then called Fort McClellan, Alabama that was my home base after basic training at Fort Lee, Virginia. Fort McClellan was closed in September 2001.

His parents and a sister survived him.

PFC. EARL SINNETT, JR.
BORN: 12 September 1923, West Virginia
Enlisted: 11 February 1943
Died: 13 March 1945

Pfc. Sinnett's IDPF contains the information that the area of death was "36°31°W—41°50°N Portugal (Azores)."

There is also a letter in the file from his mother trying to get a Burial flag in honor of her son. It was forwarded to the Veterans Administration in Washington, DC There is not a letter from the VA in response to her letter. Later on in the file there is a letter from the military that a flag would be provided if the application was completed and returned; however, I find no evidence that the application was returned.

Pfc. Sinnett was 65-3/4" tall, weighed 133 pounds, had blue eyes and blonde hair. He had taken basic training at Atlantic City, New Jersey in 1943 and transferred to Camp Polk, Louisiana, August 1943. From there Pfc. Sinnett was stationed at Esler, Florida in June 1943. From December 1943 through February 1944, he was in Great Falls, Montana and in January 1945, he was sent to Fort George G. Meade, Maryland where he boarded the "Mac."

His dental chart shows quite extensive extractions and fillings. His hospital chart shows he was a patient at Camp Polk, Louisiana from

22 July 1943 through 7 August 1943. He was also in the hospital at Great Falls, Montana from 25 October 1943 through 30 October 1943. No reason for each hospitalization was given.

This is the telegram Mrs. Sinnett received in the notification of her son's death:

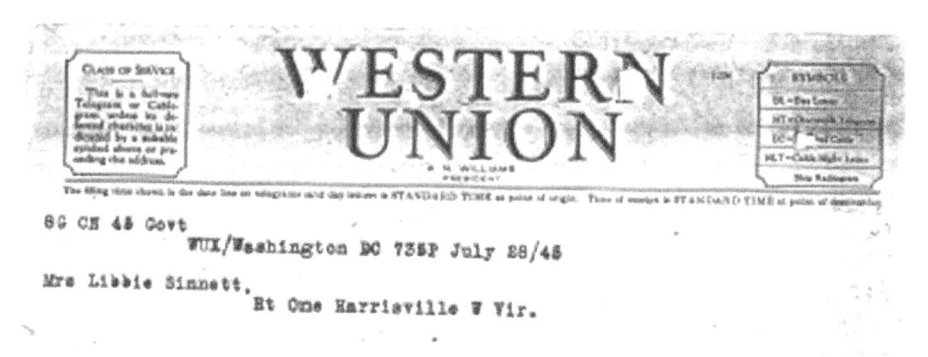

```
8G CN 45 Govt
            WUX/Washington DC 735P July 28/45
Mrs Libbie Sinnett,
            Rt One Harrisville W Vir.

It has now been Officially established from reports received in the War
Department that the death of your Son Private First Class Earl Sinnett
Jr who was previously reported missing occured on thirteen March the
Secretary Of War extends his deep sympathy confirming letter follows.
                        Witsell Acting The Adjutant General.
                                                    935P
```

I had mailed a letter to the community newspaper and here is the response received:

"I saw the notice you had put in the Ritchie County newspaper about the family of Earl Sinnett. My older sister was married to Earl's brother, Carl. I saw the parents once in a while through my sister, and they lived in a small town called Harrisville. I knew where the graves were and I took these pictures. Hope they will be of help to you. Earl had a younger brother; his name was Luttrell. He was killed in the Korean War. They are buried side by side as you can see in the picture. Notice the age on the monument, both were 22 years old. Did you know Earl was a twin? His brother's name was Burl. He committed suicide, but we do not know why. The home they had is near the cemetery, so Mrs. Sinnett visited the cemetery every day with fresh flowers. I have two nephews who are Sinnetts. They are happy to know I am sending you these pictures and information on their family. When the book is published I would like for them to get one. There aren't many family members left, but if I get more information I will gladly send it to you. Of course, Mr. and Mrs. Sinnett are now gone also, but I have sent pictures of their graves also. They are buried beside the boys. Would you please let me know if this information has been helpful to you, or if there is anything I can help to answer. I am leaving my address to you."

I received another letter that showed some changes from the letter noted above. "I have been trying to get a picture of the tombstone for you of the Sinnett brothers. I have found out a lady from Greenwood has sent you one! Earl Junior is the young man that was killed on that ship. His twin brother, Burl Raymond, was on the ship also. He survived and came home. He later took his own life. They had another brother die in the Korean War. His name was Luttrell. Some of our relatives told me he was called "Ted."

The father was generally known as "Gudgeon" or "Shing." He worked in the oil fields. He lived to be in his 90s. His wife was my great aunt and was one of the prettiest ladies you would ever want to meet. She was a very loving Mom. I wasn't very old at this time and when we went to their home, she had pictures of her sons on the wall. Below those pictures she kept "fresh" flowers made of crepe paper but Aunt Bon could make flowers out of that stuff you would not believe and that was the memorial she always kept for her sons. I don't really know how often she changed them.

Her husband thought it was a little foolish but was always ready to show off "Bon's" flowers. The last of their children died about two years ago. His name was Carl Franklin and we all called him "Tink". There were nine children in the family but only seven survived. When Aunt Bonnie was 39 she had another set of twins and they only lived 12 hours.

In fact, some of the relatives I called to ask about the boys in service didn't even know or remember her having the twins. I haven't really given you much information but hope other people have written you and it all comes together.

If there would be anything else you might need information on and I could get it for you, I certainly would try. I am also 63 years old, but my Aunt Bonnie was one bright spot in my life.

Yours truly"

CPL. DIXIE SKIPPER
BORN: 15 October 1918, Georgia
Enlisted: 4 July 1942
Died: 13 March 1945

On Monday, 20 November 2000, I received a telephone call from a young lady who works at the National Archives; she was requesting what information I was seeking and advised her regarding the IDPF, which was eventually received after a second inquiry form was sent.

The Union Recorder Newspaper and the Milledgeville Historical Society were also contacted. I was informed that Route 3 was the Skipper's previous address and that Route 3 had been changed to several named streets.

I found the Burial flag letter in the file as well as the letter requesting the flag signed by his widow. His parents survived Cpl. Skipper.

He was 67" tall, weighed 122 pounds, had brown eyes, and black hair. Assigned to Company B, Group 155(a), Infantry Regiment of the 31st Infantry Division in February 1945 out of Fort George G. Meade, Maryland. Other bases where he was stationed: Basic training at Fort McPherson, Georgia in July 1942; base not listed in Madison, Wisconsin in August 1942, MacKall; it is presumed he must have been there for some time. From there he went to North Carolina at Pope Field in May 1944, Truax Field in Wisconsin, May 1944, Baer Field, Indiana through October 1944 and finally, as noted above, Fort George G. Meade, Maryland where he joined the troops boarding the "Mac."

His dental chart shows two of his wisdom teeth had been extracted.

His widow had requested an application for the government allowance as she didn't know at the time that the government issued a monetary supplement for burial of those who died at sea and which the government referred to the Department of the Army, Quartermaster General for appropriate action. In a letter dated 15 August 1952, it is noted: "The law authorizes only the furnishing of Government headstones and markers for unmarked graves of those who die in the service or whose last service terminated honorably. There is no authority for a monetary allowance in lieu of a Government headstone or marker."

PVT. HOWARD F. SMITH
BORN: 15 January 1920, Washington
Drafted: 21 April 1944
Died: 13 March 1945

Pvt. Smith was 67" tall, weighed 126 pounds, had brown hair and eyes, and was Infantry. He left behind a wife, a sister and two brothers.

His dental chart shows all four wisdom teeth had been extracted as well as the tooth on the lower right next to the molar.

His widow signed the application for the Burial flag.

That is all the pertinent information I was able to glean from the IDPF.

PFC. PAUL J. STAYBROOK
Died: 13 March 1945

In Pfc. Staybrook's file, there is a letter from National Archives rejecting my inquiry.

PFC. HAROLD E. TATRO
BORN: 5 August 1923, Michigan
Drafted: 19 February 1943
Died: 13 March 1945

Memorialized at the Brittany American Cemetery and Memorial St. James, France

Pfc. Tatro was 5'5-3/4" tall, weighed 120 pounds, had blue eyes and brown hair. His dental chart shows four extractions (not wisdom teeth), and two cavities. His record does not indicate where he had basic or any other bases, only that he was assigned to Company B, Group 155(a), Infantry Division. We can readily presume he was at Fort George G. Meade, Maryland and assigned to the "Mac".

There is a letter in the file regarding a Burial flag to his father; his parents survived him on Royal Avenue, Berkley, Michigan.

There is also a photograph in the file showing a small church and headstones and which states: "Tablets of the Missing at Brittany American Cemetery, St. James, France." I had sent in four letters of inquiry before I received Pfc. Tatro's IDPF.

PFC. ROY W. THORPE
BORN: 6 April 1924, Michigan
Enlisted: 14 December 1942
Died: 13 March 1945

The first item in Pfc. Thorpe's IDPF was a certificate of military service but was not done until 13 November 2000.

Pfc. Thorpe was 67-1/2" tall, weighed 145 pounds, had brown eyes and brown hair. The only listed base was at Fort George G. Meade, Maryland in February 1945. His dental records show two upper wisdom teeth having been extracted.

There is a letter on file regarding the Burial flag and the application signed by Pfc. Thorpe's mother. At the time of his induction into the service, the family residence was in Michigan; on 7 November 1945, when the application was signed for the flag, his mother had moved to San Diego.

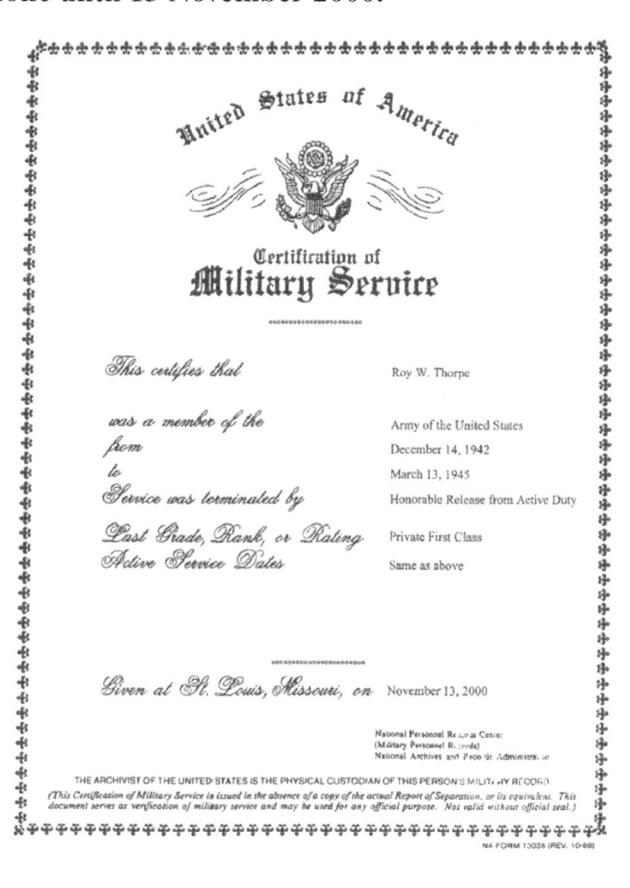

PFC. JOSEPH C. TUOHEY
BORN: 12 February 1911, Massachusetts
Enlisted: 20 August 1942
Died: 13 March 1945

There is a form letter in the IDPF file regarding the Burial flag and a copy of the application signed by the father on 16 September 1946. His parents, who survived Pfc. Tuohey, resided on Forbes Street, Jamaica Plain.

In the Station section where the bases are listed, there is the statement "Stations not of Record." Pfc. Tuohey was 5'6-1/2" tall, weighed 152 pounds, had hazel eyes and brown hair. His dental chart shows numerous cavities, 22 in all, as of 20 August 1942 with three extractions, one being a wisdom tooth.

Last organization to which he was attached is listed as Company B, 155 GP(a); in other words, at Fort George G. Meade, Maryland.

Photo courtesy of Dorothy Crowell

PVT. BRYAN TURNER, JR.
BORN: 17 July 1924, Tennessee
Drafted: 30 March 1943
Died: 13 March 1945

This is the young man who started my research into the collision between the "Mac" and the "*Bearn*". My brother-in-law sent me his journals when he served in World War II from the time his unit arrived in England until the war was over in Germany. On 13 July 1944, a Pvt. Bryan was shot and killed in France. Inasmuch as I have worked on the family genealogy for over 20 years, I immediately sent for his IDPF. Imagine my surprise when I received the one listed above.

The majority of his IDPF has been utilized in this so the reader can see in just how the reports are completed. It might also be the time to state that in almost every one of the IDPFs received, all of them have been slightly different.

PVT. BRYAN TURNER, JR.
INDIVIDUAL DECEASED PERSONNEL FILE

On May 10, 1951, a Non-Recoverable Remains Re-examination of Records was done by the case analyst, Hayden, and was approved by the Chief, Final Determination Section Mary A. Edwards, 1st Lt., Quartermaster Corps, and which states as follows:

"Area of Death: Atlantic Ocean
Name: Turner, Bryan Jr., Pvt.

Area of Death: Atlantic Ocean 41 degrees 50 degrees N; 36 degrees 31 degrees W

IDENTIFICATION DATA:
TURNER, Bryan Jr., Pvt.
Height 71"
Weight 145
Color eyes Blue
Color hair Brown
Date of Death 13 March 1945

ASSIGNED
1ST Replacement Battalion, Fort George G. Meade, Maryland, February 1945
Place of Death or Place Last Seen
Lost at sea, ship wrecked 3-13-45.
(Notice Pvt. Turner's IDPF states the ship was wrecked.)

Bryan Turner, Jr - Lost his life at sea (drowned)

List all camps in which Stationed in U.S. prior to Service Overseas, with inclusive dates at each:

Camp Grant, Illinois   April 1943
Camp Crowder, Missouri   April 1944
Champaign, Illinois   February 1944
Fort George G. Meade   February 1945

Cause of death: Drowned

Place of Death: *J. W. McAndrew* collided with the *"Bearn"* NW of the Azores Islands.

Additional information:
Age: 21 years

While the U.S. Army Transport *"J. W. McAndrew"* was proceeding to Europe from New York Harbor, it became involved in a collision with another vessel of the convoy. After the crash, a check was made of the personnel and he was among those missing lost at sea.

This incident occurred in the Atlantic Ocean.

Records also show medical treatment and other information:

Hospital
Camp Crowder, MO from 7-28-44 to 9-25-44—No reason given
Shoe size: Not of Record
Fractures and/or Breaks—None
Tattoos and/or Birthmark—None
Hurricane Mills, TN

Aboard U.S. Army Transport *"J. W. McAndrew"* when it was struck by French aircraft carrier *"Bearn"*, northwest of Azores Is. Transport received a gaping hole in No. 1 Hold where the above man was quartered and was washed out to sea. No other information on file this branch.

DEPARTMENT OF THE ARMY
OFFICE OF THE QUARTERMASTER GENERAL
WASHINGTON 25 D. C.

SUBJECT: Non-Recoverability of Remains

TO: Commanding General
American Graves Registration Command
European Area
APO 58, c/o Postmaster
New York, New York

Reference is made to Proceedings of Boards of Officers that have convened at your headquarters and have determined that the remains of certain World War II dead are non-recoverable.

Findings of the Board have been reviewed and approved on all decedents whose names appear on the attached roster.

It is requested that all records of your office pertaining to these deceased be amended to read REMAINS NON-RECOVERABLE.

CASE HISTORY FOR REMAINS DECLARED NON-RECOVERABLE

CAUSE OF DEATH: Lost at sea, as a result of a collision on 13 March 1945, between the *USAT J. W. McAndrews*[1] and the French Aircraft Carrier "*Bearn*" at 41°50°north latitude and 36°31°west longitude, about 160 miles northwest of the Azores.

BASIS FOR DECLARING REMAINS NON-RECOVERABLE

Report of Death on file indicates subject decedent was drowned on 13 March 1945 as a result of being washed out to sea when transport on which he was a passenger was rammed by another vessel.

---

[1] Please note that throughout the IDPFs, the name of the ship goes from *JOHN W. McANDREW* TO *JAMES W. McANDREW* TO *J. W. McANDREWS*.

Casualty records indicate that subject decedent was an Army passenger aboard the *USAT "J. W. McAndrews"* when said vessel was severely damaged in a collision with the French Aircraft Carrier *"Bearn"* on 13 March 1945.

A detailed account of the collision and rescue attempts that were made in connection therewith, is contained in the Status Review and Determination Report.

Of the eighty-one (81) Army personnel originally swept into the sea from the damaged hold of the transport, thirteen (13) were rescued by escort vessels, reducing the final total of Army fatalities to sixty-eight (68). These casualties are the subjects of the instant case.

One (1) Navy man was killed at his post as a result of the collision. His remains were buried at sea, and they are, therefore, not being considered non-recoverable in this case. [Carlos Inman.]

The area where the disaster occurred was thoroughly searched by escort vessels but no additional survivors were found.

There were no unknowns recovered from the area that could be associated with personnel lost from subject vessel. All remains recovered from the Azores were identified on exhumation.

The following records have been checked by this office with negative results in an effort to locate any possible burial location of subject decedent either as a known or unknown:

A-Z files of known interments in U.S. Military Cemeteries and isolated locations.

Alphabetical index file of "Believed to be" and potentially identified unknowns.

Alphabetical file of former unknowns now identified.

Geographical clue index file of unknowns interred in U.S. Military Cemeteries in the general area in which subject deceased was last report.

293 file of subject decedent.

In view of the fact that no records can be located of subject decedent's remains having been recovered and that more than three (3) years have elapsed since they were lost at sea. It is recommended that a finding of Remains NON-RECOVERABLE be determined by the identification Review Board, Memorial Division.

Dated 11 October 1948 By B. Spencer, Identification Branch

EUROPEAN AREA
APO 58 U S ARMY

Subject: Non-recoverable Remains
To: Non-recoverable Board

It is recommended that the board take action on the following case:

PLACE OF DEATH: North Atlantic, 41°50′N, 36°31′W about 160 miles Northwest of Azores
DATE OF DEATH: 13 March 1945

SYNOPSIS OF CASE: NY-634 USAT *"JOHN W. McANDREW"* was in convoy out of New York to European Theater. At about 0340 hours on 13th March 1945, French Aircraft Carrier *"BEARN"* collided with the *"JOHN W. McANDREW"* making a hole below the waterline on the starboard side; the hole was 40 feet wide and ran from deck to keel. Hold #1 was opened to the sea and it is estimated that all the men washed out into the sea and still unrecovered were in or about the vicinity of lower #1 Troop compartment. The collision occurred approximately at 160 miles northwest of Fayal Island, Azores.

Rescue work began almost immediately and after the collision by Destroyer Escort Vessels. The *"BEARN"* had suffered severe damage too as the result of the collision and was standing by. At 1000 hours the Escort Vessels gave out the search and reported the names of thirteen (13) survivors picked up. Roll calls were made several times and rescue vessels contacted to ascertain the exact number of men lost, a final survey revealed 68 were unaccounted for. One man of the US Navy Armed Guard, INMAN, Carlos A. Seaman First Class

(S-1/Cl 684-15-67), was killed while on duty and buried at sea. The damaged vessels were ordered to proceed under escort to Pointa Delgada, Azores, for emergency repairs.

Attached hereto are extracts from Armed Guard files on subject case. Two statements by Major John S. Hobbs, Transport Commander of the USAT *"JOHN W. McANDREW"* gives a detailed account of the collision and all the work done in this connection. A list giving names of 68 men lost is attached to one of his statements.

NORTH ATLANTIC—10.018

NY 634 USAT *"JOHN W. McANDREW"*
Rammed by French Aircraft Carrier *"BEARN"*, 13 March 1945
Position: 41° 50°N, 36° 31°W, NW of the Azores Islands

DEPARTMENT OF THE ARMY
OFFICE OF THE QUARTERMASTER GENERAL
WASHINGTON 25, DC

29 October 1947

In Reply Refer To
QMGMM 293
TURNER, Bryan Jr.

SUBJECT: Additional Information that may lead to the Recovery and Identification of Remains not yet accounted for.

TO: Command Officer
      American Graves Registration Service
      Mediterranean Zone
      APO 794, c/o Postmaster
      New York, New York

There is attached hereto, in duplicate, OQMG Form 371 (covering all available information in the Office of the Quartermaster General and is in addition to any previous information forwarded by this office to your headquarters) for the following deceased individual:

NAME	GRADE
TURNER, Bryan Jr.	Private

It is requested that information on the above deceased be furnished this office in accordance with provisions of Letter, The Adjutant General's Office, file AGAQ-S 293.9 (27 March 47) D-M, subject, Establishment of Boards of Review for Identification of Unknown Dead Overseas, dated 9 April 1947.

BY COMMAND OF MAJOR GENERAL LARKIN

/S/
JAMES C. MAC FARLAND
Major, QMC
Memorial Division

Incl.
Form 371 (In Dup.)

SUSPEND SLIP
Set Ser 371
Dated 9 April 1947

IT IS REQUESTED THAT THE ATTACHED FILE BE RETURNED TO: Miss Thomas

TURNER, Bryan Jr.

DATA ON REMAINS NOT YET RECOVERED OR IDENTIFIED
TURNER, Bryan Jr. Pvt.
1st Repl. Bn RDI
Fort George G. Meade Feb 45 White No Preference
13 March 45 Drowned

"*J. W. McANDREW*" collided with the "*BEARN*" NW of the Azores Islands at 41D 50 M N—36D 31 M W

ADDITIONAL INFORMATION:
Age 21
Initialed mrw
Date forwarded to Field 29 Oct 1947

WAR DEPARTMENT
OFFICE OF THE QUARTERMASTER GENERAL
WASHINGTON 25, DC

In Reply Refer To
QMGMR 293
9 April 1947
TURNER, Bryan Jr.

SUBJECT: Request for Physical Characteristics of Deceased World War II Servicemen

TO: National Headquarters Selective Service System
21st & C Streets, Northwest
Washington 25, DC
Attention: Dr. Smith, R & S Section

This office is attempting to locate and identify remains of deceased servicemen of World War II whose remains have not been recovered and/or identified.

Request the inclosed OQMG Form 371 be completed and returned to this office, indicating any physical characteristics which may lead to the identify of the late Private Bryan Turner, Jr.

BRYAN TURNER JR.

Private Turner, a son of Mr. and Mrs. Bryan Turner Sr., of Hurricane Mills was lost at sea March 13, 1945, according to a letter received from the War Department by his parents last week. Turner was nearly twenty two, a very bright scholar in high school and a very much loved young man of his community. Following is the death notice.

"Your son was aboard the U. S. Army Transport J. W. McAndrew enroute to the European Continent. On the morning of March 13, 1945 about 4 A. M., northwest of the Azores Islands, this vessel was struck by the French Aircraft Carrier Bearn, which was in the convoy and off course due to a mechanical failure. The McAndrew suffered a gaping hole in No. 1 hold in which one hundred and thirty-four (134) enlisted men were quartered. Eighty-one (81) of these were washed out to sea by the onrushing waters. The prevailing conditions at the time, heavy seas, darkness and poor visibility made rescue operations difficult. Two escort destroyers managed to rescue (13) enlisted men. The remaining sixty-eight (68), including your son perished despite all efforts to effect their rescue."

FOR THE QUARTERMASTER GENERAL:
/s/ MARTIN G. RILEY
Major, QMC
Assistant

1 Incl.
OQMG Form 371
QMGYG 293

WAR DEPARTMENT
THE ADJUTANT GENERAL'S OFFICE
WASHINGTON 25, DC

REPORT OF DEATH	29 AUG 1945
NAME	TURNER, BRYAN JR
GRADE	PVT
HOME ADDR	TENNESSEE
ARM/SERVICE	INFANTRY
DATE OF BIRTH	19 JULY 1923
PLACE OF DEATH	MEDITERRANEAN AREA
CAUSE OF DEATH	DROWNED
DATE OF DEATH	13 MARCH 1945

EMERGENCY ADDRESSEE
Mrs. Laura J. Turner, Mother
Tennessee

BENEFICIARY:
Same as above   Mrs. Laura J. Turner
Same as above   Mr. Bryan Turner, Sr.

The individual named in this report of death is held by the War Department to have been in a missing status from 13 March 1945, until such absence was terminated on 24 July 1945, when evidence considered sufficient to establish the fact of death was received by the Secretary of War.

FORWARDED TO BOARD
APPROVED BY BOARD
FIELD NOTIFIED

RECORD CARD MADE TO 293 FILE
HEADQUARTERS
AMERICAN GRAVES REGISTRATION COMMAND
EUROPEAN AREA
APO 58 US ARMY

22 March 1948

RAG 300.4
SPECIAL ORDERS
NUMBER 33

Under the provisions of AR 615-368, 14 May 47 and AR 420-5, the following Board of officers is appointed to meet at Liege, Belgium, or at such other places as the president may designate at the call of the president thereof, for the purpose of considering whether such Enlisted Man as may be brought before it should be discharged prior to the expiration of their term of service. Proceedings of the Board will be in conformity with AR 420-5. Findings and recommendations will be forwarded to the Commanding General, and entered on WD AGO Form 37.

LT COL	PARK W. BAILEY INF
MAJOR	DAVID MIMS JR FA
MAJOR	JOHN W. LONG INFANTRY
CAPT	THOMAS C. HAYDEN QMCS
1ST LT	ALVIN C. BECK INF
1ST LT	ROBERT VANINA MC

Par 3 and 4, SO 6, this headquarters, 14 Jan 48 pertaining to appointment of Board of Review for identification of Unknown Dead (European Area), are rescinded.

PAC ltr WD 9 Apr 47, subj.: "Establishment of Boards for Identification of Unknown Dead," the fol off, this HQ, are apptd. A Board of Review for Identification of Unknown Dead (European Area):

LT COL	PATRICK W. GUINEY QMC
MAJ	GEORGE M VER HULST USAF
MAJ	MARSHALL J. BLACKMON INF
CAPT	JACK C. HAYES QMC
1ST LT	JOSEPH E. McCLUSKEY INF

PAC ltr WD 9 Apr 47, Subj.: "Establishment of Boards for Identification of Unknown Dead," the fol off, this HQ, are appt a Board of Review for non-recoverability of remains (European Area):

LT COL	EDWARD D. MULVANITY QMC
MAJ	GROSVENOR W. FISH QMC
MAJ	FRANCIS P. SWEENEY INF
CAPT	OWEN F. McCANN QMC
1ST LT	GEORGE L. FREEMAN QM

HEADQUARTERS
AMERICAN GRAVES REGISTRATION COMMAND
EUROPEAN AREA
APO 58 U S ARMY
20 SEPT 1948

Proceedings of a Board of Officers appointed in accordance with letter File AGAO-S 293.9 (27 Mar 47), D-M, War Dept., TAGO, 9 April 1947.

The board convened pursuant to par 4, SO No. 33, Headquarters, American Graves Registration Command, APO 38, U S Army, 22 March 1948, at the Astoria Hotel, Paris, France on 20 Sept 1948. The purpose of the board was to determine the non-recoverability status of certain casualties now under the jurisdiction of this command.

The board reviewed report of investigation, statements of witnesses and other papers contained in the files of American Graves Registration Command, EA, pertaining to the case of the following named casualty/casualties, the remains of which have not been recovered. The case records and other data considered are attached elsewhere.

USAT *"JOHN W. McANDREWS"*

Rammed by French Aircraft Carrier *"BEARN,"* 13 March 1945 northwest of the Azores Islands (North Atlantic).

FINDINGS: The board, having carefully considered the evidence before it, finds the remains of said casualty/casualties are non-recoverable.

RECOMMENDATION: That the case concerning subject casualty/casualties be forwarded to the Office of the Quartermaster General for final approval.

End of Report

"Mr. Bryan Turner
Route #1
Tennessee

Dear Mr. Turner:

The War Department will furnish regulation Burial Flags in memory of military personnel whose remains cannot be recovered or who were buried at sea.

As the official records of this office show that the remains of your son, the late Private Bryan Turner, Jr. were lost in such a manner that they cannot be recovered, there is enclosed an application form for the flag, if you so desire it. For your convenience there is also inclosed an envelope which requires no postage for the return of the application to this office. Upon receipt of the inclosed application properly accomplished, a flag will be furnished.

May our country's flags be an everlasting symbol that these heroic men did not die in vain.

FOR THE QUARTERMASTER GENERAL:

Sincerely yours,"

JAMES L. PRENN
Major, GMC
Assistant

Gh
2 Incls:
Flag Application
Envelope

I located in the IDPF the form sent Mr. Turner, Sr., a letter regarding the Burial flag.

I do not find the form that requested one be sent the family. His only surviving sister has requested one and was forwarded the information she needed to apply for one.

I was able to locate a cousin of Pvt. Turner's residing in Waverly, Tennessee. I attended an Armed Guard National Reunion (and was made an Honorary Armed Guard Wave because of my interest in the Armed Guard) in Fort Mitchell, Kentucky, May 21-24, 2000, at the Drawbridge Inn. Inasmuch as my spouse and I were so close, we drove down to meet the cousin. She sent us out to look for the house in Hurricane Mills, Tennessee Pvt. Turner had lived in as a young man but she thought we did not find the correct one. Imagine my surprise when we learned that Loretta Lynn had bought the entire town. His cousin informed me that Pvt. Turner's sister was still alive and gave me her name and address. There is more to this story but it will be continued later on.

His cousin stated that Pvt. Turner did not go to school at Hurricane Mills as he lived a few miles on down Hurricane Creek and attended Beech Hill School. He was valedictorian of his graduating class in Waverly High in 1941.

Upon arrival home, I wrote to Dorothy Crowell, Pvt. Turner's sister. Here is her response:

"Needless to say, your letter was quite a surprise! Of course you have my permission to use any information you have that you consider to be accurate. I would like to use any information you received and I would like to buy a copy of the book.

I have only one picture of my brother. Pictures back in those days were not made very often and over time, have simply disappeared. I am sending a copy of the one I have. If this does not work let me know. I am not sure where it was made. As for a picture of the high school he attended, I am sending an article showing the building burning. He was probably a junior at this time. He was attending Murfreesboro State Teachers College (I think this name is correct) when he was drafted.

Back to the picture of the burning school, if you need to know the name of the paper that printed the article, I am not sure of the name then. It is a county weekly and the current name is the News Democrat published in Waverly, Tenn. When you go to Waverly to visit my cousin, she can get the name if she doesn't know.

I had remembered the name of the ship he was on but did not remember the name of the other ship. To me, it is amazing that you wound up with information on my brother.

Please let me hear from you in the future regarding the book.

Sincerely"

In correspondence two months later:

"To my knowledge we never received a burial flag and yes, I would like to have one if it isn't too much trouble. (I sent an e-mail months later telling how she could obtain one).

The book cover sounds great. I am anxious to see the finished product.

As I said earlier, I have thought of my brother a lot in the past few months. Such as, we lived on a farm eight miles from town and no way to travel. Junior (Pvt. Turner) played basketball and had to walk home many times after a game. I helped him when he had speeches to give, was in a play or whatever. I thought I was hot stuff helping him. He was a self-taught guitar, harmonica and Jew's harp player. Good too! Nearby were a fiddle, mandolin and another guitar player. When they got together, the roof rocked.

He was in college for several months (Army did this) before he was pulled out and sent overseas. He met a girl that he seemed to be very serious about. The only name we knew was Anne. After we received the telegram we began wondering about notifying her. Finally my mother wrote to the Dean of Women of the college on a chance she might have an idea of some sort. The Dean was having lunch one day with a teacher—and lo and behold! She knew Anne. Anne and my mother corresponded for a while and Anne and her mother came to see my parents at least once.

We heard from one man that was on the ship. He said he was in the middle and had to hold on to keep from being washed out, that Junior was on the side and washed out immediately. I have always remembered that guy saying about two hundred were lost, they were near the Azores Islands, just did not know correct figures at that time. Of course, my memory could be at fault!

There is another "saga" with Pvt. Turner but that will be given later under Mr. Hunsaker's story.

Pvt. Turner's sister and I have continued to correspond.

PVT. THOMAS B. TWILLEY
BORN: 15 June 1922, Delaware
Drafted: 3 July 1944
Died: 13 March 1945

Pvt. Twilley was 70-1/4" tall, weighed 152 pounds, had blue eyes and brown hair. He left behind a wife, mother and a brother. A War Department form is in the IDPF stating the telegram notifying his widow was sent to her on 26 March 1945. His personal effects are noted as follows:

> 1 garrison cap
> 2 New Testaments
> 1 leather folder w/picture
> 1 envelope w/pictures
> 1 Schaeffer fountain pin
> 1 belt buckle w/parachute insignia
> 2 sewing kits
> 3 booklets (type not stated)
> 1 five-cent piece
> 1 money belt without money
> 1 jacket

There is a letter from the Army Service Forces, Kansas City Quartermaster Depot pertaining to the above items:

"The Army Effects Bureau has received some personal effects belonging to your husband, Private Thomas B. Twilley.

This property is being forwarded to you in one carton and should reach you in the near future.

My action in transmitting the property does not, of itself, vest title in you. The items are forwarded in order that you may act as gratuitous bailee in caring for them pending the return of the owner, who has been reported missing in action. In the event he later is reported a casualty, and I sincerely hope he never is, it will be necessary that the property be turned over to the person or persons legally entitled to receive it.

When delivery has been made, I shall appreciate your acknowledging receipt by signing one copy of this letter in the space provided below, and returning it to this Bureau. For your convenience, there is inclosed an addressed envelope which needs no postage.

I regret the circumstances prompting this letter, and wish to express my hope for the safe return of your husband."

She signed and dated it May 4, 1945.

There is a letter in the IDPF regarding the Burial flag. A form requesting the flag is not in the file.

Pvt. Twilley's dental chart showed he had one cavity and 6 extractions, only one of which was his right upper wisdom tooth. He had received medical treatment at the ASF Regional Hospital from 12 January 1945 through 19 January 1945, and also treated at Ft. Benning, Georgia 25 January through 1 February 1945, reasons for treament not given.

His stations are noted as: IRTC, Fort McClellan, Alabama from 14 July 1944 through 15 November 1944; The Parachute School, Ft. Benning, Georgia from 16 November 1944 through 24 February 1945; then transferred to ACF Replacement Dep #1, Ft. George G. Meade, Maryland from 24 February. At the time of his going aboard the "Mac" he was listed with the G.T. 155(A) Platoon A, Infantry, Unassigned.

PVT. CARL S. WANAMAKER
Died: 13 March 1945

I received no response to my inquiry from National Archives.

PVT. EDWARD W. WECKMAN
BORN: 14 April 1912, Long Island
Drafted: 28 March 1944
Died: 13 March 1945

Pvt. Weckman was 67-1/4" tall, weighed 147 pounds, had blue eyes, and brown hair. His duty stations were as follows: Fort

George G. Meade, Maryland, from 28 March 1942 through 22 January 1942[2]. I found an obvious error between the time he was drafted and his first duty station. He was then transferred to Indiantown Gap, Pennsylvania from January 42 through 22 December 1944 and then on to Camp Reynolds, Pennsylvania in November 1944. There also appears to be an error here as well unless he was just "passing through" so to speak. His last organization is noted as Company B, 13th ASFTE. (Note discrepancies in the dates.)

Pvt. Weckman's dental chart shows 11 cavities, including all four wisdom teeth.

There is the letter on file regarding the Burial flag and his widow signed the application on October 1, 1946. A son, his father and a brother survived him.

PFC. JOHN WIECHERS
Died: 13 March 1945

I never had a response to the inquiry from National Archives.

PFC. HERMAN J. WILHELM, JR.
BORN: 7 March 1921, New Jersey
Enlisted: 6 July 1942
Died: 13 March 1945

The only information on Pfc. Wilhelm's duty stations does not show where he took basic training; however, it does show he was in Pittsburgh, Pennsylvania in March 1944 and then went to Fort Monmouth, New Jersey 20 March 1945. At some point he must have been in Camp Gruber, Oklahoma as he was hospitalized there from 19 August through 27 August 1942. He was 66" tall, weighed 123 pounds, had hazel eyes and brown hair.

His dental chart shows teeth in poor repair.

---

[2] Note discrepancies in his dates of service.

His mother signed the application for the Burial flag on September 16, 1946. A brother also survived Pfc. Wilhelm.

I have left off the cities of birth as well as the serial numbers of the men for security reasons with the exception of something unusual regarding the city/community of the birthplace.

PARTIAL LIST OF MEN WASHED OVERBOARD BUT RESCUED:

    PVT. GERALD O. BEERS
    TEC/3 JACOB E. COOK
    PFC. EDGAR FINSMITH
    PFC. ROBERT C. VanRAVENSWAAY

Tec/3 Cook was born 23 March 1922. His dates of service were from 9 December 1942 when he enlisted to 4 January 1942. His entry into the service took place in Fort Hayes, Ohio. His last known residence was also Ohio. His decorations and awards included the following: Good Conduct Medal, American Campaign Medal, World War II Victory Medal, European African Middle Easter Campaign Medal and with one Bronze Star. Additional research revealed Mr. Cook passed away in December 1992, at age 70.

The only information ascertained on Pfc. Finsmith was that he served from 19 March 1943 to 25 September 1945. His place of separation was Camp Edwards, Massachusetts. Pfc. VanRavenswaay was discharged from Boonville, Missouri.

LATER FOUND ALIVE DURING A ROLL CALL AFTER PRESUMED DROWNED:

PVT. OSCAR M. BUTLER
CPL. AUBREY R. DAILEY

MEN WHO SERVED BEFORE, DURING, AND AFTER COLLISION

ROBERT BOWMAN, ARMED GUARD
(telephone call October 12, 1999; later e-mails)
Born in 1924, reared in Farmville, Virginia
Graduated from Farmville High School, 1942

"I volunteered for the Navy on 18 December 1942, and went to Basic Training at United States Naval Training Center, Great Lakes, Illinois. I was then sent to Gunnery School for one month at Gulf Port, Mississippi. I boarded a gunboat in the Gulf of Mexico, fired one round from a 4-inch 50 [cal] World War I Naval Gun. Then I was sent to New Orleans to the United States Naval Armed Guard Center for ship assignment, then to Jacksonville, Florida to catch the first Liberty ship built at the St. Johns' shipyard where we put guns aboard the ship. The workers teased us that the ship might break up because it was the first Liberty ship they had ever built; the ship was named the *SS Ponce-de Leon*, took two days of sea trials, then sailed to New York where we took aboard four M-60 tanks.

I made two trips to Liverpool, England, one trip to Bizerte, North Africa; one trip to Palermo, Sicily, and Naples, Italy. On the return trip from Sicily we anchored at the harbor of Bizerte and one night German Dornier Bombers came over to bomb the oil dumps on the beach. That day we dryfired (without ammunition) at U.S. Fighter planes and one sailor fired a 5-inch 38 [cal] and to cut down on sunglare, he put a sunglass lens in the gunsite. During the night, as usual three bombers came right across our bow. He couldn't see the planes because of the sunglass. He got three days in the brig on bread and water. Funny thing, he got more food than we did. During some of those trips, we stopped at Gibraltar, a British "possession," Oran, and Algiers, both in Africa.

I spent 11 months on the *Ponce-de Leon*. I took a few days leave and returned to Brooklyn United States Naval Armed Guard Center for a ship assignment. I was assigned to the United States Army Transport, the *General James W. McAndrew*.

We made three trips to Naples, Italy; two trips to Glasgow, Scotland; one trip to Marseilles, France, and one trip to Cherbourg, France. I think we also made a trip to Ireland or Wales.

My 30th trip across the North Atlantic and five days out of New York, on a very black stormy night we were in a convoy of about 40 ships. We had a collision. We were the second ship in the second column on the port side of the convoy and the French aircraft carrier, the *Bearn*,[3] was the first ship in the third column of the convoy on the port side. She lost her ability to steer when her electronic steering mechanism broke down. I might mention the *Bearn* was returning to France after a refit in the United States as a result of her breakdown. We rammed her stern or fantail at the time of the collision. Having been a coxswain, I was aft waking up the 4 to 8 watch at 3:30 a.m. I did not realize we had collided with the *Bearn* until I heard screaming voices. We had a ladder or steps from the crews' quarters up to the main deck; for this reason I was able to hear the screams. It was not until I went up on open deck that I realized we had had a collision. We had aboard some Air Force personnel and a contingent of paratroops. The paratroopers were not a part of the 82nd or 101st Airborne Divisions. We lost 113 paratroopers, one Armed Guard sailor (Inman) from our gun crew, and five sailors from the *Bearn* [actually the number of men lost was four]. A destroyer escort picked up 13 of the paratroopers. Some of these numbers was told to me. I was told if the watertight doors had not been electric, the ship probably would have sunk. It was while in the Azores I learned that President Roosevelt had passed away.

---

[3] I don't know the Bearn's name prior to collision. I was told the collision was caused by a breakdown in her electronic steering mechanism. I had no knowledge of any gold aboard the Bearn. Someone told me after the war the McAndrew was renamed African Queen (should be African Enterprise). She ended up at the James River Fleet basin down in Tidewater, Virginia. One year before she was towed to Baltimore to be scrapped, I went to see her; needless to say I was one year late.

The Chaplain was a major and the medical doctor was also a major. I had to have emergency surgery for removal of my appendix and almost bled to death.

We did not sink because the *McAndrew* was a cargo/passenger vessel prior to the war and consequently, we had electronic watertight doors; otherwise, I feel confident we would have sunk. I don't know where the *Bearn* went for repairs. We sailed at about 3 knots to the Island of St. Michael or Michel, in the Azores Islands. The Azores was under the control of the Portuguese and was neutral. I do not know about the German tankers that might have been there. [This is information I received from one of the other survivors.] We stayed there about two weeks, got shored up by the Seabees. A British transport picked up all of our transit personnel and took them to France. We, at reduced speed, returned to Baltimore, Maryland where, as I understand it, the *McAndrew* was repaired and made a number of trips to South Africa. There were times when the *McAndrew* even brought back wounded Germans as well as injured American servicemen.

I took some leave, reported to Norfolk and subsequently rode a troop train to Treasure Island, San Francisco. I am quite sure I did not have to go to the Pacific; however, I had no love for Navy bases. I just wanted to be at sea. I could have stayed at Treasure Island but I chose to become a member of a Port Director's Unit at Nagasaki, Japan. I had 15 sailors under me and we hit about five islands named Johnston, Kwajalein, Guam, Iwo Jima, and Okinawa before arriving at Nagasaki.

We stayed on each island about one week and our transportation was via Marine Air Transit Systems. As you know, Nagasaki was hit by the Atomic Bomb around 1945. When we entered Nagasaki, radiation had been cleared. Needless to say it was a sight to see.

I came home on a refrigeration ship and we docked in San Francisco. I then rode the train home."

Mr. Bowman also gave me the name and address of another survivor in Gastonia, NC I wrote him 22 November 1999; the letter was not returned nor was a reply ever received. I contacted the police department and they did not recognize the name.

He also gave me the name and address of another survivor and Mr. Harris's information will be found later.

I continue to keep in touch with Mr. Bowman through his daughter.

PAUL R. BROSIUS, ARMED GUARD, New Jersey

"I am very sorry it took so long to answer your letter of October 21, 1999.

Yes, I served two tours aboard the *J. W. McAndrew*; this was after the collision. We were a new guard crew except for the gunnery officer so none of us were on board at the time.

My first trip on the *McAndrew* we brought home wounded troops from Marseilles, France, docking at Hampton Roads, Virginia; this was not a pleasant trip.

My second and last trip on the *McAndrew* we brought home a load of low point[4] paratroops that were being transferred to the Pacific; none of us were happy about this. After we left Marseilles, Japan surrendered. As we were nearing the east coast the Captain came on

---

[4] These men did not have enough points to be discharged from active duty.

the intercom and told us to look to the stern of the ship and as we watched, we saw the wake turn north and the Captain said we were being re-routed to the States. What a happy gang! All the crap games stopped and talk of going home prevailed.

We docked at Hampton Roads where the troops and gun crew debarked. My wife came down to Norfolk and several days later we headed for the Brooklyn Armed Guard Center. She left me in Philadelphia. I waited at the center for transfer to the Philadelphia Navy Yard while I waited for a transfer to Camp Perry, Virginia for discharge. This came on 6 February 1946 and I was discharged on 7 February.

Enclosed are newspaper clippings of the *McAndrews* docking with the paratroops, some of the guard crew and other information. I'm sorry I cannot recall any of the crew's names. I do remember our boatswain was from upstate Pennsylvania.

9,846 Debarks Due Here Sunday

Only 70 persons are listed as due to arrive in Newport News today at Hampton Roads Port of Embarkation, but there will be a great increase tomorrow with 9,846 scheduled to arrive. Yesterday saw a total of 9,612 debarks.

Coming in yesterday were the General Squier with 3,944 aboard; the J. W. McAndrew with 2,442; Eltinge with 3,206, and the J. D. Yeager with 20. Due in today are the J. C. Osgood with 24; and the T. Parker with 46.

A number of local and Hampton men came in on the four ships arriving yesterday. They were:

Pfc. Riley A. Arnold, 214 36th St.; Sgt. Wilbert M. Jonas, 1610 Ivy Ave.; Pvt. Carroll L. Pope, 1035 23rd St.; Pfc. Charles Avent, 1163 41st St.; Kenneth O. Grimmer, 3538 Eilers St.; Pvt. Arthur M. Urice, and the following from Hampton: Sgt. Charles A. Carter, 524 Hampton Ave.; Cpl. John B. Williams, 915 Buckroe Rd.; T/4 Gordon L. Cheek, 224 North King St.; Pvt. Odell Jackson, 435 Day St.

Ships and the total aboard each, due in tomorrow, are Noordam, 2453; P. Holland, 43; Exceller, 675; R. Amundsen, 11; Breckenridge, 5940; Escanoba Victory, 16; H. Solomon, 708; The D. S. Wright, originally scheduled for here, has been diverted to New York city.

At Newport News—(Aboard Charles Carroll) 36 casuals. (Aboard Mahlon Titney) 24 casuals. (Aboard J. W. McAndrew) 1913 troops including Headquarters and Headquarters Battery 10th Armored Division Artillery: Military Police Platoon, 10th Armored Division: 55th Armored Engineer Battalion: 90th Cavalry Reconnaisance Squadron. (Aboard Gen. Breckinridge) 5,200 troops, including several units of the 10th Armored Division: 3rd and 11th Tank Battalions: 20th and 54th

Aboard McAndrew: 2,442 troops, including 349th troop carrier group; 23d, 92d, 312th, 313th, 314th Troop Carrier Squadrons; Advance Detachment of 91st and 94th, Troop Carrier Squadrons; 107th, 109th, 161st Tactical Reconnaisance Squadron; 3548th Ordnance Company.
Aboard Eltinge: 3,206 troops including 562d, 563d, 564th and 565th Port Companies; 293d Military Police Company Type C; Headquarters and Headquarters Detachment of 614th Quartermaster Battalion; 3904th Quartermaster Truck Company; 283d Field Artillery Battalion; 48th General Hospital Group; 71st Military Police Company; 80th Station Hospital Group; 71st Military Police Company; 86th Station Hospital Group.
Aboard Yeager: Miscellaneous troops.

I also served aboard the *SS Thomas Todd* and the *SS Janet Lord Roper.*

Well, that is all for now and have a Happy New Year.

P.S. We are having a 6 to 8-inch snowstorm right now. Also, I sent Tom a copy of this information."

Mr. Brosius and I have continued to be in touch with each other at Christmas with cards.

"Received your letter of 3 February and am very sorry I could not answer sooner. I will not be coming to the reunion in May as we have a vacation planned for that time.

I'm sorry I confused you about the paratroops. We picked them up in Marseilles and were taking them through the Panama Canal when we were diverted to Hampton Roads. They were to receive a 30-day leave and then head for the Pacific.

The first trip was to bring back casualties. The photographs I sent were taken aboard the *McAndrews*; the others were taken aboard the *Thomas Todd* showing the port of Antwerp, Belgium. Also any pictures and information I send you can be reprinted unless otherwise stated.

AMERICA'S SONS COME HOME—Pictured above are the cheering troops aboard the Army transport J. W. McAndrew, as they arrived here yesterday after being diverted to an American port on their way to the Pacific war theater. In the center above the banner of the 86th Airborne, 101st Divisions, which read "From the Sky We Lead," is Capt. Curtis B. Strott of Beaumont, Texas.

I have no stories to tell about the *McAndrews*. I was an acting gunner's mate on the stern of the ship. Each time we docked in the States my wife would travel to see me or I would go home.

I did not know the *McAndrews* was formerly the 'Deltargentino'. How come the name change?"

Note: The name was changed when the military took over the ship to be used as a transport.

ARTHUR DELLEDONNE, ARMED GUARD, New Jersey

On 14 September 2000, I received first contact from Mr. Delledonne. His letter states:

"Received your letter a few days ago and I would be happy to give you any information of the collision of March 13, 1945 of the *USAT James W. McAndrew*. I believe the man who gave you my name and address must have been the U.S. Army photographer on board. My own list of men I served with disappeared somehow when I moved to my present address in 1977.

However, I still recall the events that happened approximately at 03:45 AM. My rank at that time was Signalman Third Class, and was on watch in the bridge at that time. Apparently, the French (baby) aircraft carrier lost their steering and crashed into the starboard bow.

The photos that I possess show the burial at sea of only the one U.S. Navy lookout (Armed Guard Inman) killed instantly. Our ship's position (5 column-2), the carrier was at position (6 column-1). The destroyer escorts fell back with us to pick up as many Army survivors possible. It was my belief that up to 90 armed men perished, though never confirmed. (The loudspeakers aboard always cautioned the men to sleep with their life vests on).

We were escorted to Ponta Delgada in the Portuguese-owned Azores Islands where our ship underwent temporary repairs. I'm not sure how long we were there before returning to Newport News, Virginia. The citizens of Ponta Delgada were very hospitable to all our crew. They seemed to have numerous relatives in Connecticut, USA.

Thereafter, I was assigned to a "Liberty Ship" named *SS Reinhold Richter*, carrying jeeps and other military equipment. We proceeded through Panama Canal to Eniwetok and then to Manila Bay in the Philippines. We anchored there awhile never getting ashore. The Department of the Navy then ordered us back to New Orleans without ever delivering the equipment on board. Apparently the war was over.

P.S. I will be happy to mail you the collision photos with the condition they are returned to me. Any use of the information enclosed will have my permission for your use."

Note: He did send the photographs; they were copied and returned.

GEORGE DRAGOVICH, SR., ARMED GUARD

I have had only one brief note from Mr. Dragovich. It reads as follows:

"I went aboard the latter part of September 1942. They were replacing 50-cal. machine guns with new 20-mm. I was the first loader on one 4/50[5] aft. We also had two 3/50[6] forward and eight 20-mm.

They loaded supplies, parts, and material for the Air Force Ground Personnel. One thousand five hundred (1,500)-ground personnel were brought aboard.

---

[5] The 4/50 is a four inch 50 (four inch bore and length of barrel is 200 inches (4 times 50) and is a shell gun as opposed to the powder bag/projective gun. It does not serve as an anti-aircraft gun.

[6] The 3/50 is a three inch 50 (barrel is 150 inches long,) is a shell gun, and also serves as an anti-aircraft gun.

Also brought aboard were six dual 40-mm guns and fastened them to the deck as additional firepower.

We formed a convoy in New York Harbor and moved out. We didn't know where we were going but we landed in Casablanca where I celebrated my 18th birthday.

We returned to the States in December 1942. I left the ship in the latter part of that month.

In Our Bond,"

JAMES R. GABLE, SR., ARMED GUARD, Pennsylvania

"My name is James R. Gable and not John R. (I had been given the incorrect name at the National Reunion). I served on the *J. W. McAndrew* from July 26, 1943 to May 8, 1944. I was a pointer on the bow with three 50-cal. guns and standing watch four hours on and eight hours off.

Photo courtesy of James Gable

We went into Iceland in 1943 to deliver troops to the occupying forces. We were in Oran, Algeria in North Africa in 1943. We were there when the Italians surrendered. We carried 2,000 troops into North Africa.

I was not on board at the time of the collision.

I made nine trips across the Atlantic Ocean during my tour of duty. Most of our trips were carrying 2,000 troops each trip into Scotland building up for the invasion of France in 1944.

On one trip we carried Robert Preston, the movie star, into Scotland. I think it was in 1942. Most of my trips on the *J. W. McAndrew* were just regular trips carrying troops overseas and troops returning to the States.

Photo courtesy of James Gable

The convoys were pretty well protected by destroyers, cruisers, and on one trip we had the battleship Arkansas with us."

A second letter was received on 18 June 2000:

I'm sending the photographs 56 years apart—that's a long time.

Lt. Robert Preston was in the Army Air Corps and we unloaded them in Scotland in 1943 or 1944. I never heard from him the rest of the war.

I'd like to relate a story that happened to one of our Merchant Marine personnel on board in 1942 or 1944. I can't even remember his name.

We had rough seas crossing the Atlantic in the summer. He was up topside in one of the lifeboats securing it when he fell overboard in the early morning; it was still dark. This was radioed to the Commodore of the Convoy. He dispatched a destroyer to look for him for quite some time. They radioed back that they had no luck in finding him. They were told to look for another hour. It was just getting light and lo and behold, they found him! He was not returned to the *McAndrew*.

Photos courtesy of James Gable

Some time later in the States in New York, he came aboard to visit. He was a lot less weight than he had been. I guess God took care of him. I can't remember his name or what year it was.

I can relate a story about the *McAndrew* in North Africa during an air raid. So the story goes, shrapnel hit one of our Navy Armed Guard sailors. He was unstrapped from the gun; I believe it was a 20-mm.

A Merchant Seaman who was the Officer's Steward who served their meals and took care of their living quarters laid the wounded Armed Guard sailor aside and strapped himself into the gun and began firing at the German planes. I don't remember his name. OK, how could you verify this action? I was not aboard when it happened; I heard about it after we got on board. (I have been unable to confirm this action.)

I guess there are lots of stories out there of things that happened on board the *McAndrew*. We hit a storm in the North Atlantic that was a severe storm. It damaged the *McAndrew's* forward gun tub that had two 3:50-cal guns in it. The guns and two ammunition-ready boxes were torn loose from the deck. The ammunition was rolling around, the 3-50's were damaged and had to be replaced; the gun tub was bent and had to be repaired.

We went into dry dock to repair steel plates on the bow of the ship. I wish I could remember times and dates but 56 years ago is a long time.

It may be in the ship's records (these were destroyed years ago according to information received) if they still exist.

Sure was a long time ago. How many men were killed in the collision with the French aircraft carrier? (Four)

Wish I had more news of the *McAndrew* for you."

ORELL S. HARRIS, ARMED GUARD, Tennessee

In a telephone conversation with Mr. Harris 16 September 1999, he related that he is a survivor of the collision where 68 men were washed out to sea and drowned 13 March 1945. The collision occurred approximately 50 miles southeast of the Azores (Portugal owned). Unfortunately, he did not know our young man (Pvt. Turner); however since he and his wife live so close to where he came from, they will go to the high school and newspaper trying to locate a photograph and obituary or news article about the collision and/or his death. Mr. Harris was in the Azores when President Roosevelt died.

He also believed his entire gun crew were killed at the time of the collision (one died, one lived) as they were on watch on the front gun turrets. Inman, the one buried at sea, was on the top gun turret and he fell to the deck dying on impact." Mr. Harris also gave me permission to put anything he relates or pictures he sends in this book.

Photos courtesy Mrs. Orell Harris

When I told him how blessed I felt, he said, "Well, I've been waiting all these years for someone to come along and write the story and now that you're interested, we'll help you all we can." His wife, Marjorie, also talked with me and was as enthusiastic as her husband. She's 78.

My husband and I attended the Armed Guard National Reunion in Fort Mitchell, Kentucky in May 2000. The Chairman of The Pointer, the quarterly Armed Guard Newsletter, Mr. C. A. Lloyd, told me Mr. Harris was expected. I informed him that I had already checked at the front desk about his arrival and was told a cancellation had been made.

Inasmuch as we were going to Hurricane Mills, Tennessee and Mr. Harris's home was not that far away, we decided we would go visit. Prior to arriving at the Harris home, I telephoned and that was when I learned that Mr. Harris had passed on May 11th; hence, the cancellation.

In a brief note dated 2 February 2001, Mrs. Harris would be moving to be near her daughter in Florida. I never heard from her again. Mrs. Harris requested return of the photographs she had sent me showing her husband in his uniform as a young man and then as he looked several years ago. I had to tell her I had never received any photographs. Much to my surprise early in September *2005*, I received an envelope with another envelope inside, mailed November 29, 2000. Inside were the photographs Mrs. Harris stated she had mailed. I wrote that I had finally received them; albeit four plus years later but the letter was returned as "forwarding address expired." If she is still alive and reads this, I will be more than happy to return these photographs.

EUGENE E. HOLLY, INFANTRY, Florida

"I really don't recall an accident such as you describe either going to Germany or returning. I just don't recall the exact date I went to the ETO. I did however join an infantry unit that was at several concentration camps. I continued on to Berlin, Germany where I remained until returning stateside about 13 December or 20 December 1946 aboard the *J. W. McAndrew*. I have pictures of the ship dockside in New York Harbor with us on it. I was discharged 26 December 1946 at nearby Fort Dix, New Jersey.

I have a copy of several ships' history that you are aware of and a picture of the *J. W. McAndrew*. I wish I could be of further help to you so let me know.

By the way, who was the other soldier that gave you my name? I might recall or remember running into him. And by the way, let me know about the book. Sounds interesting."

JOHN F. HUNSUCKER, SR., INFANTRY

I received this e-mail 29 December 2001:

"My dad was on the *USS McAndrews* during the collision. This has been a very emotional thing for him to talk about even after all of these years. We found your web site right before Christmas and we were so excited to be able to get the pictures and information. My mother didn't want us to show my dad until after Christmas. My father's name is John F. Hunsucker and he was in the Army. He was just being transported on the *McAndrews* as replacements to go overseas. He said that he didn't know anyone very well on this ship.

Photo courtesy of the family of John Hunsucker

My Dad received basic training at Camp Hood, Texas—tank destroyers. He took Signal Corp Training—Boehme High Speed Radio Transmission. Then he went to Camp Crowder, Missouri, Fort Monmouth, New Jersey, and Camp Gordon, Georgia. He was then assigned to the staging area for overseas at Fort Meade, Maryland. The "Mac" was in a 128-ship convoy. After the collision we drifted for about a week until we reached the Azores Islands. The British ship, "Athelone Castle" picked me up and took us to Liverpool, England. From there we went to London by train. We transferred to Southhampton, England on another train and started on the Dunnator Castle ship for LeHarve, France. This ship developed engine trouble and had to return to port. We transferred to another ship called *Sobieski* took us to France.

In France we got on boxcars called "Fourty & Eight Army trucks that took us to the front where I was assigned to the "14th Army Division".

He met Bryan Turner, Jr. on deck and they talked for hours. Then Bryan was lost at sea that very night. My father has always wished that he could find Bryan's relatives to let them know that he was with him the last hours of his life. My father has never wanted to talk about this accident because it is very emotional for him now. Your web site has provided him with pictures and he feels that he can talk and tell us things that he has never been able to talk about. Please write me back and let me know how we can get more information. We live in North Carolina. Hope to hear from you real soon. My name is Mary. Thanks!"

In another letter: "My Dad has given me some additional information that I think you had asked him for earlier. My Dad enlisted in the Army on 10 December 1942 and called to active duty on 23 March 1943. He was in a jeep accident on 7 January 1946 near Pont-A-Mousson, France. The steering mechanism went out causing the jeep to crash into a tree. The engine crushed my Dad's legs and he was in different hospitals for over one year. He was given an honorable discharge from Oliver General Hospital, Augusta, Georgia on 15 April 1947."

I received verbal permission from Bryan Turner's sister to give Mr. Hunsucker her telephone number; they did get to talk to each other about that night her brother was lost at sea.

GEORGE KUIPERS, ARMED GUARD, Florida

I received one letter from Mr. Kuipers in November 1999. "In reply to your inquiry re: my involvement or knowledge of the unfortunate collision of the *USAT J. W. McAndrew* on March 13, 1945. I'm sorry I have nothing to offer, as I was detached from the *McAndrew* after serving 13 months as the U.S. Navy Gunnery Officer. I was sent to the Naval Training (Sub-Chaser Training Center) Miami, Fla. April 1944.

I wish you better luck in gathering information that would be useful in writing your book. In the period I was aboard "Mac" we made seven round trips across the Pond (Atlantic Ocean) between the east coast of USA and either the western coast of UK or the various ports in the Mediterranean such as Oran, Casablanca, and Algiers. The ship was assigned to the British Admiralty for three months during my tenure and this entailed taking British troops from UK to the Mediterranean and returning with German prisoners (2600) to be disembarked in Glasgow, Scotland.

During my 13 months aboard the Mac, the closest we came to "action" was a granddaddy of hurricanes experienced on our return voyage to the USA at

Photos courtesy of John Kuipers

Christmas 1942. We lost one of our escorts, a Destroyer Escort, with all HANDS aboard.

Good luck with your book. I never met any of the people you mentioned in your letter.

Yours truly"

On March 20, 2000, I received a brief note from Mrs. Kuipers. "This letter is to notify you that my husband, George Kuipers, died on March 9. He is on your mailing list re the *J. W. McAndrew*. He enjoyed your correspondence and was sorry that he could not offer more information."

LEONARD S. PATRICIA, ARMED GUARD, Massachusetts

"To Whom It May Concern:

I am a survivor of the collision that occurred March 17, 1944 (St. Patrick's Day)—note he has given the incorrect date—at 3:40 a.m. I was 19 years old at the time and a member of the Navy Armed Guard Gun Crew. I was due on my watch at 4 a.m. We were in a collision with the French aircraft carrier *Bearn*. The man who I was going to relieve was killed at the starboard bow. His name was Carl Inman and he was from Indianapolis, Indiana. He was buried at sea. We lost about 200 Army men of the 101st Airborne Division (Screaming Eagles) who were sleeping in the #1 compartment at the bow of the transport of the *J. W. McAndrew*. As I was on my way to my post at the 3-inch gun, I could hear the screams of the men in the water. It was pitch dark and the ship was listing to starboard side where I was and I could hear them but could not see them. All I could hear was the sound of the mess kits banging away and the screams of "help me." I found out we were near the Azores Island of Faile.

After proceeding at 4 knots we went to the Island of St. Michael, Ponta Delgada, Azores, a Portuguese possession for temporary repairs for a month and then to Baltimore, Maryland to dry dock where I left the ship to go on furlough and then to another ship.

I have no objections of this information being contained in your book."

He referred me to Orell S. Harris whose correspondence is noted earlier.

RUSSELL A. PEACE, 74th TANK BATTALION, U.S. ARMY, Indiana

"I was born January 22, 1926, in Colman, Kentucky. I was drafted March 17, 1944, taking my basic training in the Quartermaster Corps, Camp Lee, Virginia." This information was obtained during a telephone conversation on June 9, 2000, after he had left a message to call him. As a point of interest, some twelve years later is where I took basic training at Fort Lee, Virginia.

Photo courtesy of Russell and Ethel Peace

Over the following months, Mr. Peace asked me to make sure people know that the Holocaust really happened. He was there; he witnessed first hand what happened. There will be more about this later. He also forwarded photographs of the *McAndrew* in which he shows where his bunk was in the water and where he was playing cards and "shooting the breeze" at the time. He also included a photograph of the *Bearn*. Also included is a photograph of the burial at sea of Carlos Inman (these are included with Inman's section). He has marked the location of Orell Harris and where Mr. Peace was located at that time but he is not in the actual photograph.

In a letter dated June 4, 2000, Mr. Peace states: "You probably have most of the information and pictures from the Internet but you are free to use anything I tell you. I am sure you will find conflicting information being so many people involved. Examples: 77 men lost, 9 picked up alive and the *Bearn* rammed the Mac; there would have been less death and damage had the Mac rammed the *Bearn*. The "Mac" weighed 8,000 tons, the *Bearn* 28,000 tons.

Three days and nights out from New York and 380 miles north of the Azores in convoy, the aircraft carrier *Bearn* sailing along side to our right crossed our path hitting our ship in the bow and going right through number one compartment. I was in number 2 lower compartment and the water was coming through our ceiling. They had to seal the doors between upper and lower 2 and with the men still inside in order to keep the ship from sinking and pump compressed air in where we had been to make the bulkhead strong enough to hold back the sea.

When we got up on deck the water was knee deep on deck and it was thought that some men ran right on overboard thinking the ship was already going down. I was forced over against an air vent leading to number 1 compartment and had to hear the sounds from down there just inches from my feet. By then we could feel the water hit the right side of your knee and then come back on the left side.

This happened at 4:00 a.m., Tuesday morning March 13 in black darkness and in a few minutes there was a large plane overhead flashing lights across the deck (from where I know not). The two crippled ships floated side by side for four days and nights at 4 knots per hour until 9:00 a.m. Saturday morning. A destroyer escort was front and back, out of our sight, but we could hear the depth charges being dropped, as there was an enemy submarine in the water.

We got in port at mid-afternoon, but the Azores belonged to Portugal (neutral country) and we had to lay on the deck of the Mac for another seven days. One thousand eight hundred GIs and Navy Crew.

We were picked up by a British liner said to be the third largest in the world (name forgotten) and dropped off at Liverpool, England, crossed England on train (flying box car) to South Hampton. I boarded another large ship but halfway across the English Channel, the ship burst a piston and couldn't make it through the minefields. We returned to England and boarded another ship and unloaded in LaHarve, France. Never saw much action other than at the liberation of Dachau Concentration Camp.

Some people think the Mac was a passenger ship but was a converted freighter designed to haul 1800 troops because when the water rushed in the bunks folded up like shelves with the men in them.

I don't recall the "B" Platoon, 1st Replacement Battalion. I was assigned to Headquarters Company, 47th Tank Battalion, 14th Armored Division. However, considering the problem, we were scattered all over.

Please, in your book try to help the next generation to know there truly was a Holocaust and our political leaders to understand the true cost of war.

Thank you.

P.S. The only recreation we had was during daylight hours was tossing nickels over the side of the ship to the Portuguese in canoes. We watched them dive to get the nickel before it got to the bottom and they would come up so mad because it was only a penny."

Mr. Peace also sent copies of letters he had mailed to his girlfriend at the time after the censoring of the mail was stopped. "There are so many small details that I have forgotten because from 1945 to 1994, 46 years, I tried to bury it all. You may have questions about the person I called "Fuggy" in the letter. He was my best friend, James R. Wickham from Eau Gallin, Florida. He went to Japan. I was never able to contact him because the little town of Eau Gallin was destroyed to make room for the space center, Cape Canaveral, now Kennedy. Best of luck."

The Letters

March 14, 1945

"Hello Sweetheart,

I am lying up on deck in the sun, thinking of the little woman, as usual. We sure have had a time but should hit land sometime tonight or tomorrow. We had quite a bit of trouble but I won't try to tell you about it now for I don't know whether the censors want us to write about it or not. They haven't said but I will wait until later to tell you about it. Fuggy and I are both well and doing fine. Honey, I sure would love to see you right now. I sure will be glad when we get to some land.

"Mickledorf, Germany
May 22, 1945
Hello Sweetheart,

How I wish I could write you more often but I just don't get time. Well, they have cut out censoring our mail so I will try and write about my trip over.

I left New York the 7th of March. Well, everything went along smoothly until Sunday the 11th; we had a bad storm. The ship did a lot of lurching and rocking with water coming over deck now and then, but the storm gradually broke away and the ocean calmed down some.

On Tuesday morning of the 13th it happened. A little before four o'clock in the morning I awakened with one of my nervous jittery feelings. I lay awake about fifteen minutes, tossing restlessly in my bed. Then it hit at four in the morning when everyone was sleeping. It sounded at first like we had hit ice the way the ship quivered and jerked, then a steady murmur of the engines suddenly raced.

In a few seconds I was out of bed, fully dressed, and standing by my bed awaiting orders. Then I heard water coming through the bulkhead from the compartment ahead of ours, not very much water but enough that I knew something bad had happened, and the compartment from which the water came was where Fuggy was sleeping. The next thing I knew we were moving out up on deck. It was raining and there was water everywhere. When the ship would rock, water would run back and forth across the deck. We couldn't tell so much about what had happened, it being dark.

What really had happened was a French Aircraft Carrier loaded with planes that had been along side of our ship about five hundred yards away since the convoy had left New York, had suddenly lost use of its rudder and had cut across our course. It rammed into the bow of our ship about twenty feet from the front. It completely smashed the front of our ship the front of our ship and made a hole large enough you could have driven a two and a half-ton cargo truck through it right where Fuggy was sleeping.

There I was up on deck and it so dark I couldn't see my hand before me. I could hear the water churning back and forth down in the hole where Fuggy had been sleeping. I kept asking myself over and over, "How could he have possibly gotten out." Then it began to get daylight and I started hunting for Fuggy. Well, I couldn't find a man from that number one compartment where the ship had been hit and where Fuggy had been sleeping. I heard a rumor that not a man had gotten out alive. Well, you or no one else can imagine how I felt. No Fuggy. I searched for what seemed like hours and still no Fuggy. About eight o'clock I had given up hope of finding him and was standing listening to that dreadful sound of the water churning back and forth where he had been sleeping. I decided to try once more to see if he was aboard the ship.

I went back through the ship and came to the florier, a place I had covered a dozen times before looking for him, and what did I see? There he sat, reared back like he owned what was left of the ship, half dressed with a blanket thrown over his shoulders. Well, I never was so glad to see anyone as I was, him right then as I had been thinking he had gone down with the others and then finding him there alive and well. Sixty-eight of the boys were drowned without a chance to fight for their lives. Some of them were Fuggy and my buddies. We had sat on Fuggy's bunk and talked and told yarns at ten o'clock the night before. Fuggy later told me the way things were down there when it happened, a terrible mess, and he told me how he managed to get out.

For four days we floated along at four knots speed, wondering if we would ever see land again. It had happened right in the middle of the Atlantic. At night you couldn't put your foot down on deck without stepping on someone. We were piled everywhere, not having any place to sleep. And then on Saturday morning, we sighted land, the Azores Islands, and were glad. I will never forget going down inside the ship and telling Fuggy there was land ahead. We landed that afternoon.

We spent seven days living on the crowded ship. Then on the 24th a British ship came by and picked us up. We landed in Liverpool, England. I think it was about the 28th of March. We crossed England by train to South Hampton where we got on another English boat and started to France. We got halfway across the English Channel and one of the engines burst a piston so we had to turn and go back to England.

Next we got on a Polish boat and were crossing the English Channel on Easter Sunday. We got off the boat in France the following day.

Well, I was separated from Fuggy in LaHarve, just after we landed. I was in four or five replacement depots in France, then into Germany. At long last I joined my outfit, the 47th Tank Battalion.

I can't remember the names of the towns I was in in France; I remember one was named Toul. When I get back home we will get a map and I will try and point out the route I took through France and Germany.

Well, that's the story. If I had gone into details as I went along I would have never gotten it written, but I have pretty well covered the story, and a long letter, too.

Say hon, you can make this public. Be sure and let Mom and them read it for I don't want to write the same story over.

It is getting late so Bye for now. Good night. Sweet dreams. Love forever."

In a note dated July 17: "Here are a few samples of material to help you verify dates, towns, etc.

Again, I'm sorry I worked with so many outfits, but you don't have a choice as to where you are being sent. I sent you e-mail last night. From time to time, I'm sure you will notice me repeating myself. Just use the material you need. My closest buddy's name was JAMES R. WICKHAM, nickname "Fuzzy—not Fuggy."

Dachau, Germany
July 28, 1945
Monday 7:50 p.m.

"Hello there Honey,

Well, I started receiving my mail today. I got four letters from you, one V-mail and three airmail; the latest was written the 9th. I sure was glad to get them after waiting for over a week. I don't see why I haven't heard from Mom before now. It has been a long time since I heard from her. I guess I will write her and Pop tomorrow night.

I spent most of yesterday searching for water for the company. I am hauling water from Munich now. That was the closest water point I could find. I went for a walk last night and ended up at a dance. Of course I didn't do any dancing, but I watched. Oh, they sure had a time. The people were all Polish, Russian, Rumanian,

Hungarian, Checs, etc., except for a half dozen American soldiers.

Hon, about the chewing gum. Don't bother to send it. You use it. After all, he didn't get it for me. How's everyone getting along? Tell them all I said hello.

I am sitting up on the upper porch and it sure is nice and cool. I have a little writing table to write on. Hon, tell "Hotshot" I said 'Yes, I need all the chocolate I can get. Ha Ha.' Well, I sure was glad to get the mail today and I hope it continues to come okay.

I guess this is about all the news for now. Take care and be good night and Sweet Dreams.

Love always,"

Dachau, Germany
July 31, 1945

"Hello Sweetheart,

Well, well. What are you doing tonight? It is eight o'clock here right now so I guess it is along in the afternoon back home, so I guess you are sleeping, huh?

I got a letter from Mom today. Sure was glad to get it. I heard from you yesterday; maybe I will again tomorrow.

Things are still dull around here. Nothing new ever happens. Maybe an SS gets shot now and then, but that isn't news. Another last night; they haven't sense enough to act right and stay alive. I was on guard from two to four this morning."

Haag, Germany
November 8, 1945
"Thinking of You

Hello Sweetheart,

I will drop you a few lines this morning to say hello and let you know I am still getting along okay and feeling fine. I hope this letter finds you getting along okay.

It will soon be dinnertime but I thought I would knock out a few lines to you before I eat. It is twenty minutes till twelve right now.

Honey, I got four letters from you yesterday and I sure was glad to get them. I also got one from Mom. Hon, I sure am looking forward to that box of candy you are sending to me. I hope it gets here soon. I look for it every day.

Well, I guess everyone is stripping tobacco now. I sure wish I was there helping you, don't you? The weather here is cool and cloudy, rains a little now and then and then not any too nice weather. I guess the snow will be flying soon."

I have continued to receive e-mails from Russell and Ethel Peace. He has not been at all well the past three years and rarely goes out of their home. He has continually asked me to make sure I write about Dachau Concentration Camp. I have continually responded that I couldn't write about something that I had only heard on the news or in the movies. After about six months of coaxing, he finally sent me the following.

"On the last Sunday of April 1945, the first Allied soldier, an American scout of Polish descent, came through the gate of the main Dachau camp. The few Nazis in the tower watched apprehensively. They were no longer there as guards; they had been ordered to stay on merely to complete the formalities of surrender. The upper ranks had already fled, to blend in among the German civilian population. The young American's first impression, later detailed in an interview, was one of 'glaring chaos', thousands of ragged skeletons in the yard, in the trees, waving little rags, climbing over one another, hysterical, completely out of control.

The scout went back for support and returned with a small detachment. The flags of many allied nations had suddenly appeared. Apparently the prisoners had been secretly piecing them together over the months from tatters and patches and strips of cloth. One prisoner, a Polish priest, exuberantly kissed an officer, learning later to his glee that she was Marguerite Higgins of the New York Herald Tribune, the first American war correspondent to report on Dachau. A military chaplain came forward and asked that all who could do so to join him in a prayer of thanksgiving.

Soon the advance scouts were joined by other Allied soldiers and one of the German guards came forward to surrender with what he believed would be the usual military protocol. He emerged in full regalia, wearing all his decorations. He had only recently been billeted to Dachau from the Russian front. He saluted and barked, 'Heil Hitler.'

An American officer looked down and around at mounds of rotting corpses, at thousands of prisoners shrouded in their own filth. He hesitated only a moment, then spat in the Nazi's face, snapping 'Schweinebund' before ordering him taken away. Moments later a shot rang out and the American officer was informed that there was no further need for protocol.

Some of the Nazis were rounded up and summarily executed along with the guard dogs. Two of the most notorious prison guards had been stripped naked before the Americans arrived to prevent them from slipping away unnoticed. They too were cut down. General Eisenhower sent a laconic communiqué from headquarters: 'Our forces liberated and mopped up the infamous concentration camp at Dachau.' Approximately 32,000 prisoners were liberated, 300 SS camp guards were quickly neutralized.

During the next few days as the burials went forward, the sick and the dying were transferred to hospital facilities, makeshift as they had to be, and food was carefully distributed. Prescribed might be a better word, for the starving had to adjust their food intake with medical discipline. Only then did the American command turn to review the files that the Germans, with characteristic meticulousness, had maintained.

The full record of the pseudo-medical experimentations came to light. Prisoners had been used as laboratory animals, without the humane restrictions placed on vivisection. The camp was itself, a vast laboratory in which the Nazis proved that there is no limit to human depravity. It must be remembered that these experiments were not planned or conducted by identifiable psychopaths. They were performed or supervised by professional scientists, trained in what had been once considered peerless universities and medical schools. Indeed, they were called 'technically competent barbarians.'

In the last weeks before the liberation, the prisoners had to live under inhuman conditions, conditions that even they had thought to be impossible. The gigantic transports continually arriving from the camps evacuated in the face of the advancing Allies brought human beings that were, for the most part, reduced to skeletons and exhausted to death. From each railway carriage it was necessary to remove the corpses of those who had died en route.

Those prisoners incapable of work were taken to the "invalid barracks" where they received only half of the allotted ration. This meant awaiting death by starvation. They were not set to work, neither were they allowed to remain in the barracks during the day; considering the cold winter weather, this amounted to a death sentence. At night up to 1600 people crowded into barracks originally intended for 200. Daily over 100 people, and for a time over 200, fell victim to the typhus epidemic, which had been raging since December 1944. The steadily growing number of sick prisoners crowded into a very small space, as well as the lack of medicines, made it impossible to bring the epidemic under control.

The town of Dachau had not been bombed but numerous armament factories where men and women in the subsidiary camps worked, were partially or completely destroyed through bombing. Since the prisoners were not permitted to use the civilian bomb shelters, many were killed in these air raids.

After the bombing raids on Munich, groups of Dachau prisoners, labeled as death squads, were sent to search for unexploded bombs and to do the initial cleaning.

Every day the prisoners saw the allies' bombers in the sky. The mood in the camp vacillated between hopeful impatience and anxious despair. The dominating questions became: What did the SS intend to do with the prisoners who numbered over 30,000? Would the prisoners all be slain before the arrival of the allies?

After the war it was revealed that the plans had indeed, existed to kill the inmates of the concentration camp by bombs and poison. On April 14, 1945, Himmler telegraphed the following command to the camp commanders of Dachau and Flossenburg: 'There is to be no question of surrender. The camp must be evacuated immediately. Not a single living prisoner must fall into the hands of the enemy.'

Mr. Peace also sent me names and addresses of other men to contact and I heard from only two of them, Mr. Delladonne and Mr. Holly, both have submitted their stories and they are contained in this book.

In August 2002, I visited the Peace family in Osgood. While visiting my sister and her daughter they drove me to Indiana to meet Russell and Ethel. We certainly had an enjoyable visit. He has one tiny room, almost like an alcove, from which he works and has a lot of World War II memorabilia on a corkboard.

They have spent years in collecting clothing, toys, food and many, many other items to take to the poor children in Appalachia. In fact, they've been doing it for so long, they have begun to take the items collected to the children of the original children. They took us to their basement which had three rooms filled with donated items. What a wonderful couple! Their home was comfortable and full of love for others. They celebrated 56 tears of wedded bliss March 21st. Another interesting fact about this marvelous couple is that Mrs. Peace is a Hatfield lady—you know, the Hatfield vs. McCoy feud?

She has sent me some interesting Hatfield family photos and one newspaper article.

They also have several ponds where they grow trout, koi and other fish to sell to markets.

Photo courtesy of Russell and Ethel Peace

ROWLEY, William H., Armed Guard, Pennsylvania

Photo courtesy of William H Rowley

My first contact with Mr. Rowley was by telephone on 23 September 1999, although he had called earlier at my office at 3:30 p.m.; inasmuch as I was working on exhibits for a case going to court, I told him I would call him back after I got home.

Mr. Rowley explained that the Mac had been a Grace luxury liner prior to World War II when she became an U.S. Army Transport. He relayed there were Merchant seamen, Navy gunners, and Army nurses aboard as well as U.S. troops.

He reports although I have not discovered it elsewhere, including from his sister's correspondence, that this was Carlos Inman's second trip and he was getting married when he got home.

The copies of photographs he sent me he believed, had been taken by an Army photographer, who also took the photographs of the funeral of Carlos Inman, but he would not receive the photographs until after the war was over.

Four days out of New York there was a collision between the *McAndrew* and the *Bearn*. He was two decks down drinking coffee at the time. The ship continued on to the Azores. Mr. Rowley is the only one presently located who stated there was a German tanker there but there was no fear on the personnel's part as the island was Portuguese-held. He stated the military personnel could not wear uniforms.

The "Mac" was in dry dock in Baltimore, Maryland for approximately four to five months for repairs.

He was discharged in 1946.

We talked again on the telephone on 16 October. He stated the doctors and nurses took care of the wounded picked up in England. Paratroopers slept in mailbags (used as sleeping bags) and when one was asleep, it was difficult to tell which bags were mail bags and which contained the sleeping men.

In the small community where Mr. Rowley lives, he stated that a portion of the cemetery in the front had been donated for World War II vets. He also gave me the name and address of the Armed Guard magazine that he had received in 1991. However, when I sent a post card to them, it was returned. He would like to get together a reunion for just the guys who still survive but I was unable to get a firm commitment from any of the men.

App. not Req.

Prepare in Duplicate

Local Board No. 2 — 22
Indiana County   063
    43 002
12 Indiana Theatre Bldg.
Indiana, Pa.

(LOCAL BOARD DATE STAMP WITH CODE)

November 6th, 1943.
(Date of mailing)

ORDER TO REPORT FOR INDUCTION

The President of the United States,

To _WILLIAM_   _HUGH_   _ROWLEY, JR._
   (First name) (Middle name)   (Last name)

Order No. __12,283__

GREETING:

Having submitted yourself to a local board composed of your neighbors for the purpose of determining your availability for training and service in the land or naval forces of the United States, you are hereby notified that you have now been selected for training and service therein.

You will, therefore, report to the ~~induction station~~ at **Bus Station**, Main St., Homer City, Pa.
(Place of reporting)

at __6:15 A.M.__ m., on the __16th__ day of __November__, 19__43__.
(Hour of reporting)

This local board will furnish transportation to an induction station. You will there be examined, and, if accepted for training and service, you will then be inducted into the land or naval forces.

Persons reporting to the induction station in some instances may be rejected for physical or other reasons. It is well to keep this in mind in arranging your affairs, to prevent any undue hardship if you are rejected at the induction station. If you are employed, you should advise your employer of this notice and of the possibility that you may not be accepted at the induction station. Your employer can then be prepared to replace you if you are accepted, or to continue your employment if you are rejected.

Willful failure to report promptly to this local board at the hour and on the day named in this notice is a violation of the Selective Training and Service Act of 1940, as amended, and subjects the violator to fine and imprisonment.

If you are so far removed from your own local board that reporting in compliance with this order will be a serious hardship and you desire to report to a local board in the area of which you are now located, go immediately to that local board and make written request for transfer of your delivery for induction, taking this order with you.

Pearl Kennedy
Member or clerk of the local board

D. S. S. Form 150
(Revised 1-15-42)

On 6 January 2000, I received a letter from Mr. Rowley's daughter. She gives his biography as follows:

"I was born on August 23, 1925, in Pennsylvania and have continued to live there through my childhood. I was drafted into the Navy in 1943. My first full day was Thanksgiving Day. Boot camp was in Sampson, New York and went to Gunnery School in Camp Shelton, Virginia. I spent nine and one-half months on the *SS Amos Kendell* hauling ammunition to Europe. (Burned the candles at both ends!) and had to report back to the Armed Guard Center in Brooklyn, New York on Christmas Eve 1944. Upon arrival at the Center, the Navy was making up the gunnery crew. I was chosen, transported by truck to the *McAndrews*. My first memories of the Mac was finding my assigned bunk and collapsing! When I awoke on Christmas morning, we were out to sea in convoy. Destination was South Hampton, England. Once there, we took off troops, gathered up casualties, turned around and headed back for the States. Round trip was made once every 26 days.

Second trip: back to South Hampton, unloaded troops, then headed to Marseilles, France to pick up casualties. Memories of Marseilles is of an older warehouse type building, built of red brick, advertising on the side "White Star Lines." Unfortunately, most of the building had been bombed away. A safe return was made back to the United States.

Third trip: March 1945. Eighteen-knot convoy out of New York once again heading to South Hampton, England. Four days out of New York, early on the morning of the fifth day, we were rammed by the French Aircraft Carrier, *Bearn*. I had been serving watch from 4:00 a.m. until 8:00 a.m., every two hours, had a 20-minute break. I was on a break down in the chow hall drinking coffee when we were rammed. My first thoughts were of sealed compartments filling with water; therefore, I headed for "daylight!" Not knowing what actually happened, I headed for the upper deck. Once on deck, I looked overboard and remember seeing a huge hole in the starboard bow with interior lights shining out through the hole into the darkness of the ocean. Everything was total chaos! Every man went to his gun presuming it was [an] enemy attack. Several days later we transferred troops, doctors, and band members onto a ship from Australia heading to England. The only people remaining on the Mac were the Merchant Marines and the Navy gun crew, of which I was included.

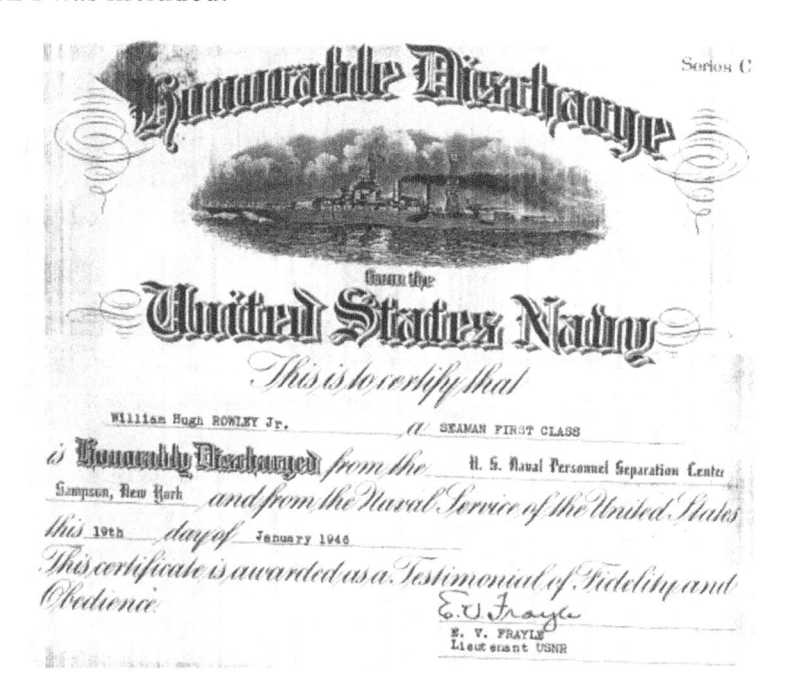

We "limped" to the first available port, which was Ponta Delgada in the Azores that belonged to Portugal who was neutral. The Navy flew in Seabees from North Africa to re-enforce the bulkhead of the torn ship so that we could return home. Repair time to the Mac took approximately three months. We were permitted ashore but not in uniform. While being in port for the repair time, I remember a German tanker directly beside the Mac. The German crew from that tanker was interned for the duration of the war due to a large gun on the bow of their tanker. Once we were ready to leave port, we traveled alone heading back to the States, traveling at only one knot per hour due to the damage to the bow of the ship. Took us 21 days from Ponta Delgada to Baltimore, Maryland where we came to port at Bethlehem Steel's dry docks. I was in Baltimore still on the Mac when the Japanese surrendered.

After serving on the Mac, I was chosen for a gunnery crew on the *SS PanAm*, which was an American tanker. [We] Went to Naples, Italy with a load of gasoline. The war was over. Upon return to the States we were shipped back to the Armed Guard Center in Brooklyn. From there I was sent by train to Shoemaker, California. We often pulled liberty in Oakland, California. I was sent back to Sampson, New York for my formal discharge on January 19, 1946.

I've talked with Leonard Patricio and he informs me that any and all information he has sent to you, you are more than welcome to use in your book, as is all the information I've also provided you. (See Leonard Patricio's correspondence given earlier).

Have appreciated your letters and concerns with the Mac and look forward to keeping in touch with you. Please let me know the opinion of the above.

Thank you again,

Sincerely"

In another letter received 12 February:

"Hello!

This letter is a follow-up to the one dated January 1, 2000, and in response to the questions left unanswered. I've tried to answer them in order that you have asked them. Hope I make this understandable for you.

First full day of boot camp was Thanksgiving Day 1943 for a 6-week period ending approximately January 7, 1944.

Home for one week of leave.

Returned to Sampson, New York for a few days to be assigned to gunnery school in Camp Shelton, Virginia that lasted approximately 6 weeks into the early part of March. With several days off I then boarded the *SS Amos Kendell* heading for Europe.

First trip took me to Italy that took a month traveling time, plus one month to unload with Army trucks on the deck and ammunition in storage. The second trip was from Baltimore, Maryland to Halifax, Nova Scotia where the convoy was made up, running three weeks in the fog. We ended up in Oban, Scotland. Once there we learned of the upcoming European Invasion. Ten days after the invasion we went into Omaha Beach, Normandy, France. I was scared to death, sitting on 8,000 tons of ammunition that the Army needed badly. After a week of trying to unload onto Army "ducks", they beached the *Kendell* where they could unload onto tractors/ trailers. After leaving Normandy, our first stop was Belfast, Ireland. Ireland to us looked beautiful and green after seeing all the destruction of war-ridden France. We headed back to the U.S., loaded up and headed back across the Atlantic to Naples, Italy; this time, my third trip, unloaded and headed back once again to the U.S. at Norfolk, Virginia. We went into dry dock. We had served enough time on the *Kendell* to be excused from the ship and go home on leave.

Once we left the *Kendell*, it was sent to become a refrigerator unit to ship beer to South America!

The leave that ended December 24, 1944, was a 21-day leave, which began on December 3, 1944.

Once assigned to the Mac and finding my bunk, located on the "B" deck, which was the second deck down. The main deck is always "A" deck. Upon awakening on Christmas morning (hour unknown) by simply another Navy man of the gunnery crew. Guard duty was a 4-hour shift one with 8-hours off, and this was done in continuation.

Casualties came from all over Europe as result of the on-going war.

Seabees [are] equal to the construction people of the Navy.

While being in port during the repair time (Azores), the German tanker that was interned was exactly that, because of the large guns on its bow and therefore it was considered a "man of war" ship.

With the ship and the crew being so large, I did not personally know any of the 68 that were drowned, nor did I know any of the 13 men rescued. The man you mention as Carter (sic) Inman, I believe was Charles Inman from Indianapolis, Indiana. The remaining troops had only been on board the ship for about a week, so not a lot of friendships had yet been developed.

Please find enclosed a copy of my "you have hereby been drafted" notice and discharge papers. If you have any more questions or I can be of any more help, please don't hesitate to let me know."

In a telephone conversation 26 February, Mr. Rowley stated that cigarettes were 5-cents a pack and a box of Hershey's with almonds—25-cents. He didn't like chocolate so gave or threw it away; however, he did eat the almonds.

When he returned home from the war, he built his own car, as there were none available. He now has a Corvette that he uses in parades. The gas tank holds only three gallons of gas but ran out of gas only once. He stated he loves the way the story is shaping up.

In another e-mail from Mr. Rowley's daughter, she states her father never graduated from high school; instead he went and served his country. He does not read well at all. He is thrilled with the idea of being included in your work, and has certainly enjoyed the "reliving" of his adventures.

Since my father's involvement with you and your book, my boyfriend has become very interested in the Mac story. In his free time he loves to "surf" the web and has done a lot of this in regard to the Mac. In his searching, he came up with some information on the 11-crew members that were rescued by the *Roche*. In the process of talking about this the other evening at my parents' home, father explained that in the very bottom (belly) of the ship, they carried mailbags. The crewmembers of the ship, when sleeping, slept in "fart bags" as he called them, which is zippered up to the chin kind of sleeping bag. When the ship was hit everything became tossed to sea and it was very difficult to tell the mail bags from the humans in the fart bags . . . thus, why so many probably were not rescued. And to top this off, he says it was dark and "we were at war" . . . I guess they didn't go around with super duty, blinding headlights of any kind."

Photo courtesy of William H Rowley

JAMES B. TYLER, Armed Guard, Mississippi

I received two letters from Mr. Tyler. Although I've written several more times, I've not heard from him again.

"Sorry I am late with the answer to your questions concerning the *James W. McAndrew*.

I went aboard the Mac 3 March 1942, made a trip to Casablanca and returned to Staten Island, New Jersey. I stayed aboard the Mac until 27 January but am not sure of this date.

Can't give you any information concerning the Mac being rammed. I never saw any German tankers in the Azores.

I am 77 years of age and in great health. I have been married to Jeanie 53 years last July 21st. We have two daughters, two granddaughters, and one great-granddaughter.

My granddaughter got some pictures from Tom Bowerman's web site.

I have a long list of first names of shipmates when I was aboard the Mac, but don't have addresses.

The Mac was a converted cruise ship-fine ship.

I served aboard five ships: *SS Nemaha*—went aboard March 3, 1942; *SS McAndrew*—went aboard September 3, 1942; *SS Felipe de Neve*—went aboard April 23, 1943, and the *SS Alcoa Guard*—went aboard April 23, 1944; and the *Amphibious Personnel Demolition* (A.P.D.-131)—was aboard from March through November 2. I received my discharge November 15, 1945.

I appreciate your correspondence. Please let me hear from you after you get your information on the *McAndrews*."

On 5 April 2000, I received another letter from Mr. Tyler. At the top of the page he lists the following: Foster (Michigan), Kuhen (Pennsylvania), Ferris, Raffer (California), Dawson (Kentucky).

"Hope these names will be of some help to you. I do not know anything about German tankers or German POWs.

I have no objections to being quoted in your book.

In the Armed Guard History, Volume I, you will find pictures of three Water Valley, Mississippi boys. Page 94—Rayford N. Edgar; Page 194, James B. Tyler; Page 154, Bruce J. Myrick.

I appreciate your interest in this project. Let me hear more from you. Enclosed is a copy of a letter I received from David Wilson on December 30, 1987."

"Shipmates aboard the *USAT J. W. McAndrew*, early 1943:
Lt. S. D. Smith
Sears, B.M. (New York)
James Francis Cotter B.M. 2/c
Griffin, Coxon 2/c (New York)
Green RM 2nc
McCaskill Signalman 2/c
Allen E. Johnson—SM 2/c
David H. Wilson SM 3/c
Todd—North Carolina
C. Quincex—Florida
D. Quincex—Florida
Jerry Bailey
Jack Bailey
Felker—North Dakota
Dummett—Ohio
Elliott
Ebbole—Illinois
Farnett
Ferraden
Chistrusky—Illinois
Copeland—Ohio

Dear James,

I have your name and address from the Armed Guard book and see that you served aboard the *J. W. McAndrews*. I also served aboard her at Casablanca and for several trips afterwards as a signalman with Johnson and McCaskill; also signalman, and James Francis Cotter, BM 2/c.

I know where Johnson is and correspond with him. He is in the book, page 122. I would sure appreciate hearing from you and any information you may have any others who served on the *McAndrews*.

I remain your shipmate,
In Christ,
David H. Wilson[7]"

DAVID H. WILSON, Armed Guard, West Virginia/Washington
A friend who responded on Mr. Wilson's behalf contacted me.

"Dave Wilson was interested in responding to your recent letter regarding the *USAT McAndrews*. His health is declining and he resides in a Moses Lake rest home. His mother was also in that rest home with him, but she died earlier this year. Being unable to write due to a hand problem, I offered to assist. I am a friend of Dave's helping him with a ride to church on Sundays. I am a writer and avid World War II history buff with a large library.

Dave has a clear memory of his service on board the *Battleship Tennessee* at Pearl Harbor. They were berthed behind the *Arizona*. Dave's battle station was in a forward magazine. There was concern that the fires from the *Arizona* would engulf the bow of the *Tennessee*. Dave was standing on powder bags trying to stuff rags in the

---

[7] I wrote to the address of Mr. Wilson in West Virginia; it was returned. I contacted Mr. Bowerman who sent me an address for him in Washington State. I wrote him at that address in July and finally had a response in late September. Inasmuch as he was aboard the Mac, he will have his own section.

magazine vents to keep smoke out. Very tense. The *Tennessee* took bomb hits but was protected from torpedo strikes by an outboard battleship.

Dave's service in the rest of the war was very busy. I believe he had ships sunk from under him twice. I had not heard of the guard unit he served in as a gunner on transport ships. Unfortunately, with so many ship changes, it is hard for Dave to remember particular ships. He remembers a little bit about the *McAndrews*."

His story: "I made 19 trips on a variety of ships as a member of the gun crews. It is hard to remember particular details of specific ships. I do remember the *McAndrews* as a good ship. The captain was a very tough man. We made a two week stop in a Caribbean port to off-load sugar. I certainly remember that stop. A boat brought a harbor pilot out to the ship. He was a very dark black man. When he climbed to the bridge, the captain really went into a rage. He wasn't about to let this black man pilot his ship. He threw him off the ship.

I thought we boarded a company of Seabees for that crossing to North Africa.

I remember that the ship was hit in a collision, probably during a course change at night. We were hit by a French jeep carrier that ripped a big hole in the side of the ship above the waterline." (That puzzled me that Dave said "a French jeep carrier." I was sure they never had one. I checked my copy of Roger Chesneau's excellent "Aircraft Carriers of the World." The description and photos of the French carrier *Bearn* answered that question. She was a full-sized pre-war carrier—actually a World War I unfinished battleship hull completed as a carrier in the 1920s. Too slow for World War II carrier task force service; she had her flight deck shortened and was used as an aircraft transport. So she looked like a jeep carrier—a large jeep carrier!)

"I don't remember any details of the collision. I do remember that 65 men were killed. We still made it to North Africa with the convoy. Because of our shallow draft, we were the first ship sent into Casablanca harbor. There was concern about potential ship blockage of the channel.

There was a large French battleship in the harbor that we went closely by. It was so well camouflaged in sand-colored paint that you could almost run into it without seeing it because it blended so well with the background. It had damage from several shell hits."

Mr. Garnant: "My first thought was that this would be a French battleship damaged by the British in July 1940 when they attacked the French fleet in an anchorage near Oran. But Siegfried Breyer's "Battleships of the World 1905-1970" has the story and a photo of the French battleship Jean Bart. It was nearing completion in St. Nazaire in March 1940 when it had to hurriedly put to sea ahead of the Nazis. German planes bombed the ship as it left the harbor. That was the damage seen by Dave. In particular the forecastle was torn open by a bomb hit. The ship sailed to Casablanca where it stayed throughout the war."

Mr. Wilson: "After landing our troops and equipment, the *McAndrews* sailed for Staten Island where I left the ship for another assignment."

I e-mailed Mr. Garnett but never received a response.

JOHN W. WILDE, Armed Guard, Maine

"I am in receipt of your letter of 1 December 1999 and received it on 7 December 1999, a fitting day.

After serving in the North Atlantic for two years, I was transferred from the Armed Guard Center, Brooklyn, New York, to Baltimore, Maryland.

The ship seemed to be completely finished and I just casually heard about a collision. We picked up troops and took them to Naples, Italy, which was a bombed-out world. We picked up a sunken ship that had "turned turtle," unloaded the troops and sailed for Marseilles, France. Here we picked up the 82nd and 101st airborne troops destined for the Philippines for replacements for the 11th Airborne Division.

The saddest part of this story is about a young Russian boy, 18 or 19, very talented, who played the ukulele and sang in broken English. He was freed from the Germans and adopted by the troops. He wore the same uniform they did and had fought beside them. We were almost to Panama when the war ended and we went to Newport News, Virginia and unloaded the troops. At that time someone squealed about the Russian boy and the MP's picked him up and put him in our brig. We were allowed to bring him cigarettes, food, etc., and he told us then that if he goes back, the Russians would kill him but we still had to take him back. The last I heard through the grapevine, he was turned over to the Russian delegation in France and was probably executed.

I didn't not make the trip back as I had enough points to get ready for discharge.

In answer to your questions:

I was a 20-mm 350, 450 gunner; the voyage I was on was uneventful; we were fast and alone due to speed.
Regards pictures—I had a lot but can't seem to find them, but about a year ago C. A. Lloyd called and asked me for some and I did send him a half dozen or so. He is a real fine guy and I'm sure he will send you copies if asked.[8]"

In a telephone conversation with Mr. Wilde 5 January, Mr. Wilde stated he would write other stores regarding his tour of duty on other ships and requested that I send them to Mr. Bowerman. He stated he would not be attending the National Armed Guard Reunion. I never heard from him again although I wrote additional letters, postcards and sent Christmas cards. Also when I retired, a

---

[8] When I attended the National Armed Guard Reunion in Fort Mitchell, Ky., I did ask Mr. Lloyd for some of the photos. I have, for whatever reason, never received any from him.

change of address was forwarded to each of the men and/or family members in this book, Armed Guard, Connecticut.

WILLIAM A. YOUNG, SR., Merchant Marines, Connecticut

Mr. Young wrote his letter as follows: "I received your letter a few days ago. I can hardly remember the "Mac". I sailed on her as an Ordinary Seaman. I know we went to England and maybe to Iceland, Oran, and North Africa. I was told it sailed in the South Atlantic before the War. I saw the "Mac" once again when I sailed to France. She was at a dock and she had a large hole in her side. We were told she was torpedoed. I guess from your letter the hole was because of a collision. I don't recall if I made one or two trips on the "Mac". I remember the trip from England to Iceland was rough. The submarine alert went off about every half-hour. I don't know what happened to the "Mac" after the War.

The "Mac" sailed out of the port of New York and as far as I know, always stayed in the North Atlantic. I was on the "Mac" before the collision. At the time I was on the "Mac" the men in the Merchant Marines had no uniforms. We only had the uniforms from the Maritime Training station. If I remember correctly, we were all young fellows in our twenties, and knew little about the sea.

I am sorry I can't be of more help to you. I am 78 years old and going back that far is hard to remember everything.

Yours truly,"

I never heard from Mr. Young again. You will note in front of his name in the list of men, who served aboard the Mac, are the letters OS, that is the beginning level of the deck crew. They are later promoted to Able Bodied Seaman (AB).

U.S. NAVY ARMED GUARD AND THE MERCHANT SHIPS

When one writes about the Armed Guard, one has to automatically include the Merchant Marines. One could not operate without the other during their dangerous crossings to deliver material and supplies to the allies during World War II.

"Since I had never heard of the Armed Guard, I asked the counselor to explain. 'The Armed Guard', he said, 'is a special arm of the U. S. Navy that defends cargo ships from enemy air attacks and submarines. On average, there are between fourteen and twenty gunners, one signalman and maybe a radio operator in each Armed Guard crew. The rest of the ship's company is made up of civilian Merchant Marine personnel'.

'It's volunteer duty at this time', he added, 'due to the extremely hazardous Murmansk run to Russia. Allied convoys run the gauntlet of German U-boats, aircraft, and surface raiders and about twenty (20%) percent of the ships never make it back. But if you like guns, are eager to see action, and want to go to sea almost immediately, it should be just the ticket'.

The Navy provided merchant ships with ammunition, magazine storage space, splinter protection for the bridge and radio shack, berthing (sleeping area), and messing space (eating area) for the gun crew.

During the early days of the war, some innovative Merchant Marine skippers had their carpenters build gun tubs fore and aft, containing creosote-soaked poles that looked like broadside guns to discourage enemy submarine commanders from surfacing to use their deck guns, a common practice then, to save torpedoes. Merchant ships were highly vulnerable to attack owing to their low speed, lack of armor, and few watertight bulkheads. Hence the all-out effort to increase their surface and anti-aircraft armament.

The first training was in a small arms classroom. There we learned to break down, clean and reassemble pistols, rifles, and Thompson submachine guns. In time, we were expected to do the entire "drill" blindfolded.

Part of this training included working the bigger surface and dual-purpose guns mounted in the back of the classroom building. We practiced simulated loading and firing with dummy ammunition. We also learned how to take the breechblocks and firing mechanisms apart, and how to clean and reassemble them.

Armed Guard crews usually included one or two people with the communication skills of signalman and/or radioman. When ships are grouped together into convoys, the need for communication between ships becomes obvious. A signalman deals in Morse code, semaphore (any apparatus for signaling, i.e., by lights, flags, etc.), and international code flags; a radioman with radio. Unlike gunners, communication personnel take orders concerning most of their work directly from the civilian captain. For responsibilities relating to the Navy, they take orders from the Armed Guard Officer. Communications personnel are also taught to operate the guns in case a gunner is injured. In addition, they serve as phone 'talkers' for the gunnery officer during enemy action.

Signalmen and radiomen also served in a little-known special Armed Guard service called Convoy Control meaning they were assigned to foreign flag merchant ships. In most cases, they sailed with ships' crews who often spoke no English, with the exception of the captain and senior officers, ate bad food, and suffered abominable living conditions. Sometimes, the Armed Guard gunners were included in these special teams depending on the ship's armament.

Petty officers wore rating badges on the left arm for the trades, on the right for those who worked on the deck, like gunners, boatswains, and quartermasters. A white stripe around the right shoulder meant seamen deck hands, red around the left for below-deck firemen—a reflection of hierarchy and skill.

The quality of food was generally good the first two or three weeks out until the ship got low on fresh supplies. Breakfast, for example, might be a choice of bacon or sausage with eggs fixed to order, plus hot cakes and orange juice. Lunch and dinner might include a choice of meats and vegetables, and a desert of some kind. The baker made fresh bread almost daily and one could count on a selection of cold cuts and cheeses in the pantry refrigerator day or night for sandwich makings before or after standing watch. Coffee was almost always available, too. Some said it was loaded with saltpeter (a common name for potassium nitrate) to curb the men's sex drive.

The relative few books available were passed on from man to man. Armed Forces Radio Network broadcasts when available, were piped in to the crew and gunners mess compartments' as well as the wardroom, a welcome addition for many of the men. Some men worked on their tans while on deck, others slept the time away between meals. The two most popular 'time killers' were gambling and bull sessions. The bull sessions could take place any time, anywhere men gathered but since there might not be a deck load, most were held on and around the No. 4 hatch after supper. Subjects ranged from reflections on events of the recent past to future plans.

One of the favorite topics of conversation on the ship was which branch of the Armed Forces had the best deal. Since the majority of passengers were Navy men, one can guess who won that debate. Four U.S. Navy advantages no one questioned:

A clean, dry place to sleep;
Daily showers, even if they were sometimes salt water;
Hot meals three times a day; and
Burial at sea in a worst case scenario.

Reflecting on Armed Guard experiences, one of the Gunner's Mates summed up his feelings: "The men in the Armed Guard didn't get the carriers, battleships, or destroyers of their dreams, but they got something else from their time in the Armed Guard. The pride and satisfaction of knowing they fulfilled the Armed Guard motto: 'We Aim To Deliver.'" The Armed Guard and their Merchant Marine shipmates delivered the troops and everything needed for their support—from food, medicine, and clothing to bombs and ammunition—to theater of operation around the world. And in doing so, they grew up and became better men while the Navy was fulfilling its long-standing promise, 'Join the Navy and See the World.'

Intercepted Mail:

Dear Ma:

I joined the Navy because I admired the way the ships were kept so clean and tidy. This week I learned who keeps them so neat and tidy.

With love,

Junior[9]

During their training, the Armed Guards were trained what conditions meant:

CONDITION 3[10]

One-third of the crew was on watch; four men were on lookout and three on standby status. The Petty Officer supervised the lookouts moving throughout the ship.

CONDITION 2

One-half of the crew was on watch with six on lookout and five on standby. As in Condition 1, the Petty Officer moved about the battle stations supervising the lookouts.

CONDITION 1

The entire crew was at their battle stations in the event of an enemy attack. At sundown and during the night as well as at sunrise, all hands became lookouts, which was when the enemy would usually attack. The men and guns were prepared for any possibility.

---

[9] With author's permission, William L. McGee, **Bluejacket Odyssey—Guadalcanal to Bikini—Naval Armed Guard in the Pacific,** The Glenncannon Press, 1997

[10] Taken from the Armed Guard Training Film.

Private steamship companies, owners of the Liberty Ships, were taken over by the War Shipping Administration to run the ships, accomplished by the civilian

Merchant Marines. They would carry munitions, food, and supplies to Russia, England, and other allied destinations during the war years.

With specific and important jobs aboard a ship, including but not limited to, manning the guns, ammunition, protection of the ship, ship's crew, and cargo from the enemy, the United States Navy Armed Guard did it all. Their orders were to stay aboard a ship and fire the guns as long as the ship was afloat. This was to keep the enemy from crippling the ship, then boarding her for provisions the enemy needed to stay on patrol longer. The Armed Guard succeeded in this endeavor. When the German Naval Officers knew they were losing the war, it was then that the enemy was also known to kill the ship's crew before sinking the ship.

Headed by one officer, gun crews generally consisted of 8 to 24 men.

At first the gunners perhaps received as little as one or two weeks of training before going to sea. Some ships only had creosote (oil covered) poles as "guns." Later, more effective armament such as the 20mm and 40mm, 3"50s and 5" 38s were installed. As war was getting closer to the U.S., training was expanded to six weeks, which was controlled by centers in Brooklyn, New York, New Orleans, Louisiana, and Treasure Island, California.

The Armed Guard was organized during World War I when Allied and American shipping was being attacked and sunk, mostly by the enemy U-boats. This branch had been deactivated after the

war ended with Germany's defeat, as Merchant ships were free to deliver goods and supplies whenever and wherever needed; other governments and companies purchased many.

During World War II, the Armed Guard was again activated and served on over 6,000 ships as compared to 384 ships during the First World War. Their own officers were in charge of the crew with radiomen and signalmen operating all transmission of codes and messages; however, the radioman was occasionally a Merchant Marine.

In the event of war, in April 1941, the first Armed Guard crew was taken from the regular Navy and sent to Little Creek, Virginia to set up and train gunners. Availability of guns at that time was so scarce that casualties among the ships and its crews were high. Both ships and crews were shipped out without guns or escort protection. The U-boats ruled the seas at this point, particularly in the Atlantic.

Our ships were sitting ducks. Many men lost their lives even in the vicinity of the American coastline. Earning the name of "Torpedo Alley," the skies were lit at night by the burning Merchant ships off the coast of North and South Carolina. On 28 April 1942, a "dim-out" or "black-out" was ordered to be observed every night along a 15-mile area of the Atlantic coast in order to stop the German submarine activity.

Shopkeepers and owners all up and down the shoreline from Texas to Maine were afraid they would lose their customers should they close their stores. The glow of the lights on shore made the men and their ships easy targets.

Much attention has been given to the Murmansk Run (see Appendix I) and the Battle of Leyte Gulf; the general public is not aware of the real battle for life that took place in the lifeboats of the Merchant Seamen and the Armed Guard crew as they tried to hang on, sometimes in unbearably cold wind, rough seas, hot sun, and the darkest nights with little food or water . . . and many did not.

To give the reader an idea of how laden with cargo a ship could be; i.e., was on D-Day. Picture this: When the jumping 82nd Airborne paratroopers left the airplanes, their supplies were on board a ship, including their trucks, tanks, and everything else they would need to carry on the fight.

The crewmembers had a great feeling of accomplishment when their merchant ship arrived at the homeport for more cargo, and justifiably so. Not only had they seen thousands upon thousands of tons of war supplies come safely through the perils of the weather, the sea, and the enemy, but they had come through it themselves. They had every right to feel more than proud of their branch of the service.

Coming home for leave or extended liberty gave them the opportunity to talk about worthy seafaring traditions and sharing their experiences. They had ridden camel back in Egypt, climbed the Eiffel Tower in Paris, eaten water buffalo meat in South Africa, or visited the burning ghats (broad wide steps) along the Ganges River, tasted fish and chips, ginger beer, and porridge in England or bouillabaisse in Marseilles, France, bargained for rare sapphires and rubies in Ceylon (now Sri Lanka).

The Armed Guard was deactivated again after World War II. Some of the men would become regular Navy making a career of the service to retirement. However, most returned to the places from whence they came—farms, factories, schools, service stations, small towns, large cities; some even became politicians. I have discovered over the years they never gave up their love of the sea or any water, settling near the ocean, lakes, or rivers.

When peace came, the men returned to become a part of a society that was about as strange as the people of distant lands; those who spoke different languages, practiced different customs, having a difficult time readjusting. They had watched the sinking of a ship, seen the mate they might have shared breakfast with, played cards with, die a horrible death, and had heard the sound of the big guns being fired. Returning from years of combat readiness and the vigor of war, the Armed Guard became the forgotten heroes of a conflict that took them to almost every port in the world. Just under 2000 men went to their resting places beneath the sea, whether it was on a ship that sunk, jumping overboard from a burning ship, or for any other reason necessary to leave the ship in the middle of nowhere, and not always with a rescue ship in sight.

We should remember our heroic Merchant seamen and Navy gunners; those who have been long forgotten and unrecognized, long left out of the history of World War II, and the war at sea. And, in our quiet moments of reflection, we must remember those who did not come home.

U.S. NAVAL ARMED GUARD AND MERCHANT SHIP CROSSINGS
MURMANSK AND ARCHANGEL, RUSSIA RUNS

In early December 1941 and early 1942, the United States sent out many ships destined for Murmansk. The crewmembers had unsuitable clothing and nonworking guns. In order to disguise the fact that the ships had no guns, the crews even placed creosote poles on the bow and stern until real weapons were available. Some weapons were placed on the ships after they arrived in England. Before going on to Russia, as armaments became available, the poles were replaced by small caliber weapons. Over the next several months, the Armed Guard and the merchant crews were fortunate not to have lost more of their ships and personnel going to and from the Russian ports, due to the lack of weapons.

On 6 December 1941, the *SS Larranga* left the Port of Boston on a trip that would take her to Murmansk. Christmas Eve the gunners got their first taste of battle when they fired their guns three times at a surfaced submarine, scoring a possible hit on the sub with the second round. These few rounds were the first to be fired by the Armed Guard at the enemy. Thousands more rounds of ammunition were to follow before the war ended in 1945.

Approximately 350 merchant ships were sent to the Russian ports through 26 April 1945. Most of the 46 ships lost were between 5 January 1942 and 14 March 1943. The Navy made every effort to give these ships the armaments and large quantities of necessary ammunition. As the gun crews gained experience, they became experts in protecting the merchant ships, merchant crews, and the cargo the ships carried.

Floating mines were spotted on 5 March 1942. The convoy was caught in a severe winter gale and scattered all but five of the original 20 ships during the 2-day storm. A German plane began shadowing the convoy on 8 March during which five other ships and a destroyer joined the convoy. Two ships, the *SS Raceland* and *SS Bateau* were lost; the *Raceland* was torpedoed or bombed, and the latter from unknown causes. Four more destroyers and a cruiser joined them on 29 March. They had arrived in time to protect them from a surface battle with German destroyers.

The battle took place approximately 150 miles northwest of Murmansk, was fought in a heavy snow squall with shells falling and exploding all around the ships. Some of the escorts were damaged, but they also inflicted damage that included the sinking of one of the enemy destroyers. An enemy scout bomber dropped its bombs into the sea after the *SS Dunboyne* fired back with all of its nine guns.

On 4 March the *SS Expositor*[11] left Pier 98 in Philadelphia and headed to New York where she took on cargo of 5,000 cases of TNT.

The *SS Effingham*, while on her way to Murmansk, was torpedoed 150 feet astern of the *Dunboyne* during the morning of 30 March 1942, but was able to launch two lifeboats. The Chief Merchant Marine Officer was in charge of the lifeboat. This man stayed at the main oar most of the time for 32 hours in frigid weather. The survivors were picked up by the *HMS Harrier* (British ship) but not before five men died in the boat due to exposure to the harsh weather and high seas. The survivors owe their lives to the officer for his courage and leadership. He should have been recognized for his efforts beyond the call of duty but this was not to be.

When the convoy was abeam[12] of Kildin Island, approximately 20 miles north of Murmansk, enemy aircraft dropped four bombs ahead of the *SS Eldena* [later sunk in July 1943], and dropped two near the *SS Mormacmar*. Entry was made into the Port of Murmansk with only nine of the original 20 ships.

---

[11] See Appendix III for a copy of the Ship's Log for the SS Expositor's run to Murmansk.
[12] At right angles to the ship's length or keel.

Submarines were also in the area but were heavily attacked by the escorting vessels. The Russian planes and the effective firepower from the anti-aircraft guns in the hills were welcome sights to the battle weary men who had not slept in three days as the ships slipped through Kola Inlet and anchored on 30 March.

On 3 April, Armed Guards aboard the *SS Mauna Kea* claimed four hits on a German sub by blowing off the conning tower and presumed sunk. Most of the convoy went to Murmansk but the convoy split up 29 May with some going to Archangel, another northern Russian port.

The crew of the *SS Pancraft*, built in New Jersey, boarded the ship. For four days crew cleaned and mounted a 4:50 surface gun that was so old, they were afraid to fire it. The ship sailed for Nova Scotia on 13 April 1942, going on to Scotland and Iceland in time to be in the Convoy PQ-17[13] to Murmansk via the Barents Sea. The ship, making eight knots, was loaded with coal and TNT; 36 other vessels were in the convoy. German planes from occupied Norway started circling the convoy on 2 July to test the firepower of the ships.

For the *Pancraft*, the long Murmansk nightmare was over on 28 April. They then left on the return trip for Reykjavik, Iceland arriving on 7 May. Before they arrived in Iceland however, the convoy faced mines and another serial attack on 1 May as well as enemy surface ships.

Under constant daily attacks, the convoy was in Murmansk until 28 April. The convoy survived 110 alerts and 54 actual bombings. The Russian government credited the *Eldena* crew with shooting down three enemy bombers and the crew was awarded with an extra months' pay. The *Dunboyne* was also credited with two enemy planes going down and assistance on bringing down another.

Approximately 125 or more planes were engaged in dogfights.

---

[13] One of the mostly costly battles in World War II in the loss of lives, ships, cargo. There is still some debate as to whether PQ-17 was deliberately allowed to be destroyed by Churchill and Roosevelt in furtherance of the war; it simply depends on which book one reads.

Only two American ships, the *SS Yaka* (later sunk) and *SS Cheswald* (later deliberately sunk), had Armed Guard crews on board in PQ14-[14]. Leaving Reykjavik on 6 April in the convoy, many ships were turned back due to fog and snow. An enemy "shadow" plane (a plane seen in the distance not doing anything to cause any damage and yet not close enough at which to shoot or could have been an enemy scouting plane relaying information regarding the ships' location to their subs), circled out of range. Escorts made contact with three enemy destroyers. The following day, a German plane appeared but left. The Commodore's ship was torpedoed and sunk in about one minute.

On 15 April about 50 enemy and allied planes were in the air at one time that occurred again later that same afternoon.

Other ships in the convoy picked up 31 survivors from the icy waters. Heavy clothing gave no protection. More bombs were dropped and torpedoes were seen. Much to the happiness of the crew, the escorts sank a submarine ahead as they entered Murmansk harbor on 19 April. They shared in daily attacks that PQ-13 was receiving. Due to the damage to her bow and propeller, the *Yaka* missed sailing when the convoy left on 28 April.

On 12 May and again on 14 May, the *Yaka* was again damaged from near misses. A bomb hit her No. 2 boiler on 15 May. On 27 May her crew shot down one enemy plane but more bombs missed the ship. Later, bomb fragments on 13 June opened her deep tank and made 14 holes in her port side while in Murmansk, the *Yaka* experienced 156 air raid alarms and yet somehow managed to survive.

Sixteen American ships were included in the PQ-15 convoy when it left Iceland for Murmansk on 26 April. On 30 April and again on 1 May, the convoy-encountered mines and enemy scout planes. One enemy plane was shot down. Their bombs fell wide. On 5 May three

---

[14] These convoys (the PQ series) went from Iceland to Russia; return convoys from Russia to Iceland were designated QP convoys.

Merchant ships sank in rapid order. The attack took place after midnight and one of the enemy planes crashed in flames.

A lookout on the *Expositor* sighted a conning tower in the center of the convoy a few yards off the starboard quarter. The 4:50 gun on the ship was brought to bear and the top of the conning tower was blown off as the submarine changed course. A torpedo was avoided by backing up the ship at full speed. The Armed Guard on this ship consisted of only four gunners, a signalman, a striker, and an officer. The officer was awarded the first Silver Star Medal presented to an Armed Guard Officer. He had been assigned to the ship in February 1942.

Most of the ships left Murmansk on 21 May and arrived in New York 28 June, leaving ships behind in Murmansk that continued to receive constant bombings.

This time it would worsen.

The *Expositor* delivered another cargo to Russia. She was torpedoed and sunk 22 February 1943 in the North Atlantic in Convoy ON[15]-166. She left Liverpool on 11 February 1943 bound for New York in a convoy of 48 ships. When the *Expositor* sank, she took along the lives of six Merchant Seamen plus three Armed Guards. Of the 48 ships in convoy, 11 were sunk and one damaged. Of the 48 survivors from the *Expositor* were picked up by *HMCS Trillium*[16] that included L. Whitsun Lloyd, Armed Guard, later killed in the sinking of the *SS Black Point* 5 May 1945 by the German sub U-803, just three miles off the coast of Port Judith, Rhode Island. Mr. Lloyd[17] was the last Armed Guard to be killed in the North Atlantic Theater of War.

---

[15] ON convoys were from Liverpool, England to North America.

[16] Commissioned at Montreal on 31 October 1940. She was unique in that she spent her entire career as a mid-ocean escort, participating in three major convoy battles: SC.100 (September 1942), ON.166 (February 1943) and SC. 121 (March 1943). She was sold in 1947 for conversion to a whale catcher and further entered service in 1950 as the Honduran-registered Olympic Runner. In 1956 she became the Japanese Otori Maru No. 10, and last appeared in Lloyd's list for 1959-60.

[17] In May 2000, I met Mr. Lloyd's brother at the National Armed Guard Reunion held in Fort Mitchell, Kentucky. We have e-mailed each other on occasion since then.

Attacks on this convoy were heavier than previous ones. At this time, the sun never set and the enemy could attack around the clock.

On 25 May the *SS Carlton* was hit and had to return to Iceland. German planes (approximately 108) attacked the convoy sinking six ships, three more were listing, and two on fire. Many of the ships were strafed or damaged by near misses.

Survivors of the *SS Alamar* were rescued when the ship sunk on 27 May 1942. The survivors from this ship were aboard the *SS Massmar* as it sunk on the return trip when it ran into a minefield. Twenty-four of the 36 survivors of the *Alamar* were known to have died.

Also, sunk in the minefield were the *SS John Randolph* with five crewmembers killed and the *SS Heffron* with one crewmember killed. Some of the foreign ships also sunk when those ships hit mines.

On board a Liberty ship, the crew was ordered to proceed to the shipyard in the Port of New York on 9 June 1942, where it dry-docked. Imagine the crew's surprise when the ship's bow section below the waterline was reinforced with heavy steel plates. No one had an answer when they inquired as to the reason for the bow's reinforcement. It was later discovered that those plates were to be used in plowing through solid ice. No one then had any doubts as to where the ship was headed.

She proceeded to sea after being loaded with cargo at the Brooklyn Army Base. The crew was told their destination: Halifax, the capital of Nova Scotia. The ship anchored in the bay and waited for a week for the convoy to get ready for departure before heading across the Atlantic.

Going by way of Greenland and Iceland, the convoy left Halifax sailing the northern route. After passing Iceland, the convoy came under attack by German submarines. The subs lined up inside the convoy's columns; the weapons could not be fired without hitting their own ships. The ship ahead of them that was carrying ammunition was hit by a torpedo and exploded. After a hard right turn, another Liberty ship avoided the sinking vessel as another torpedo just passed the bow. She would have been next in line for a torpedo if she had stayed the original course.

A British long-range bomber arrived for the defense of the convoy, and started to bomb the German subs. One of the ships mistook the British bomber for a German bomber and started shooting. (This is known as "friendly fire.") Hit, the bomber's last maneuver was to turn his plane away from the convoy before crashing into the sea; no one survived. A very unselfish act and in order to save lives, the pilot and crew died.

With the first excitement in the North Atlantic over, a convoy was headed for the Norwegian coast and the North Cape, where the brutal action really began. The Germans sent dive-bombers and U-boats to attack. It was all over by the time Murmansk was reached—half the convoy was destroyed.

What a tragic sight watching ships go down and the men struggling in the icy cold water before going under. One of the ships went down by the stern and the bow was way up in the air. A man was crawling out of the porthole from the forepeak[18] and was most likely doomed since he had no life jacket, and a sinking ship's pressure and suction would take him down.

Finally, the ship arrived and moored at the dock, having the opportunity to relax and take it easy.

Some of the crew decided to go to town. As they walked out the gate it was noticed a KGB agent followed them. The crew decided to keep walking until trolley tracks were seen. There was a sharp bend so the trolley had to slow down on the bend; the men ran for the trolley and jumped on. They looked back at the KGB agent. It appeared he seemed surprised and disappointed that they had managed to elude him.

---

[18] This is the extreme forward lower compartment that was used for storage.

After walking around downtown, the crew returned to the ship without the KGB.

The following day the crew went to the local International Seaman's Club ("ISC") located on the dock. The club was provided by the Soviet Government to discourage seamen from wandering away from the ships and going into town.

The crew enjoyed their drinks even more when two young ladies joined them. Drinks were ordered. As the ladies did not speak English, the men kept their conversation in Lithuanian. The ladies were given four pairs of silk stockings to make a good impression and to show them kindness. The ladies were excited and grateful. Silk stockings were worth more than gold. They thanked the men in Lithuanian. However, they advised that the crew should avoid talking politics as they had been engaged by the KGB to observe all foreigners, and to report conversations to the KGB.

The cargo was completely unloaded after ten days in port and the ship departed Russia to form a convoy that was to return to the United States by way of Iceland. The ship arrived in New York after 15 days at sea and moored at the Brooklyn Army Base for another load of cargo.

Due to the fact that the escorts were called away on 4 July 1942 to meet the larger ships of the German Navy, over three-fourths of all merchant ships in the Convoy PQ-17 were sunk. This left the Merchant ships at the mercy of the subs and enemy airplanes.

The Armed Guard shot down eight of the German airplanes. Torpedoes sank the *SS Christopher Newport* and *SS William Hooper* with both ships losing three crewmembers each. The Armed Guard gunners from the *SS Daniel Morgan* [later bombed and torpedoed losing four crew members] fired at and hit a torpedo only 20 yards from the *Carlton* thus only temporarily saving that ship.

Axis Sally[19] broadcast that the planes were going to give them a good 4th of July celebration. The planes, as promised, showed up on America's Independence Day. As enemy planes circled the convoy, the subs jockeyed for position and took aim on special ships. Orders were received by the Convoy's Commodore to split up the convoy and proceed on their own to Murmansk, which they did, leaving the ships at the mercy of the enemy. Some of the ships sailed north into colder waters near the ice floes as did the *Pancraft* who had survived the July 4 attacks. Because of the high latitude and the season, the sun never set. The vessels were never cloaked in darkness so some crews decided to camouflage their ships to make them look like big chunks of ice from the air and sea by painting them white.

On 5 July, the following day, the report was given that seven JU-88s (German dive bombers) attacked but only three dropped their bombs as the gunner fired the .30-caliber weapons at them, hitting them, only to see the expended bullets ricochet off the armored planes. The dropped bombs hit near the starboard bow in the coal pile next to the TNT. One bomb hit amidship.[20] Abandon ship orders were given. Coal was all over the place and the ship split at the seam.

The *Pancraft*, another victim to the enemy, sank on 7 July 1942. Strafing killed one Merchant seaman. One seaman, hit by shrapnel, lost his grip and was killed when he fell between the ship and lifeboat. *HMS Lotus*, a British ship, rescued the men from the *Pancraft*. When the attack was over, 153-Armed Guardsmen and Merchant seamen

---

[19] Axis Sally broadcast for Germany just as Tokyo Rose broadcast for Japan. Both tried to lower the morale of our troops. Axis Sally would say things such as, "Roy Smith with the 79th Division . . . Thought you would like to know that your wife Mary, who lives on Stradbury Street in Oakland, California, is having good times with the recruiting sergeant who sent you away so they could play."

    Jane Anderson, born in Atlanta, Georgia, also served up propaganda for Hitler's "cause". She had once been a respected journalist. There is still some mystery as to why she became a German spy in Germany.

[20] In or toward the middle of the ship.

were dead. Twenty-three Allied ships had been sunk. The Russians reported the surviving ships reached the Port of Archangel safely going by way of the islands of Novaya Zemlya.

Although great losses had been suffered, the delivery—a huge mass of planes, tanks, guns, goods, medicine, and machine tools for the hard-pressed Russian people, was accomplished and contributed to saving the country from the enemy.

After being at general quarters for more than 18 hours, the *Morgan* crew witnessed the sinking of the *SS Fairfield City* when she was bombed with a loss of eight crew and an Armed Guard crew of nine, on 5 July. Prior to sinking, the *City's* gun crews shot down two of the five planes that attacked her with bombs. The *Morgan* was so damaged by bombs that she also sank.

In addition to the sinking of the *SS Carlton*, others sunk on that day were the *SS Pancraft* which suffered the loss of two crew members, the *SS Washington*, the *SS Peter Kerr*, and the *SS Honomu*. The 31 *SS Carlton* survivors and 5 from the *Honomu* became prisoner-at-war victims in the German camps and were liberated in 1945. Nine Armed Guardsmen from the *Carlton* were also liberated.

The *Washington* crew spent 10 days in their lifeboats. After 7 cold days with most of the crew suffering from exposure, they went ashore on the Novaya Zemlya Islands and managed to cook up seagull soup. Later, meeting with a group of survivors from a British ship and having snared 100 ducks further down the coast two days later, they enjoyed a feast. They finally came upon the *SS Winston Salem* grounded on a sand bar and they had their first really good meal in many days. When they reached Archangel on 24 July, one-third of them had frozen feet. Many of them survived the sinking of the *Washington* and returned on other ships. Unfortunately, some of these ships were also sunk and several of those men were killed as these ships were hit.

Late in the evening of 2 September 1942, Convoy PQ-18 left Loch Ewe, Scotland with supplies in which a total of 8 American and 2 Russian ships and a total of 40 ships were sunk. Convoy PQ-18 was the landmark or turning point of the war as bigger and better guns were supplied to the gun crews. With the barometer falling and by the evening on 3 September, the convoy faced gales that were high with 90-foot waves.

The first contact with the enemy was made on 5 September when the weather was better, and again on the 11th of September.

Enemy scout planes appeared on all sides of the convoy two days later in the early morning hours. Enemy subs struck twice and two ships went down. During the same afternoon planes that numbered from 20 to 50 came in for a second attack. They were painted black with green and orange wing tips, a weird and awful sight to behold. They skimmed above the ocean at about 20 feet. With a thousand guns blazing at them, they would dart up and down to confuse the aim of the gunners. More planes flew in dead ahead and from the starboard side 30 minutes after the initial attack.

The *SS Mary Luckenbach* disintegrated upon impact when one of the bombers, on fire and rapidly losing altitude, flew his plane with its deadly cargo onto the forward deck. There were no survivors, although before going down, the crew of this ship was credited with the downing of 5 to 7 enemy planes.

Fifteen enemy bombers returned to drop bombs from a high altitude at the carrier and other ships on 15 September. Wave after wave of approximately 60 to 70 planes in each attack flew over, unloading their bombs that lasted almost four hours. The gun crews could only gaze upward in hopes of hitting the planes and the men almost dropped dead at the guns from lack of sleep. One report stated an Armed Guard officer reportedly had not slept 2 out of 72 hours and had even refused to leave the bridge for any food. It was 21 hours out of 24 on duty for the Armed Guard if they wanted to live.

Finally, the ships arrived in Archangel later that month. The Armed Guard gunners had shot down more than 45 German planes, but they lost 13 ships in the convoy. The gales and huge waves were the ships' ally since it kept the enemy planes away.

There were many convoys such as SC[21]-107 that left New York City with 41 ships 24 October 1942, of which 15 were sunk before they reached Liverpool. The convoy arrived there 10 November but has never gained any recognition for its Murmansk Runs although many of the ships were sunk. All Armed Guardsmen in this convoy proudly wear the Combat Star on their American Theater ribbons for their work.

A trickle movement of ships was tried at the end of October 1942 by sending out 10 ships: 5 American, 5 British, braving the hazards to Murmansk without an escort. In order to travel 100 miles apart, they left one ship at a time, at 12-hour intervals. Due to the high loss of ships and personnel it would not be tried again.

Convoy JW-51A[22] consisted of Merchant ships plus escorts and left Scotland on 7 December. Among the 10 American ships was one veteran ship, the *Jefferson Meyer*, which underwent and survived a ferocious German sub attack 10 days earlier. In a convoy from London to Hull, she was attacked by "E-boats" in "E-boat Alley" east of Dartmouth on 12 December. Five ships were sunk there.

Young boys became old men in a very short time and many of them in this and other convoys to follow, lost 10 to 20 pounds in merely a few days. Other ships would sail to Russian ports; they suffered equal or worse fates. The men who sailed and survived consider themselves blessed and extremely lucky.

The entire bottom of the ship, the *SS Olney* on the port side, was found to be bent in numerous places. She reported that she might have run over a submarine on 3 November. The *SS L.V. Stanford* had a torpedo pass close by her. Later she fired the machine guns at a periscope and the sub dove, but as there was an oil slick, it was believed the sub at least was damaged.

---

[21] Convoys sailing from New York City to Liverpool.

[22] JW-51A departed from Loch Ewe, Scotland to Kola Inlet, Russia in December 1942 and not a one of the 16 ships survived after the enemy detected them. It should be added here that the JW series replaced the PQ series to Russia.

Many other episodes such as this occurred in the Battle of the Atlantic. There was always the worry about the return home. The loss of 4 ships in Convoy QP-13 after being led into an allied minefield due to bad weather and poor visibility was the cost on 5 July 1942. This had prevented the Convoy Escort Commander from getting a good fix before entering the minefield. Other ships had to face U-boats on the way home. The stress and uncertainty of strikes was very hard on the nerves of the men.

Due to rough seas and continuous fog that limited seeing distance to a few feet, the extreme bitter cold, rain, turbulent seas, or a combination of all three, many ships collided in the convoys. As a safety measure, a 300-foot line with a towing fog buoy was attached as a warning from the stern of the ship so the ships' watches, fore and aft, could see if they had closed in on a ship ahead. This was designed to send a pattern of water about 5 feet into the air.

The winter ice in the waters off Murmansk made the required course of the convoys very near the North Cape of Norway and within the range of the JU-66s (also German dive bombers), and the waiting subs, which were guided in by the long range aircraft.

One convoy (PQ-13) headed for Murmansk and after leaving Iceland, ran into very bad weather causing the ships to get badly scattered. When weather cleared a little, the long-range German planes found the ships and attacked the destroyers with bombs.

Many times without food, the survivors were given Vodka to drink which "went right to the feet" when Russian sailors picked up the men of sunken or damaged ships. When Murmansk was reached these young men would be put into a Russian hospital. If one of the men died, especially with great dignity, it wasn't until the following day crewmembers would find out about the death. They might not have known each other's names or where they were from but even to this day, the pain and suffering these men endured and about which they never complained, has not been forgotten by their mates.

This was the case in Convoy ON-166 when the *SS Chattanooga City* and the *SS Expositor* were torpedoed before midnight on 22 February 1943. The crews aboard the *SS Jonathan Sturges* and *SS Hasting* saw those ships hit and the latter two were hit a few hours later with the loss of nine crewmen aboard the *Hasting*. The *Sturges'* crewmen were the only ones not picked up within minutes. One Armed Guardsman would spend 16 days in the cold North Atlantic before the *USS Belknap* rescued him. One of the Merchant seamen died of exposure one day prior to the rescue, even though he had been huddled next to a rescued individual.

Three Armed Guardsmen and two Merchant seamen suffered through an ordeal lasting 41 days, not only suffering from the bitter cold, but also the shortage of food and water. The other 17-crew members would die.

On 7 May 1945, while discharging cargo in Murmansk, word was received that the war was over in Europe as Germany had surrendered. The Russians did not believe the "rumor." On the following day, the United States and Britain were celebrating V-E Day; however, the Russians maintained that the war was not over until Stalin said it was over. The Russians finally accepted the fact on 9 May that the war was over in Europe.

As the reader has gathered, the runs to Murmansk/Archangel were often tragic and terrifying trips.

U.S. NAVAL ARMED GUARD AND MERCHANT SHIPS ATLANTIC CROSSINGS

Consisting of up to 100 or more ships, the convoys appeared to spread out from horizon to horizon. Being assigned locations in the center to provide additional protection were tankers and ammunition ships, but submarine commanders countered by moving inside. Easily recognized by their silhouettes, tankers, when set ablaze, lit up an entire area, giving a better choice of targets for the enemy. Although tankers were hard to sink, they could burn for hours or even days.

Five knots was about as slow as convoy speed could be and it was easy for the faster moving ships to get lost or outdistance the convoy. U-boats generally had a field day when stragglers or damaged ships became sitting ducks. Until late in the war there was a large area in the mid-Atlantic where no air power could be delivered. The U.S. East Coast was a great hunting ground for subs, as ships were silhouetted against lights on the shore. A common sight was of burning ships. German sub packs infested the Atlantic.

Occasionally, the Merchant ships would run out of fuel. They would burn anything that would keep them going. Enemy subs were seekers of ships in difficulty and had no great problem sending many of them to the bottom. Tremendous explosions from torpedoes rocked many U.S. ships.

Men would run through fire with face, hands, and ears badly burned, sometimes barefoot, sometimes with hair burned off during these trying times. It is hard to imagine them living beyond a day or two. Many had the tenacity and the will to live, and did so.

The first and last ships sunk by the enemy were with the first being the *SS Cynthia Olson,* sunk on 7 December 1941, 1200 miles west of Cape Flattery, Washington, with the loss of all hands including 33 crew and 2 U.S. Army. The last was the *SS Black Point* sunk in the Atlantic off Rhode Island on 5 May 1945, with 11 Merchant seamen and one Armed Guard killed as noted earlier. (See Footnote 17.)

Sometimes the men had to spend days and nights in lifeboats when ships in the frigid Atlantic were torpedoed. Some of the men froze to death, some went mad, and others just barely made it when rescued. With nothing to eat for days on end, they caught what fish they could, would cut them into small pieces for each man to have a portion, then eaten raw. Others had only small amounts of water to drink, having to catch rainwater as best they could.

Living on sandwiches and water, it is important to remember that during battle the gunners were unable to leave their stations, required to stay by their guns, sleep next to them and relieving themselves in buckets.

Attacks by water and air were always a threat. The Mediterranean was the most violently contested of the oceans and seas due to its proximity to land and was involved in many battles between the Allies and Axis nations.

In November 1942, the Liberty ships began the invasion of North Africa making history in Sicily, Salerno, Anzio, and southern France. The hazards of war faced these allied ships. There were subs, guns, and other weapons on the shore, enemy aircraft in the air, and underwater mines. Enemy frogmen setting explosives, and radio-controlled glide bombs in the air were two additional new problems encountered by the Merchant vessels, and therefore, the Armed Guard.

Convoys in the Mediterranean would have been annoyed by enemy planes/bombers were it not for the British planes. Their planes matched in ferocity that which our ships had received from the enemy on the way to Murmansk.

British ships, many of which carried American troops, were torpedoed. At times they would explode and sink within minutes. Many troop replacements headed for the battlefield never made it. Some jumped overboard from the burning ships to save themselves only to be killed by depth-charge concussions.

One night as a convoy neared Algiers, torpedo planes and bombers attacked one ship that knocked down an enemy plane. Two hours later another attack occurred. Under cover of night the ships sailed from Algiers hoping to forgo attacks. However, attacks occurred any way, which were so intense that three of the gunners aboard one of the ships had ruptured eardrums.

The Germans attacked again once past the Rock of Gibraltar when the ships were on the way home. This time a ship limped to Liverpool for repairs after a near-miss bomb hit, which knocked the propeller shaft out of line.

The North African landings were merely a prelude to the long-awaited invasion of Europe that became known as the invasion of Normandy. Allied toeholds in Africa simplified the matter of staging the greatest military amphibious operation the world had seen up to that point. Two huge invasion armadas moved across the stormy Mediterranean toward the Island of Sicily.

Assembled in African ports over a period of many weeks were scores of Liberty ships to lend a helping hand to these armies and their vast impediments. Each Liberty ship had temporary accommodations for 200 troops.

Ships passed shattered pieces of airplane wings and fuselage when designated anchorages were approached. One tug had tied on one tail section of a half-submerged plane and was trying to pull it ashore. Bodies were seen floating in the water. It was later discovered they had been airborne troops from gliders that had been mistakenly shot down by "friendly fire."

It was difficult for the men to believe this was real, as at times it was so peaceful. It was surreal to the point that it was more like a dress rehearsal than a war except for the occasional shelling by warships. High-level bombers and dive-bombers began what would become more than 50 air attacks in a week beginning in the late afternoon. When these events happened, the men knew this definitely was not a dress rehearsal.

Being too busy, the seamen did not see the airplanes diving or flaming down during an air attack. What appeared to be glittering tinfoil were bursts of shrapnel in the air and bombs falling. The fires and explosions of ships created indescribable terror.

Drenched by water was a new Armed Guard gun crew that had some near misses when raiding dive-bombers flew over. In one of the Navy logs from that 8-to-12 watch ended with, "Army stevedores discharged cargo between bombs, bullets, and barges," so even in war, there can be humor.

Time after time during the week of one battle, a ship would move but soon after, the German shells followed. Gunners knocked down four planes and a glide bomb. Gunners also got the bomber that had dropped a bomb. The plane blew up leaving nothing but a carburetor that landed on the deck. It was hung in the Armed Guard mess room as a symbol of their marksmanship. The Armed Guard gunners fired approximately 750 rounds of 20-mm shells and got one of two planes during another air raid.

The "black gang" men (firemen, oilers, wipers[23], water tenders and engineers) were marked men, but during the war there was never any evidence that these men missed a watch in time of attack. Many of them went below knowing there was a 50-50 chance they might not come up again. Subs and torpedo-bombers always aimed for the engine room.

Frequently, the last line in the obituaries of Merchant ships in the Mediterranean and elsewhere was "Torpedo hit in the engine room. All men on watch were killed." If a ship could be crippled there was always a chance to finish it off later. In the strain and stress of battle, the shock of frightening explosions and fire, men sometimes made on-the-spot decisions to abandon ships that under "normal"

---

[23] Water tenders assure the water level is maintained in the boilers. Often the Firemen and Water tender jobs are combined. Wipers wipe off excessive oil. They constantly oil the bearings and rods.

conditions could have been saved. Time and weather would have permitted ships that appeared badly damaged to move to dry dock for repairs. This was particularly true for some cargo ships that refused to sink despite tremendous damage.

One of the most costly engagements of the war in the Mediterranean and one seldom mentioned in World War II histories, occurred at the Italian port of Bari, on the Adriatic Coast (near the "heel" of Italy), the night of 2 December 1943. One will find Bari mentioned ever so briefly in several books but as of this writing, only two thus far, have been written detailing the entire story.[24]

In this engagement, the British 8th Army was pushing the enemy back along the coast. Thirty freighters and tankers were at the brilliantly illuminated docks in Bari, discharging ammunition, bombs, gasoline, and other supplies needed for the drive north. Aircraft engines were heard in the early morning hours. Winches were stopped as stevedores searched the moonlit sky. Guns on all ships were manned; gunners waited for the command to open fire. The command never came.

The ships at Bari had been instructed not to fire on attacking aircraft until a designated gun ashore opened the action by firing tracers. Parachute flares lit the harbor and the planes were overhead in what seemed like minutes. The Battle of Bari lasted only 20 minutes. Seventeen ships were sunk or damaged beyond all repair: British 4, Italian 3; American Liberty ships 5; damaged but repairable: American Liberty 1; British 2; Dutch 1; Norwegian 1.

Unknown to many, including the ship's officers, at least one of the American Merchant ships was filled with mustard gas tanks. When

---

[24] Glenn Infield, "Disaster at Bari", wrote the first book about Bari. (See Bibliography.)

the ship exploded, mustard gas was released into the atmosphere and the ocean. President Roosevelt had ordered that mustard gas be taken to Italy in case the Axis decided to use it. Many civilians on the shore and many of the men who jumped or fell into the water suffered terribly and died horrible deaths from the mustard gas. It took some time for the medical facilities' staff to discover what caused the sloughing of the skin and they were hard-pressed to give comfort to the sick, the injured, and the dying.

The Armed Guard is still looking for American survivors of this bombing who suffered from the effects of the poisonous mustard gas.

U.S. NAVAL ARMED GUARD AND MERCHANT SHIPS NORMANDY

Although this invasion was costly for those troops who would go ashore and advance on the enemy, it was not as costly to the Merchant ships and the Armed Guard personnel due to the allied air and sea superiority as had been anticipated. The pre-planned bombardment of the enemy by allied airplanes and warships confirmed the belief that the Allies had come with the intent to stay.

Ports at Omaha and Utah Beaches were made "modern" by scuttling 22 Merchant ships. The Armed Guard gunners manned the Merchant ships' guns toward the beach and on the beach. They endured the fury of the German counterattacks for days. They gave protective firepower for the allied invading forces and the men unloading ammunition, guns, and hundreds of other necessary material.

Courage was required, as was the ability to go many hours without sleep. It didn't take long to discover the Armed Guard was such men.

Having stripped the ships of unnecessary gear, the large guns aft were substituted for four 20-mm and a 40-mm gun since airplanes strafing them would be more of a menace. The larger guns had been installed for surface attacks, hence the smaller guns' removal. Having placed explosive charges in the holds and large holes cut in the transverse bulkheads, the ships were ready to be scuttled in order to provide protection to the troops landing on the beaches at Normandy. Food and ammunition was moved topside as some of the decks at times were under water. German long-range guns fired on them by day with the enemy bombers taking over at night.

The lead ship, the *SS James Iredell*, which had been bombed 23 October 1943 with no loss of crew, was scuttled at her appointed position 7 June 1944. Enemy artillery was so intense during the evening that the Armed Guard had to be evacuated from the ships. The men returned the following day and stayed until 17 June, long before being relieved by a fresh crew of gunners.

Although a dangerous project, enemy planes were shot down at both installations, which proved the plan worthwhile. The Merchant ships and men came under all kinds of attacks; however, they suffered no loss of life and returned to the United States on the *Queen Elizabeth*.

While shuttling from trips between Great Britain and Normandy, Armed Guardsmen experienced just about every form of attack from planes: subs, fast E-boats, mines, artillery, and the dreaded new V-2[25] rocket.

Ships taking part in the Normandy invasion and afterwards are too numerous to list. The Armed Guard crews and other personnel taking part in this enormous task will go down in history as a symbol

---

[25] V-1 rockets were commonly called "buzz bombs" by the Allies and came before the V-2 rockets—the first missiles; both were long-ranged, radio-controlled glide-bombs, and were sent to destroy London because of Hitler's hatred of the British people for Germany's loss in World War I. The 'V' stood for vengeance.

of courage. They lived by their motto: "WE AIM TO DELIVER" and THEY DID!

U.S. NAVAL ARMED GUARD AND MERCHANT SHIPS
THE MEDITERRANEAN SEA

World War II had come early for the people in the Mediterranean Sea. For the U.S. Navy Armed Guardsmen, the action started from the moment the first ship entered the Straits of Gibraltar. Six Merchant ships, in June 1942, formed the Malta Convoy. Armed Guard units were on the Dutch ship, *Tanimbar* and the United States flag ship, *SS Chant*, which was bombed 15 June 1942 with the loss of 3 Merchant crew. Both ships were lost, but the ships' gunners fought fiercely before sinking, by shooting down several enemy planes.

Supplies had to be delivered. The gunners faced a determined enemy to see that they were unsuccessful in delivering said supplies. They knew they were in for a battle when they were required to attend the Defensive Equipped Merchant Ship Schools (also known as DEMS). More armament was added to the ships before leaving Great Britain on 4 June 1942. The escorts included ten destroyers and 2 cruisers.

On the night of 11 June the convoy entered the Straits. As dawn broke on the 12th, these ships were joined by others making up a convoy of two carriers, five cruisers, 21 destroyers, four minesweepers, and 6 motor launches to escort the 14 armed Merchant ships to Malta.

Launches were towed behind the other vessels in the convoy part of the way in order to conserve fuel so they would be fully fueled against the possible dangers of the fast E-boat attacks.

It should be mentioned here that a gentleman in Missouri is trying to save one of the last minesweeps in the United States. The other surviving minesweep is in a museum in Kansas, of all places! As of this writing he has had very little success. He was born after World War II so his effort has to be a labor of love.

Laid out on the decks was ammunition so it was available for quick use. Only five of the 14 Merchant ships reached Malta and from June 12 they had to fight all the way in. Serious action began on 14 June when one reconnaissance plane dropped 3 bombs. Decks were wet down on all ships to keep the ammunition from exploding.

Fifty enemy aircraft approached from the north with 3 being shot down. After the first attack, more planes attacked and 12 more planes were shot down, but not before one flaming plane had unleashed a torpedo and sunk the *Tanimbar*, as noted above. She went down quickly without any Armed Guardsmen being killed. The *Chant* was strafed and the *Liverpool* was hit.

Eating at their guns, the tired gunners suffered another attack with near misses. One dive-bomber was downed. Hours later 40 dive-bombers attacked without any success. Another attack was attempted with another dive-bomber lost.

The convoy was attacked at dawn on 15 June by two Italian light cruisers and three destroyers. Our ships sustained no damage. Later that morning dive-bombers began to attack again. The *Chant* was hit amidship blowing part of her hull plating away and also sustained other damage. She was carrying coal on her deck with coal dust being everywhere. When the flames spread, the crew abandoned ship.

British Spitfires appeared during an attack by Italian ships. The ships did not return. More planes attacked during the day but the Spitfires drove them off. Other attacks occurred but little damage was sustained.

Armed Guardsmen were on board the *SS Almerica* and *SS Santa Elisa*. Those ships were also sunk, both torpedoed 13 August 1942. When the gunners were rescued, they joined the gun crews on other ships that happened time and time again whenever ships were lost. None of the Armed Guard crews were lost but 3 men did receive serious burns when they had to jump overboard into flaming gasoline that had been a part of their cargo.

As the battered convoy prepared to enter Valetta Harbor at Malta, enemy mines took their toll. One Polish destroyer was sunk. As the convoy remnants entered the harbor, the grateful people of Malta and gun crews stationed high up on the fortification sites, cheered while a band played, "God Save the King" and the "Star Spangled Banner."

U.S. NAVAL ARMED GUARD AND MERCHANT SHIPS PACIFIC ARENA

With the bombing of Pearl Harbor at 7:55 a.m. Hawaiian time, war started for the United States. The war also began for 33 Merchant crew and two U.S. Army soldier passengers aboard the *SS Cynthia Olsen* when a shore radio picked up an SOS that a Japanese submarine that had surfaced was shelling her. Being that the *Olsen* was unarmed, she was the first U.S. Flag Merchant ship sunk in World War II. There were no survivors as all 33 Merchant Seamen and the two U.S. Army soldiers were killed.

At anchor in Manila Bay on 6 December 1941, the *SS Capillo* came under attack by Japanese planes. She was moved near Corregidor upon hearing that the United States had declared war on Japan and came under attack again on 8 December. She was hit with bombs and strafing attacks, killing one crewman. She, too, was not armed. Of the 35 crewmen captured by the Japanese on 2 December, six died while prisoners of war.

While serving on the *SS Grant* one man was injured. He was hospitalized, captured, taken prisoner and repatriated in September 1945. Fifty-nine Japanese planes raided the unarmed ships in the harbor on 8 December 1941. Before guns could be placed on the ships for any protection, many such incidents occurred in the Pacific.

One of the best kept secrets of the war involved the Japanese balloon bomb offensive, prompted by the raid on Tokyo 18 April 1942, as a means of direct reprisal against the U.S. mainland. Some 9,000 balloons made of paper or rubberized silk and carrying anti-personnel and incendiary bombs were launched from Japan during a five-month period, to be carried by high altitude winds more than 6,000 miles eastward across the Pacific to North America. Perhaps a thousand of these reached this continent, but there were only about 285 reported incidents. Most were reported in the northwest US but some balloons traveled as far east as Michigan. Japanese bomb-carrying balloons were 32 feet in diameter and when fully inflated, held about 19,000 cubic feet of hydrogen.

Two days after 3 November 1944 a US Navy patrol boat spotted a balloon floating on the water 66 miles southwest of San Pedro, California. As more sightings occurred, the government with the cooperation of the news media adopted a policy of silence to reduce the chance of panic among residents and to deny the Japanese any information on the success of the launches. Discouraged by their apparent failure of their effort, they halted their balloon attacks in April 1945.

The captain of the *SS Benjamin Harrison* deliberately grounded her with 167 crewmen aboard. Twelve died while prisoners of war. When torpedoed on 16 March 1943, three were killed when their lifeboat was sucked into the turning rudder, including two members of crew and one Armed Guard. The Japanese salvaged the *Harrison*.

Being torpedoed on 2 May 1943, the *SS William Williams* had an unusual story to tell: Orders were issued to abandon ship; she was. The men decided to re-board her and did so. Under her own power, she finally made her way to port.

On 12 September 1944, the *Harrison,* was being sailed by the Japanese, was sunk by the submarine *USS Pampanito* in the South China Sea while en route from Singapore to Japan. Nine hundred allied prisoners of war were aboard. Over 500 prisoners were saved by submarine rescues.

On 24 October 1944, a suicide plane narrowly missed the *SS David Dudley Field*. Another Kamikaze hit the tugboat alongside the *SS Augustus Thomas* while a third suicide plane hit the No. 7 gun tub of the *Field*. A wing of the plane was ripped off. Amazingly, the loader of the No. 7 gun tub had his shoe cut by the propeller but escaped any injury. As this same plane passed over the *Field*, it swept away the ventilators and burned the gunners in the No. 6 gun tub. Three Armed Guardsmen were injured and fragments hit others but there was no loss of life.

Unfortunately, little history was kept on the Merchant ships or the crews until 7 August 1942, when the allies began their first offensive at Guadalcanal. The Merchant ships had carried supplies there but experienced little action. Ships were soon armed and U.S. Armed Guard crews were placed on board to man the guns. Attention was mostly focused on the "North Atlantic runs" to England and Russia.

The Marines and Army military suffered many casualties. The *SS James Ramsey* fired only one shell; reported 8 air raids while there; however, there was plenty of danger.

The Battle of the Philippine Islands that started 20 October 1943 is now known as the big "Battle of the Pacific" for Armed Guard crews. The Battle of Leyte was the most comparable as far as experience went on the way to, and, in Murmansk, Russia. Again, as then, the Merchant ships, Merchant crews, and the Armed Guard gunners stood up to the worst the enemy could offer and came out victorious. The Kamikaze pilots were introduced to the crews here. The first Armed Guard gunner reported wounded was on the *SS Joseph Wing*; his injuries were caused by falling flak.

Taking a lot of punishment, the *SS Benjamin Ide Wheeler's* Armed Guard had general quarters (Condition 1) 353 times in 76 days before being hit by a Kamikaze pilot on 27 October 1944. It was at this time one Armed Guard and one Merchant Seaman were killed. Also aboard were 267 Army engineers, their equipment, and cargo of high explosives and gasoline. According to the signalman on board the *Wheeler*, she sank in 36 feet of water, but the gunners continued to down the four enemy planes.

Although suffering 50 constant enemy attacks with some 40 bombs dropped near her, the *SS Adroniram Judson* and other ships survived. The gunners were credited with two planes downed before the bombers arrived and added two more downed planes with four assists prior to leaving on 30 October.

Reporting 137 "red alerts," the *SS Clarence Darrow* kept firing at the enemy over a period of 19 days, shot down two planes, and assisted on three more.

The *SS John Page* shot down two planes with two assists.

As she anchored in Dulag Harbor, Leyte, on 12 November 1944, the *SS Thomas Nelson* exploded when a Kamikaze hit her. Her cargo consisted of bombs and gasoline as well as 633 U.S. Army troops, 38 Merchant Seamen and 27-Armed Guard. Three Armed Guards and 80 Army men were killed and 164 injured. The same airplane was strafing the ship when it hit the jumbo boom. The impact exploded the bomb carried by the plane, which started a fire that took two hours to extinguish.

The Army volunteers assisted the Armed Guard gunners in fighting the fire. It should be noted that this was not a sole incident with Army volunteers. They offered assistance where needed time and again. According to one of the volunteer ammunition loaders, the aft guns were put out of action but others continued to defend the ship.

The *Nelson* was not abandoned. Doctors and medical supplies were rushed in from shore to treat the wounded; the wounded were then taken ashore in small Navy crafts.

On 3 January 1945, the *SS William I. Chamberlain*, the *Allen Johnson*, and the *Lewis L. Dyche* were credited with several planes shot down in a convoy for Mindora. Suddenly a Kamikaze hit the *Dyche*. The ship disintegrated killing all personnel that included 41 crew and 30-Armed Guard. There were casualties on a nearby fleet ship. The Armed Guard death toll for Mindora: 63 missing and dead, 23 wounded.

The gunners were credited with 8 enemy planes shot down, 16 assists, plus a possible 3 more credits. A Kamikaze plane hit at the water line of the *SS Emira Victory* while she was at Langayen Gulf. Flying fragments injured six of the Merchant seamen.

Another suicide plane crashed on the *SS Otis Skinner*; the fire burned for 36 hours.

On 12 January a Kamikaze hit the *SS Kyle V. Johnson*. This ship had been named for a Merchant Seaman (Kyle V. Johnson) aboard the *SS Maiden Creek* in the Mediterranean Sea on 17 March 1944.

The suicide plane hit the No. 3 hatch, starboard side, after being hit by 20-mm gunfire. There were 500 Army troops and 2,500 tons of vehicles and gasoline in drums aboard the *Johnson* as she steamed toward the gulf in a 100-ship convoy about evenly divided between ships and LSTs ("Landing Slow Targets" was what the men called these). At 0130 hours, 6 or more airplanes attacked the convoy. The engine of the plane plowed through the hull plating into the 'tween decks crowded with troops and finally coming to rest in the lower hold.

The *Johnson* dropped out of the convoy to fight the fire, extinguished the flames, and rejoined the fleet. The death toll was one Armed Guard killed, 128 Army casualties, and many injuries sustained by the crew and military.

Said a survivor of the *Johnson*: "There was a blinding flash and an explosion so heavy it blew the steel hatch beams higher than the flying bridge." The Armed Guard was restrained from shooting unless directly attacked while at Okinawa due to the superior air coverage of the allies. Because so many allied planes were in the air during these attacks, restrictions on shooting stopped the risk of being shot down by friendly fire. Having to endure the strain of the attacking enemy, the Armed Guard had some close calls. They could do nothing but wait.

The first ships to arrive in the Okinawa area arrived on 6 April 1945, at Kerama Retto Bay.

Anyone who served aboard ships during the war can tell you that a ship takes on its' own personality and becomes as a living, breathing entity.

A new era in warfare and a new era in history dawned on 6 August 1945—the nuclear age—ushered in by the first atomic bomb drop on Hiroshima. Military technology continued to accelerate with the improvement of tanks and planes, reappearance of rocket weapons from the simple hand-carried "bazooka" to the highly complex long-range German V-2 rockets, improvement of radar and radio communications. Warfare would become three dimensional with strategic and tactical combinations. Civilian science and industry on one hand, military competence and genius on the other depended on the success of closer affiliation.

Unprecedented pooling of leaders, staffs, troops, and resources by the British Empire and the United States encompassed the theaters of war with integrated armies, navies, and air forces, which had never happened before. Each country willingly subordinated individual national characteristics, doctrine, and training of a unified command directed against common objectives.

The United States Navy solved one of the most logistic problems of naval warfare was that of vessels having to return to a land base for fuel, supplies, and repair. The Navy's Seabees[26], the Army's port troops and railroad, and airborne Engineers reduced routine supply problems to a minimum whereas a quarter-century before, these would have been insurmountable obstacles.

The war did not end for many at the signing of the surrender treaty on 2 September 1945. The Armed Guard stayed on and mopped up the enemy holed up in caves on some of the islands.

When you see the flag of the United States of America, admire it. Had all the brave young men not been willing to die for the cause of peace, for us; yes, for you and for me, and for the opportunity for the lives we lead today, today we might not be the English speaking country that we are. We owe them our gratitude, respect, and to always remember what they did for us—long after the last World War II veteran has gone to his "greater glory."

---

[26] Seabees is a name coined for Construction Battalion members. CB's/Seabees built bases, airfields, storage facilities, etc. Swabee, often confused with CB, is just another name for a sailor, coined from swabbing (mopping) decks.

U.S. NAVAL ARMED GUARD AND MERCHANT SHIPS NORTH AFRICA

By manning the guns and communications of Merchant ships, their crews, and their cargo, the Armed Guard played an important part in the invasion of North Africa on 8 November 1942. Some ships were defended which brought men, food, munitions, and other essentials with which to fight a war. Compared to approximately 1500 Merchant ships in the area in the battles of Sicily and Italy that were to follow, these 30 ships were just a few. Not a single ship that was defended by the Armed Guard was sunk at the invasion of North Africa.

The *Edward Rutledge* came under attack by shore batteries and machine gun fire. By mistake, a British Spitfire also fired at her. Later, the gun crew shot at two more enemy planes and downed one, a Spitfire that was being used by the Vichy French. The gunners stayed at their battle stations 7 November to 10 November as planes were sighted with some being fired upon.

While unloading their troops at Casablanca, the U.S. Army Transport (U.S.A.T.) *J. W. McAndrew, Santa Monica*, and the *Santa Elena* experienced no serious attacks. Later however, the *Santa Elena* was aerial torpedoed on 6 November 1943, and 3 Merchant crew were lost. The gunners aboard the "Tawali" shot down a British patrol bomber when it appeared that it would attack her. Enemy frogmen placed small explosive charges along the ships' keels at Algiers, where more serious damage was done.

The *Exceller* fired at a plane that afterward the gunners learned was "Free French". However, she was attacked later by some German Heinkel 111 airplanes but sustained no damage as she was using Army 40-mm and .50-caliber machine guns, which was a part of her cargo, to defend the ship.

Armed Guard crews were in a Malta-bound convoy aboard three Merchant ships that entered the Mediterranean Sea from the Suez Canal on 16 November 1942. The *Mormacmoon, Robin Locksley*, and the Dutch ship, *Bantam*, came under aerial attacks with near misses. The *Agwimonte* became engaged with a British armed ship on 12 January before the men discovered they were on the same side. Later, on 28 May 1943, the *Agwimonte* was torpedoed suffering no casualties.

The first American ship in Bone, Algeria, North Africa was the *William Johnson*. Experiencing a hell on earth with 47 alarms and 21 air raids by German planes from 18 December to 6 January 1943, she sustained damage to her aft gun that was machine-gunned and her flag was pierced with bullets. The bow gun was covered with debris and shell fragments were flying everywhere. The Merchant Marine crew and the Armed Guard had helped fight three fires among the ammunition piles stored on the quay.

While awaiting orders at Algiers to proceed to Bone, the gunners of Italian frogmen with Limpet mines witnessed a daring raid. The frogmen sank one ship and damaged three others. The *Arthur Middleton* disintegrated except for a 40-foot section of the stern but this part sank a few seconds later. Killed were 11 Merchant crew, 3 Armed Guards, and 1 U.S. Army personnel. Only 3-Armed Guards survived.

The Armed Guard and the Merchant crews, many times during the battle, performed heroic deeds and from the Mediterranean conflict, none of which could be documented because of the censorship involved.

At the beginning of 1943, enemy subs concentrated on the mouth of the Straits. Raids and attacks occurred many times as the Germans stepped up their attacks, as in one convoy which had left New York on 4 March 1943 bound for ports in the Mediterranean Sea. Men who witnessed them have told stories of these deeds, by others who did them. The most that could be said was, "I looked over at the next ship and when I looked back, she was gone, blown to bits." The Armed Guard performed many jobs that should have been written in the logs but were not allowed to be at the time because of security reasons.

Armed Guard Replacement Centers were soon established in ports that the Merchant ships supplied for those who had been injured and others who became seriously ill. These replacements had to adjust to new gun crews as soon as they arrived. Many Armed Guardsmen volunteered to assist in guarding the prisoners of war. They felt it was their duty when prisoners were taken and had to take them back to the States.

On 12 May 1943, with the North African Campaign over, allied bases were established in order that the war could be fully carried back to the enemy's soil that had achieved another stepping stone toward victory. The agony of battle and desert heat was over for the Allied Forces.

At last, another continent with its people had been liberated!

U.S. NAVAL ARMED GUARD AND MERCHANT SHIPS SICILY

On 11 July 1943, Merchant ships started arriving at Gela, Sicily one day after the invasion began.

After the *SS Robert Rowan* arrived and was approximately one-half mile off the beach, an enemy shore battery began shelling the ship, injuring one soldier but no loss of life. Many of the shells straddled the ship. One enemy attack did no damage but when 3 bombs hit the ship bombs shortly thereafter, orders to abandon ship commenced.

Leaving at the very end, when the Armed Guard and all hands were clear of the ship a few minutes later, the No. 2 hold exploded. Dive-bombers strafed other ships and boats. After the first explosion, the *Rowan* was blown in half by another. Initially, the attack consisted of 32 bombers.

Hindsight being what it is, the *USS Boise* was most likely the real target, for earlier she had silenced the enemy shore batteries. Transferring the Armed Guard gunners from the *Rowan* to the *Arizaba*, the latter ship arrived on 15 July in time to witness the disintegration of a Norwegian freighter that blew off rooftops and killed many civilians.

When a Canadian ship carrying ammunition broke into flames, she was towed out to sea and beached. Before the gunners left, Gela was more or less cleaned of enemy troops; many ships going there later saw no action whatsoever.

The crew of the *William W. Gerhard* shot down a plane at Salerno on 1 August. The plane was very close to a train of ammunition that blew up on the dock. Shells flew around the *Gerhard* and many shells fell on deck. Just prior to a shell being thrown overboard, it exploded, injuring three Armed Guardsmen. The *Gerhard* was later torpedoed on 21 September 1943, with two Armed Guardsmen killed.

Sicily could be called the final stepping-stone to the invasion of southern Europe and final victory. Many stories could be told about this battle. For instance, the day paratroopers were to fly into Sicily but due to a sandstorm in Africa, takeoff was delayed. Later, being airborne, they could not send out the message that they were on their way. As they came over the ships following an air raid, some were shot down before the shooting could be stopped. This is the price that is sometimes paid in war.

COLLISION COURSE

While doing research on this ship and the French Aircraft carrier who rammed her, I decided that the more important issue here was the men who served aboard the "Mac" and the troops who were aboard her at the time of the collision as well as the little known Armed Guard. It was with this in mind that the format and information required began to take form. I knew it would be a tremendous undertaking after all these years, but knowing that so many of our World War II veterans are dying daily, decided it was imperative; so my mind and path were set. Knowing the research might take many months, even years, I refused to let that keep me from trying to find as many of the men or surviving relatives as possible.

Every letter, every photograph, every telephone call, even e-mails have been a treasure. After all these years, I am still in contact with many of the men, their wives or widows, and other relatives. What a blessing this has been for me! And I must admit I am truly blessed.

One of several new vessels of the Mississippi Shipping Company to be drafted into military service, the *Deltargentino* still carried that name when first acquired as a troopship by the Army. Renamed the USAT *J.W. McAndrew*, she was home-ported in New York during the war, and made numerous crossings to Europe and North Africa carrying about 1,900 men per voyage. (National Archives)

THE *DELTARGENTINO*

This ship was built in 1940 by Bethlehem Steel Company, Sparrows Point, Maryland. It was of the "Delta" type, owned by the Mississippi Shipping Line Company, Inc., and was launched in November 1940. Her routes included New Orleans, Port Arthur, Mobile, Gulfport, Pensacola, Tampa, Pernambuco, Rio de Janeiro, Santos, Montevideo, and Buenos Aires. Inasmuch as she was built in the United States, she was registered here in this country and would carry 67 first class passengers.

Her funnel was yellow with a yellow Greek delta on a green disk separated from a black top by green over yellow over green bands. The hull was black with red boot topping.

One of several new vessels of the Mississippi Shipping Company to be drafted into military service, the *Deltargentino* still carried that name when first acquired as a troopship. Her overall length was 491 feet 10 inches, her beam was 65 feet 6 inches, had a speed of 10 knots, and turbine propulsion.

USAT JAMES W. McANDREW

The *Deltargentino*[27] was renamed the *James W. McAndrew* in honor of James William McAndrew, having gone through a hasty conversion from a luxury cruise ship to a troop ship in June 1941 when she was assigned to the U.S. Navy but was not taken by them. Instead her completed conversion enabled her to carry 1,891 troops for the Army. The reader will note in later correspondence that she still had her fancy chandeliers and steel steps instead of the rope ladders Navy men were used to using. She made four voyages from New Orleans to Cristobal before being assigned in 1941 to New York as her homeport. From her new homeport she made cruises to Puerto Rico, Jamaica, the Canal Zone, Trinidad, and New Orleans.

Photo No. 80-G-30488 USAT J. W. McAndrew in November 1942

---

[27] The names of this ship used throughout the IDPFs are *John W. McAndrews, John W. McAndrew, James W. McAndrews,* and *James W. McAndrew.*

James William McAndrew was born in Pennsylvania on 30 June 1862. While growing to manhood, he made quite a name for himself in the military. He graduated from West Point in 1888 and continued his military education by attending the Army School of the Line, completing his studies in 1910. He graduated from the Army Staff College in 1911 and the Army War College in 1913. Neither of these colleges is now functioning.

McAndrew was commissioned a 2nd Lieutenant of the Infantry on 11 June 1888. He moved up through the ranks and was promoted to Brigadier General, National Army on 5 August 1917; Major General, National Army 16 April 1918; Brigadier General, U.S. Army on 8 November 1918; and finally to Major General, U.S. Army, 5 May 1921. (Note the name changes the Army undergoes throughout his military service.)

He saw action in the Sioux Indian Campaign, 1890-91, and at the Battle of El Caney, Cuba, 1 July 1898. During the insurrection of the Philippines, he served a tour of duty from 1899 through 1902. He served with a regiment in Alaska, 1905-07, and was a member of the General Staff Corps from 1916 to 1917.

During World War I, he served in France from 26 June 1917 through 8 June 1919, as Chief of Staff with the American Expeditionary Forces. From 6 May 1918 through 26 May 1919, he was Commandant at the General Staff College in Washington, DC

Major McAndrew died in Washington, DC on 30 April 1922, and is buried in Section 3 of Arlington National Cemetery.

NOTE: I wrote the Pennsylvania State Historical Society for additional information and as amazing as it might seem, they stated in a response to my inquiries that they have no information, not even a photograph. I also wrote to the Department of the Army, United States Army War College and Carlisle Barracks where he not only attended but also was supposedly a department head, and according to them, "They also have no information".

In January 1942, the "Mac" left New York for the Panama Canal and sailed to Australia. In May 1943 she sailed to Iceland and Glasgow, Scotland, continuing on to Capetown, South Africa, and then returned to New York in August. The "Mac" was used to drop off supplies, replacements of military, and pick up wounded in Southampton. She made one trip to Glasgow, Scotland with 2,600 German prisoners of war.

After participating in the invasion of North Africa in November 1942, she left for Casablanca, Morocco. She returned to New York where she made many trips to Europe and Africa with the principal ports of call being Oran, Algeria, Casablanca, Algeria, Gibraltar, Belfast, Northern Ireland, Naples, Italy, Cherbourg and LeHavre, France, Plymouth and the Clyde (Northern England), Southampton. Only major voyage repairs by Todd-Brooklyn interrupted this service during May and June 1944.

While en route to Europe in convoy in March 1945 the *McAndrew* was involved in an accidental collision with the French Aircraft Carrier, the *Bearn*, and put in at Ponta Delgada, Azores Islands[28] for temporary repairs by their maritime service but conducted under Navy supervision. Additional information about the collision will be

gleaned from the survivors, the crew, and the testimonies. According to the men who were aboard at the time of the collision, she traveled at about 4 knots per hour, taking several days to make the 50 to 160 mile trip, depending on whose letters one reads.

Arriving back in the States, between April and June 1945, the ship

---

[28] The Azores Islands were controlled by Portugal that the Allies sought to occupy as a forward base for the defense of shipping against U-boats. Negotiations with the Portuguese government opened in May 1941, but it was not until October 1943 that Britain gained the use of an airstrip. The U.S. Navy joined forces with Britain in extending the airfield and occupying the islands the following January.

underwent permanent hull repairs at the Bethlehem-Key Highway Plant in Baltimore. She left the Hampton Roads Port of Embarkation for Naples in July. Following her return to Baltimore, she mad several miscellaneous voyages, such as Hampton Roads, Virginia to Marseilles, France; Newport News, Virginia to Naples, Italy; and New York to LeHavre, France.

C3 (Modified)
8,602
17 knots

THE cargo-passenger vessel S.S. AFRICAN ENTERPRISE operates between New York and ports in South and East Africa. She carries 80 passengers and general cargo. The run from New York to Cape Town—her first port of call—takes seventeen days, the longest non-stop commercial run made by any line today. The round trip takes about two months.

AFRICAN ENTERPRISE

The U.S.A.T. *James W. McAndrew* was purchased by the American South African Line, Inc., and delivered to the Port of New York on 5 May 1947, at noon, Eastern Daylight Time ("EDT"). She was then sold to the Farrell Lines, Inc. with delivery to the Port of New Jersey on 22 December 1948, at 12:45 p.m. EDT, at which time title passed and she was converted back to a passenger/cargo line.

She was renamed the *African Enterprise* and was laid up by the Maritime Administration in Baltimore, Maryland by the Farrell Lines, Inc., on 22 September 1960, at 12 noon.

Next she was put in the Reserve Fleet on the James River near Lee Hall, Virginia on 19 October 1960, at 9:00 a.m., with the Department of the Navy receiving temporary custody on 28 September 1966, at 11:00 a.m. This temporary custody was granted in order for the Navy to remove the spare tail shaft.

On 9 April 1969, the Boston Metals Company ("BMC") purchased this grand ship that had been involved in many historical moments. If she could have spoken she would have delivered some tall yarns about her heyday.

[Vessel Status Card for DELTARGENTINO, O.N. 240124, Type Sgl.So.Pass., Gross 7997, Hull No. 50, Built by Bethlehem Steel Co. at Sparrows Pt., Md., Completed 11-1940. Basis to W.S.M.C. 5-5-47 Noon EDT @ New York from War Dept. - Surplus]

Date Allocated	Operator	Form of Agree.	Port of Delivery	Date and Time Delivered
Oct 1936	Amer. S. African Line, Inc. FARRELL LINES INC.	GAA	New York	5-5-47 Noon EDT
See Pink Card for old information	Deld to Farrell Lines Inc. Oct 1944 Title Passed 12-22-48 12:45 PM EST Renamed "AFRICAN ENTERPRISE"	PUR	Jersey City	12-22-48 12:45 PM EST
	Maritime Administration (Trade in) (Preparing for lay-up by Farrell Lines Inc.)	Title	Baltimore, Md.	9-22-60 12:00 Noon EST
	Reserve Fleet	-	James River	10-19-60 9:00am
	Dept. of Navy (Temporary custody) (For removal of spare tail shaft)		James River	9-28-66 11:00am EST
	The Boston Metals Co. (Scrap) (Physical Delivery)	Purchase	James River	4-9-69 5-8-69 10:55AM EST

She was sold for scrap metal and was delivered to BMC on 8 May 1969, at 10:55 a.m. In February 1972, she was broken up for scrap at Baltimore, Maryland. And thus ends these sad stories of a beautiful ship.

BEARN

The *Bearn* was one of five battleships of the "Normandie" class begun in 1912 by FC de la Mediterranean, LeSeyne, and laid down 10 January 1914. This was suspended at the start of World War I as steel was "used for more important construction." At the end of World War I these ships were considered obsolete and four hulls were scrapped.

Regarding the *Bearn*, she was launched in April 1920. The postwar plans were to turn her into a battleship but these plans were canceled, as she was too slow; instead she was converted to an experimental carrier during 1923 through 1927, and commissioned in May 1927. British assistance was needed in this design. As in carriers of other nations, she spent her early years in experimental trials. At trial the speed of 21.5 knots was reached with over 40,000 horsepower but was quickly made obsolete by advancing carrier design.

The *Bearn* was converted as follows: The basic battleship hull was retained but the armor greatly reduced. Her boilers were upgraded but the original steam/reciprocating plant was retained. There was a single-level hangar with repair shops and spare aircraft storage below. A large island projected out to starboard. The elevators from below were small, oddly shaped, and inefficient. Her speed was too slow causing her to be ineffective as a fleet unit.

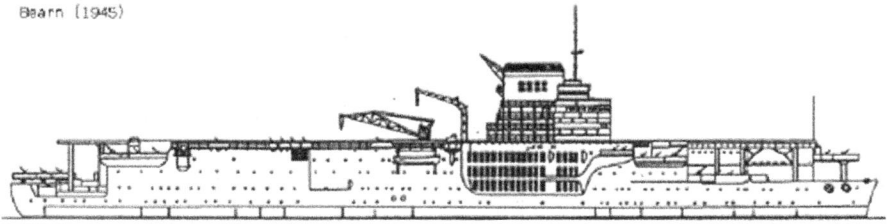

Bearn (1945)

Soon after completion the *Bearn's* flight deck, which was 600 feet long and with a height of 51 feet from the waterline, was modified and rebuilt with a downward slope at the bow completion.

She was again refitted and generally upgraded in 1935. By bringing the external gangway to a level of three feet nine inches lower, this allowed personnel to move about clear of the flight deck. The central hangar underneath the flight deck could house five torpedo planes, five reconnaissance planes, and seven fighter planes, which was only a portion of the total of 36 aircraft it carried. Under this hangar were the workshops for assembling and repairs as well as the accommodations of partially equipped planes. By means of asbestos curtains, the hangar and workshops could be divided into two portions.

The hangar and workshops were equipped with overhead transporter cranes for the rapid manipulation of heavy weights, and a special type of derrick was fitted on the starboard side of the ship, abaft[29] funnel.

Planes were carried up to the flight deck by means of three electric lifts, the smallest being 27x40 feet and the largest 50x50 feet. On a lift, forward, was the chart house, which could be raised above or dropped below the flight deck. She was capable of accommodating over 40 planes.

Smoke was diluted with cold air to avoid eddies[30] in the surrounding atmosphere.

Other items of equipment included 3530 cubic feet of petrol, under inert[31] gas and 530 cubic feet of oil.

It was stated that owing to the lack of space on the flight deck, only about one-fourth of the total number of planes carried could be employed simultaneously.

Her operational abilities were limited by the poor selection of aircraft available as well as her slow speed. She spent several years ferrying aircraft from Canada to France. Her service as a carrier ended with the fall of France in 1940. At

---

[29] Aft, at or near the stern [rear end] of a ship.
[30] A current or circular current similar to a whirlpool.
[31] Few or no inactive properties.

Fort-de-France in Martinique, she came under the command of Admiral Robert, Governor of Martinique, who remained loyal to Vichy France until the United States broke off relations with Marshall Petunia. By previous arrangement with the U.S. approval, Admiral Robert demilitarized her at Martinique. Her only wartime and postwar service was as an aircraft transport, as she was too small and slow to function as a fleet carrier.

It should be noted that in December 1940 when President Roosevelt took a cruise aboard the *USS Tuscaloosa*, and took aboard Churchill for a secret conference, the *Bearn* lay to just outside the territorial waters of Martinique. Many on board were focusing their binoculars during this brief conference on the *Bearn* lying in the harbor of Fort-de-France, an ominous symbol of the French "fleet in being" which was still under the flimsy control of the Vichy Government. Admiral Robert resigned 30 June 1943 and turned the colony and warships over to the French Committee of National Liberation under Charles deGaule. When this occurred, the *Bearn* became available to the Allies.

Proceeding to the French West Indies in June 1940, she remained inactive until 1944. She went to the United States (Puerto Rico) for refit and conversion to an aircraft transport, where she was completely re-armed with four 5-inch/38 cal. weapons, twenty-four 40mm anti-aircraft weapons and twenty-six 20mm anti-aircraft guns.

U.S. and local French authorities agreed on measures to form Allied bases in Martinique, and three French warships, including the carrier *Bearn*, were immobilized. The *Bearn*, too small and slow to function as a fleet carrier, would enjoy an unglamorous but important second life as an aircraft transport. From 1945 through 1947 she was still used as an aircraft transport in French Indochina.

The French Marine Nationale Etat-Major Service Historique sent their "collision report" on 27 March 2000, which states:

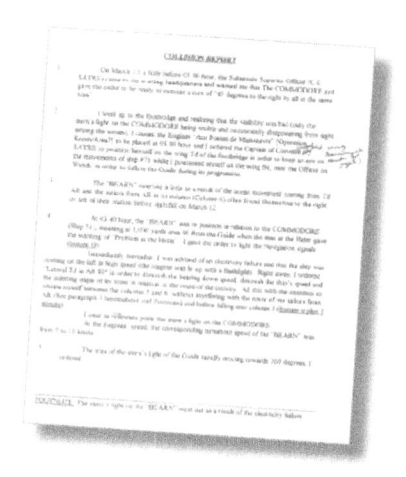

"On March 13, 1945, a little before 03.00, the Substitute Superior Officer came to my evening quarters and warned me that the Commodore just gave the order to be ready to execute a turn of 45 degrees to the right by all [ships] (zig zag course) at the same time.

I went up to the footbridge and realizing that the visibility was bad (only the stern's light on the Commodore being visible and occasionally disappearing from sight among the waves), I caused the engines' [Aux Postes de Manoeuvre] operation room/area to be placed at 0.300 hour and I ordered the Captain of Corvette Satre[32] to position himself on the wing Td[33] of the footbridge in order to keep an eye on the movements

---

[32] A Corvette is a small escort and patrol vessel built by British and Canadian merchant shipyards from 1940 until the end of the war to an adapted whale catcher design. These were planned by the British in 1939 as an answer to their desperate shortage of escort vessels and were intended for coastal work. Mr. Bowerman states: "I will always remember the tiny Corvettes dashing around our convoys warding off the submarines, giving skippers hell when a porthole was open with light shining out, picking up survivors, and giving up their own bunks and blankets to them. God Bless Great Britain."

[33] I have been unable to locate these abbreviations although it is presumed to be a directional order of the ship.

of ship #71 while I positioned myself on the wing Bd[34], near the Officer on Watch, in order to follow the Guide during its progression.

The *Bearn* swerved a little as a result of the ocean movement coming from Td AR[35] and the sailors from AR[36] in its column (column 6) often found themselves to the right or left of their station before nightfall on 12 March.

At 03.40 hour, the *Bearn* was in position in relation to the Commodore (Ship #51), meaning at 1,000 yards of area 90, from the Guide when the man at the helm gave the warning of a "problem at the helm." I gave the order to light the navigation signals (Instant O[37])."

Immediately thereafter, I was advised of an electricity failure and that the ship was coming on the left at high speed. The magnet was lit up with a flashlight. Right away I ordered "Lateral Td in AR 80" in order to diminish the bearing down speed, diminish the ship's speed, and the sidelong angle of its route in relation to the route of the convoy. All this was with the intention to situate myself between [convoy] columns 5 and 6 without interfering with the route of my sailors from AR, herein above and before falling into column 5 (Instant plus 1 minute). The stern's light on the *Bearn* went out as a result of the electricity failure.

I used as reference point the stern's light on the Commodore (lead ship in convoy).

At the engine's speed, the corresponding turnabout speed of the *Bearn* was from 9 to 10 knots.

The area of the stern's light of the Guide rapidly moving towards 360 degrees, I ordered:

---

[34] Ibid.
[35] Ibid.
[36] Ibid.
[37] I have talked with people who spoke French, were born in France, written to French schools here in the U.S., the Internet, and these terms must be related to the old French Navy as no one seems to have any idea what they mean or where to locate them. Please see author's note at the end of this chapter.

Central Engines Stop

Lateral Bd Stop (Instant 1 mn 30) and these orders were transmitted by the telephone operators: 'All lateral engines in AR (Instant 1 mn 45 to 2 mns'); this sequence was followed in order to avoid any confusion in the orders transmission which could only be made by telephone; the Martini (electronic order transmitters) being non-functional as a result of the complete electricity failure.

At 03.45 hours (Instant O plus 3 mns) the collision took place with one ship of the convoy (ship #52—the U.S.A.T. J. W. McAndrew). The estimated positions of the footbridges of the two ships are indicated below:

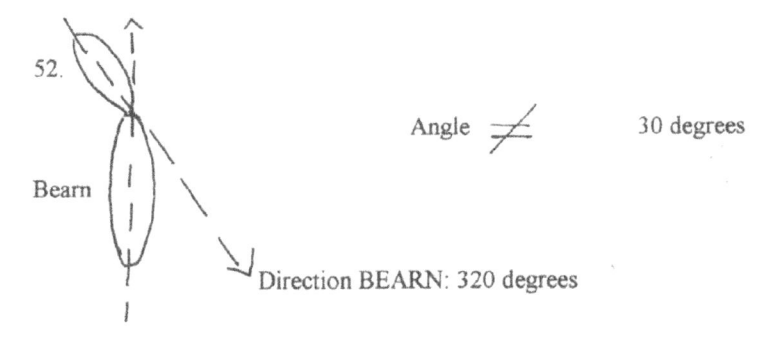

Angle ≠ 30 degrees

Direction BEARN: 320 degrees

The *Bearn*, which was still slowly bearing down on the port side must have been without considerable deviation in AV as proven by the fact that it immediately freed itself from the hole in the U.S.A.T. *J.W. McAndrew* which remains in area O and the reverse direction towards Bd of the sheet metal forward of the *Bearn*.

While my order: "All Lateral engines in AR" was transmitted, I noticed the stern's light of the Guide was in area 60 Td.

At the time of the electrical failure, the course of the *Bearn* was 85-86 (swerving to the right) and the helm was to the left 10.

Four young sailors were lost because of the collision: Machinist Jean Lorrain; Crewman Albert Egault; S/Spte Georges Derrien; and S/Spte Didace Rivas. Three of them were killed aboard the *Bearn* and one washed out to sea; his body was never recovered.

On Board, March 15, 1945
Frigate Captain Lamy
Captain of the Aircraft Carrier *Bearn*"

The reader will find the names of the lost French sailors listed at the bottom of the list containing the names and ranks of the lost American military personnel.

The *Bearn*, from 1948 to 1966, served as a training ship and an accommodation ship for submarines.

In 1966 she was deleted from the Navy list and was scrapped in Toulon, France, 31 March 1967, and the hull sold to Italian breakers.

NOTE: I have also written several French schools regarding the AR/T/TD and other abbreviations with no response. My interpreter could not locate anyone either.

April 9, 1945

FRENCH NAVAL MISSION
In the U.S.A.
****
Aircraft Carrier BEARN

8 222 S.G.

ACTIVITY REPORT
****

ADDENDUM TO CHAPTER M

CHART OF LOSSES
INCURRED SINCE MARCH 1st

UNIT	* NAME * FIRST NAME * Middle Name	* RANK	* SPECIALTY	* WOUNDED * DISAPPEARED, * DECEASED OR * PRISONER	* CAUSES
P A BEARN	* LORRAIN * Jean * 1653 C 33	* Q.M. 1C1	* Machinist	* Killed	* Collision 13.3.45
Same	* EGAULT * Albert * 4311 B 39	* Mot (?)	* Crew	* Killed	* Same
Same	* DERRIEN * Georges * 432 L 44	* Mot (?)	* S/Spte (?)	* Killed	* Same
Same	* RIVAS * Didace * 224 BIZ 39	* Mot (?)	* S/Spte (?)	* Killed	* Same

TESTIMONIES

MAJOR JOHN S. HOBBS
TRANSPORT COMMANDER

A radio casualty message from the *USS Earl K. Olsen* reported escorting the *USAT John W. McAndrew* and *FSN Bearn* to Ponto Delgado, Azores for emergency repairs. Both vessels were badly damaged in bows by collision at sea. The *Bearn's* stem was broken and *J. W. McAndrew* was badly holed below water line.

A radio message from the Commanding Officer, Lagens Field, Azores, dated 20 March 1945 reported U.S. Army personnel listed in this book as casualties, reported as missing non-battle since 13 March 1945 as the result of the collision at sea of vessels *John W. McAndrew* and the French Aircraft Carrier *Bearn* which struck the *McAndrew* about one point off the starboard bow in the #1 hold, when we were located at 41°, 50°N latitude and 36°, 31°W longitude in the Atlantic Ocean. The position of this vessel, while in convoy was 52, immediately behind the Commodore's ship. The position of the *Bearn*, which rammed us, was 61 while in convoy, ahead of our position and abeam of the Commodore's ship to the starboard side.

A statement by Major John S. Hobbs, Transport Commander of the *USAT John W. McAndrew* contains the following pertinent information:

"Prior to my retiring at about 2400 hours, 12 March 1945, the weather was misty with heavy black clouds, and the sea was moderately rough.

At about 0340 hours, 13 March 1945, a loud rending crash awakened me. I immediately jumped out of bed and awoke 1st Lt. John W. Ferrick, Troop Commander, who was quartered in his cabin, #2, located on the port side of the shelter deck, immediately aft of #3 hold. When we were about to leave the cabin, M/Sgt. John O. Lorimer, Troop Commander, came to the cabin to find out what was wrong. I then sent Lt. Ferrick and Sgt. Lorimer to the troop compartments with verbal instructions to keep all troops quiet while I investigated the crash. Lt. Ferrick and Sgt. Lorimer left the cabin and proceeded to the #1 hold where the crash had occurred.

I then left the cabin via the port side exit and proceeded along the port side of the vessel to #1 hold where it seemed the crash had been. Upon arrival at the #1 booby hatch, I found that the ship's emergency crew had arrived before me. The emergency crew was holding a rope down into lower #1 troop compartment and pulling the passengers up to the shelter deck by use of said rope.

Looking down into #1 hold, I saw that the ladder from the shelter deck to the main deck was hanging in a vertical position and that the ladders from the main deck to the 'tween deck had been completely washed away. Two men were hanging from the cargo ladder in the lower #1 troop compartment and were apparently frozen to it. Seeing a possible chance to assist them, I immediately turned about, entered the upper #2 troop compartment of the main deck and opening the forward starboard watertight door, went into the damaged hold, closing the watertight door after me.

Upon entering the damaged hold, I found that I had to enter the damaged truck. By crossing a narrow ledge to the cargo ladder, I was able to get a rope around the body and under the armpits of one of the men, thereby permitting the emergency crew to raise him to safety. The other man dropped from the ladder and was washed to sea before I could assist him.

The lights were on in the hold so that I could see all that was happening quite well. The waves were as cold as ice water and at times I was completely drenched by the sea. I looked around for any personnel that might possibly be left in the hold. As I looked, [I] saw that the entire hold from a point below the cargo hold to a point as high as the shelter deck had been opened to the seas for a width of about 70 feet, fore to aft, along the starboard side.

Everything at that time that may have been in lower #1 troop compartment and every man, except himself, had been washed to sea, ascertaining afterwards, the 4,475 bags of mail stowed in #1 hold, had also been washed to sea.

After the troops were quieted down, a roll call was ordered which was to be made by all shipmen and Company Commanders. Those officers who reported personnel as missing were ordered to make a roll call at least twice that same day. While rosters were being called, the ship was searched throughout and the public address system was used in an attempt to locate missing personnel. There were 134 enlisted men quartered in lower #1 troop compartment at the time of the collision as well as one Flight Officer posted on duty in the compartment.

Of those quartered in the troop compartment, 81 of the enlisted men could not be located, and one enlisted man who had been posted as a member of the ship's guard on the forward starboard shelter deck could not be located.

While the *McAndrew* and the *Bearn* were standing by, destroyer escorts, the *USS Earl K. Olsen* and the *USS Roche* searched for survivors commencing immediately after the collision. Everyone worked with skill and determination. Confusion was practically nil. The U.S. Army medical staff aboard the *McAndrew* worked steadily from the time of the collision until about 1000 hours caring for the injured. I had a second and a third roll call made as noted previously, hoping that more of the missing personnel would be discovered aboard our own vessel.

At about 1013 [in one of the testimonies the time is given as 013] hours 13 March 1945, the escort vessels signaled us, giving names, ranks and serial numbers of rescued. The *Olsen* reported two men rescued and the *Roche* reported 11 men rescued. All vessels in the area searching for survivors was discontinued at this time, it being my opinion that all personnel reported missing at sea may now be considered dead.

As soon as the troops were quieted down, the survivors were issued all of the available POW equipment, and all excess hospital patients' clothing that was aboard, including comforters and blankets. The Steward's Department then served breakfast with hot coffee at 0600 hours. I was then compelled to quarter troops wherever I possibly could, resulting in their being quartered in the troop mess, the troop galley, the dining salons, and in all passageways located on the main and shelter decks. At this time orders were received by the Master of the *McAndrew* and the *Bearn* to proceed to Ponta Delgada, San Miguel Island, Azores under the escort of the *Olsen*. The *Roche* then proceeded to rejoin the convoy giving up further search. Both the Deck and Engine crews worked steadily to keep the vessel afloat and under headway.

Upon arrival at Ponta Delgada, the *Olsen* transferred the two men whom she had rescued to the *McAndrew*, thereby deleting their names from the "Statement of Casualties." These two men were Pvt. Oscar H. Butler and Cpl. Aubrey R. Dailey.

There were two U.S. Navy Armed Guard gun crewmembers stationed in the forward gun tubs at the time of the collision. One of these, Carlos Inman, Seaman 1C1, was killed almost immediately. The other survived. A funeral at sea was later held for Inman at the request of the Senior Gunnery Officer.

Final survey left me with 68 enlisted men missing at sea.

Proceeding to Ponta Delgada, where we arrived at 0827 hours, 17 March 1945, I then received from the *Olsen* the two survivors, which she had picked up. The *Roche* did not stop at Ponta Delgada with the eleven survivors that she had picked up.

While anchored at Ponta Delgada, I also took aboard from the *Bearn* 9 U.S. Navy Officers, 13 U.S. Navy enlisted men, 2 U.S. Army officers, and 123 U.S. Army enlisted men. One U.S. Navy officer passenger from the *Bearn* had secured passage and flown to his destination.

The British steamship "*Athlone Castle*" arrived on 23 March 1945, and anchored outside the breakwater, in the open sea. I boarded her to find out if she was ready to receive passengers, and whether or not she could take our cargo. I found that she was ready to receive the passengers and that she could not take our cargo, so I immediately returned to my own ship. While making the trip to the *Athlone Castle*", I found that the seas were quite rough. The passengers would have to climb a pilot ladder, entering the vessel via a side port, making the transfer dangerous. I then ordered all passengers to wear a life jacket when transferring to the *"Athlone Castle"* and then proceeded to transfer all passengers and the officer's baggage from #4 trunk. The transfer commenced at about 1630 hours, 24 March 1945, the *"Athlone Castle"* sailing at about 1215 hours 24 March 1945."

/s/ John S. Hobbs

The following is taken from statements made by some of the survivors rescued by the Destroyer *Roche*.

PFC. ROBERT C. VanRAVENSWAAY

"My bunk collapsed over my feet and all the tiers of bunks were mashed together. I managed to crawl out through wreckage. I reached the hole of the ship. At that time the ship listed and the water carried me out. I was sucked under the water and when I came to the surface, I got caught under some kind of a net but finally escaped. I had no life jacket but grabbed a plank and joined with another survivor who went out of his mind and finally drowned. The man with me also got weak and drowned. The weather was very heavy at that time. I passed several dead bodies in life jackets who were just being beaten back and forth by the waves."

PFC. EDGAR FINSMITH

"All the pipes, including the staircase, came down and I never thought I'd get out. The water was coming in very fast. I was about to resign myself to my fate when I felt a small object hitting me and I realized that I must have been floating. I opened my eyes and took a breath and saw the stars shining above me. I tried to get away from the ship as fast as possible because I thought it was going down. I swam about ten yards and noticed two fellows that seemed to be on a raft. One of them I recognized as a fellow by the name of Wilhelm and later found that the other was Jacob Cook. I was too weak to climb aboard the group of boards so the other two helped me. At this time I noticed that my hand was ripped open. I rested for about five minutes and then the waves broke the boards apart that we were on and I drifted away from the other two fellows. The waves kept turning the board over and I had to keep climbing on. I kept reaching for life preservers in the water but couldn't find any. I finally got a board and stuck it across the board I was on crossways so that it wouldn't turn over. That held for about five minutes and then the board I was on started twisting again. After about a half-hour I noticed a flash of lights from the Destroyers turned on. They seemed quite far and every time they came my way I got on my hands and knees and kept waving at them. I later learned from the crew of the vessel that through this method the Captain of the ship was able to see me and finally picked me up.

I remember grabbing the rope from the destroyer escort. Two members of the crew went over the side with ropes around their stomachs and about that time I passed out. I regained consciousness in the sick bay. I was in the sick bay for about seven hours, during which time I had two blood transfusions. I then saw Jacob Cook who was on the same transport."

TEC/3 JACOB E. COOK

"My legs were pinned down between two beds and water came in. I then went back out and there was another great bang and water came in again. This time the water went out and there was a big crash again and the last I saw falling down to the bottom. At this time I was washed out of the ship and when I came up, I grabbed ahold a piece of wreckage and floated around for two hours. A destroyer escort picked me up."

On the informational sheet author received in 2000, it states S/Sgt. Cook was born 23 March 1922. At the time of his entrance into the service on 9 December 1942 at Fort Hayes, Ohio and was discharged 4 January 1946 as a Staff Sergeant. According to a CD I have for research, Sgt. Cook passed away 2 December 1992. As of this writing I have not been able to locate any surviving relatives.

His awards and decorations included the Good Conduct Medal, American Campaign Medal, and the World War II Victory Medal,

European African Middle Eastern Campaign Medal with one Bronze Star.

PVT. GERALD O. BEERS

"As soon as I hit the water I submerged and probably would have drowned if it had not been that I was buoyed up by a barracks bag that I managed to grasp. I had no life jacket. When I came up I grabbed ahold of some wreckage and tried to pull myself out of the water. However, the water was so violent that I was merely tossed around and the next time I went down I went through the hold in the bottom of the ship and came up in the ocean. I must have injured my leg on the jagged edges of the hole in the ship when I went through. The water was very rough and I could never have stayed afloat if I had not got ahold of the barracks bag that I hung on to. I was close to a rescue ship several times but the waves were so high that it was impossible for them to see me. Long after daylight I finally succeeded in making them see me and was picked up approximately seven hours after I hit the water by the destroyer escort, the *USS Roche*. I talked to four or five fellows in the water but I didn't recognize them. I lost consciousness as soon as I reached the deck of the destroyer escort."

The foregoing facts and statements describe the conditions that prevailed after the collision of the two vessels:

The accident occurred during darkness in the early morning hours and search for the missing personnel began immediately as soon as the word was flashed. Lights were turned on and the two destroyers that picked up all survivors began searching the sea for survivors. The high seas, darkness, and poor visibility made rescue operations difficult. Nevertheless, the destroyers picked up thirteen of the eighty-one missing personnel. Some were picked up before daylight, others after daylight, while still others were lost due to the roughness of the sea and their own physical exhaustion when on the verge of being rescued. The search lasted for approximately seven hours after the accident and two hours after the last survivor had been rescued, when, in the opinion of the Commanding Officer of the *USS Olsen*, no one alive was in the vicinity to be rescued.

A number of dead bodies were sighted and it was deemed inadvisable to recover them. In view of the conditions described and the opinions of those responsible for the safety and rescue of the missing personnel, the only logical conclusion is that subject personnel are dead.

It is recommended therefore, that pursuant to authority contained in Section 9, Missing Persons Act, the foregoing information be accepted as an official report of death and that casualty reports be initiated stating that the personnel aboard the *USAT J. W. McAndrew*, were killed (non-battle) on 13 March 1945 in the Atlantic Ocean, that all personnel were in pay and duty status at the time of death which occurred in the line of duty and was not the result of their own misconduct, and that evidence of their death was received by the War Department on 24 July 1945.

JOHN T. BURNS, LT. COL., AGD

Officer in Charge

Status Review and Determination Section

Approved. Recommended action will be taken.

Subscribed and sworn to and before me this 7th day of April 1945.

S/t/RAFAEL R. HURTADO, Capt. T.C.

>Marine Casualty Investigating Officer
>TRUE COPY
>S/t/ EDWIND J. SULLIVAN, 1ST Lt. Inf.
>A TRUE COPY

A report from the Commanding Officer of the *USS Earl K. Olsen* contains the following pertinent information concerning the collision and rescue operations:

The convoy consisted of 38 ships in nine columns proceeding on base course, 083 T., speed 14 knots. Wind was from 220 T., Force 6 decreasing to 5 by mid-morning, with seas of 5 decreasing later to 4. Visibility was poor, approximately 2000 yards with slight rain falling but improved by daylight. Water temperature 60, air temperature 58. At about 954OZ (Zulu time), 13 March 1945, in approximate position 41-58N 36-OOW, the *USAT J. W. McAndrew* (ship #52) reported over TBY that she had been in collision with another ship which later proved to be *FNS Bearn* (ship #61).

The Escort Commander almost immediately requested Convoy Commodore to have all vessels turn on side lights which was done and at 0545 directed the *Olsen* and the *Roche*, then trailing escorts, to stand by damaged vessels and render all possible assistance. It was some six to eight minutes after the collision that *Bearn* stated over TBY that she had been involved in the collision and had not been under command at the time as a result of a complete electrical power failure. No information concerning casualties or possible men in water could be obtained from either the *Bearn* or *McAndrew* at this time.

At 1106 [the] *McAndrew* gave first accurate picture of her total casualties, and the *Bearn's* was received some 15 minutes later.

While the *Roche* was engaged in picking up her first group of survivors, the *Olsen* was sweeping area immediately around and between the two damaged ships. By this time 12 and 24-inch searchlights were being freely used by both the *Roche* and *Olsen* and at about 0730, in the near vicinity of the *Roche*, the *Olsen* sighted first a body and then a man nearby clinging to a plank. This man was utterly incapable of helping himself even to the extent of grabbing thrown lines lying over his body, which made rescue attempts in the terrific seas and high wind extremely difficult. He was eventually brought immediately alongside through conning the ship to him and his board. Three volunteers went over the side with lines about them tended from the deck to guide him to a cargo net. This was an extremely hazardous operation due to the heaving rolling and tossing of the ship that created a terrific suction at the ship's side tending to drag men under the surface with each roll. The man, apparently unconscious but still alive, could not be prided loose from his board for a considerable time but eventually was and was being lifted aboard when he was sucked from the grasp of rescuers by a tremendous roll to drop from sight not to return. The three *Olsen* men were brought aboard suffering from slight shock and exposure.

Shortly afterward, it now being daylight, two other men clinging to wreckage were sighted nearby and were successfully brought under the same conditions as described above. They were in fair condition but were unable to help themselves to any extent. One had swallowed a quantity of salt water as a result of his buffeting alongside the ship and was brought aboard unconscious to be revived after a half-hour of artificial respiration by the Chief Pharmacist Mate. During the course of this rescue the *Olsen* sighted another group of men nearby to whom the *Roche* was directed to rescue four more men. These were the last men alive to be located though thorough sweeps of the entire area were made for approximately two more hours.

It is believed that it can be stated with certainty that no men still alive were left in the area. There were approximately ten floating bodies sighted, which were deemed inadvisable to recover.

Of the 11 men rescued by the Destroyer *Roche*, two were wearing life preservers at the time of the incident, and two managed to find them in swirling waters. Seven were without life preservers and kept afloat by grabbing floating wreckage or swimming.

THOMAS "TOM" ROY BOWERMAN, Armed Guard, Alabama

"I was born in Florida. I thought I was born April 5, 1922 and celebrated my birthday April 5th until I needed a birth certificate to join the Navy when I was 20 years old. I found there was no record for a Thomas Roy Bowerman anywhere but there was a record for a male child, surname Bowerman, no given name, April 6, 1922. What a shocker! You know all your life that all great people are born on April 5th and suddenly you have to readjust your thinking. I had a sneaking suspicion all along that April 6th was really the greater day, and I was right, of course.

For a brief history of how Mr. Bowerman ended up as an Armed Guard and I quote: "We finally ended the three weeks and were given a comprehensive test and assigned a grade. One could make as high as 150 and I made something over 140. We then went to a huge room and a Chief Petty Officer announced there were openings in a high tech school and those interested, with a grade above 140 should stand up. He did not get enough applicants and lowered the grade requirement to 130. He got too many and raised it to 132 or 133 and finally got the number he needed. He continued the process with various schools and assignments. All this time, my best friend kept telling me to wait, as the best would be last. Finally, there were about 25 or 30 left from several hundred and the Chief announced: "Okay, you dummies are Armed Guard gunners." The next day we were taken to the Balboa Zoo Park and assigned quarters in temporary buildings and began gunnery training at the San Diego Destroyer Base.

There were a few good features of life in the Navy Armed Guard. On most ships we had a Simmons innerspring mattress, linen service, including sheets, pillowcases, towels, and our own mess with our own mess boy and terrific food.

To do our laundry we just put water, soap and clothes in a bucket and set it down and dropped a steam pipe in it. Go back later and rinse a few times and hang it up. When our mops got dirty, just tie a line around it and throw it over the stern and drag it a few miles.

In one of our many e-mails over the years (from September 1999 to the present), a couple in the United Kingdom (England) asked the question regarding rank.

They did not understand the ranks of the different military with the exception of the three lowest grades of the Navy, the Coast Guard, and the Army specialists. He not only explained the difference to the couple in the UK; he also explained it to me.

The seamen wear one, two, or three stripes on their sleeves. These stripes first appeared on the cuffs of sailors' jumpers in 1886. Petty officers and Seamen First Class wore three stripes (S1/C Carlos A. Inman who died in the collision between the *USAT James W. McAndrew* and the *Bearn*) wore these stripes. Seamen Second Class had two stripes and Apprentice Seamen had one stripe."

Regarding awards and decorations, Mr. Bowerman received the campaign ribbons for the American Area and the European-African Middle Eastern Area, as well as the Asiatic-Pacific Area and had crossed the equator on his first ship as an apprentice seaman.

Mr. Bowerman has maintained the Armed Guard web site for all the Armed Guard veterans. He has devoted a lot of time and his own costs to this service. He constantly receives letters, e-mails, telephone calls from "ol' salts" and/or their relatives seeking information. He enjoys looking at the pictures and reading the stories of all you Armed Guards. "We were so incredibly young, so incredibly under gunned, so incredibly willing and able to do anything we were asked to do. We served on ships with telephone poles painted to look like guns, or even with the old 3 inch 23-1/2 six pounder that had been designed to be dismantled and hauled across country on mules. Every time I fired that one, I got a nose bleed."

"There are an estimated 30,000 to 40,000 living Armed Guard Veterans I have not been able to locate for our web site. Most of them have no earthly idea that our Armed Guard Association even exists. We need to be their 'Whistling Man' and bring them into the fold. The lives of many of our veterans, once young and stalwart and fighting for our country, now in many cases, dumped along the highway of life and neglected or treated as second class citizens.

Mr. Bowerman saw no service aboard the Mac but did serve aboard five separate Merchant Marine ships: the *SS Charles M. Hall; SS Esso Nashville; SS Charles*

Sumner; SS Lewis Luckenbach; and the *SS Esso Providence*[38]. Being around the firing of the weapons aboard ship has played havoc with his hearing. We've never met, never talked on the telephone, writing on occasion via snail mail, but he has become not only my mentor but also my best ex-military e-mail buddy.

He wrote his autobiography "Fireclay".

One of the stories in his book mentions that his mother fried him up some chicken and corn bread, placed them in jars and it took 17 months for them to catch up with him. The food was not edible after all those months . . . real treasures from home, but too long in transit.

"Pay was raised when World War II began and entrance pay was $50 a month." He thinks that as a Gunners Mate 2/C his income was $117.00 per month. "While I was in England and out for a few drinks, I would just put all the money I had on the bar or counter and they took what I owed them. A pound was $4.32 in those days; in the year 2000, it was probably around $1.75."

"The gun crew's prime duty was standing lookout duties. As a Gunners Mate, I was not required to pull lookout duty but on all five of my ships, I stood lookout like everyone else. We were on watch four hours and off four hours, plus about two hours around sunrise and sunset where the entire gun crew was on lookout. Usually either

---

[38] Mr. Bowerman gives very good details about his ships in his book.

the sunrise or sunset would fall within our regular four hours. That means we stood lookout duty fourteen hours a day. In addition to lookout, we had to clean our quarters, clean the guns, keep all the gun tubs painted, attend training sessions in such things as military articles of war, survival at sea, and signals. I found that this left three and a half hours a day for sleeping."

"The typical Armed Guard gun crew consisted of Gun Captain, Pointer, Trainer, first loader, second loader; there was a hot shellman on a shell gun (projectile in a brass case). On a bag gun there is no hot shellman. On a bag gun there was a man who dipped a brush on the end of a long rod in water and then used it to ram the projective in after it was loaded. The wet brush cleared any smoldering remains of the previous silk bag of powder. On the bag gun, the gun captain would insert a primer in the breech and on the shell gun the primer is already in the case. On 20-mm guns, there was one who fired and one who loaded the magazines when needed."

"I was too busy to pay much attention to what all the merchant crew did, but a good many of them were trained as gunners, loaders, and ammunition carriers. They helped load the guns and took over when gun crewmembers were wounded or killed. I should also mention that the merchant crew also stood lookout duty and they generally manned the lookout post in the crow's nest, which was the least desirable watch station."

"An interesting point is that duty with the Navy Armed Guard was qualifying time with the Merchant Marine. One good friend on one ship went into the Merchant Marine after the war and earned his third mate's license in a very short time. He was in the Merchant Marine five years and left as a Second Mate."

Mr. Bowerman has never attended one of the National Armed Guard Reunions. He states the reason is this: "I do not know what holds me back from going to the reunions. I think that sometimes it is just the idea of seeing the old gang at their present advanced ages. Something inside me tells me to hang on to the memory of them as teenagers, running like crazy to the guns when the general alarm sounded, climbing vertical ladders with two five gallon cans of paint in their hands, and a paint brush between their teeth; alert, healthy, lean and mean fighting machines."

After 15 years of dedication in maintaining the Armed Guard Web Site, effective 28 May 2007, Mr. Bowerman has forwarded it to Project Liberty Ship and the person who will now maintain it, Ron Carlson. However, if you still wish to contact Mr. Bowerman I'm sure he will direct you appropriately. If you wish to contact him via e-mail, go to armedguard@cableone.net.

After all his assistance and being my mentor for many years, Mr. Bowerman passed on to his "greater glory" on 16 December 2008.

ACKNOWLDGEMENTS

I owe a debt of gratitude to Magali LaCousse, Consevateur Director of Archives of the Marine National Historique Service of France for her answering my questions and sending the report for this book regarding the collision between the *McAndrew* and the *Bearn*. By the same token, I owe a debt of gratitude to Monique Miller for the translation of the collision report regarding the accident as well as the report giving the names of their dead and the history of the *Bearn*.

If it had not been for Erick E. Estrada, a young ex-Navy man with whom I worked, what you read in this book is because he gave me such marvelous assistance in getting started. His eye for detail when reading correspondence I received, including close scrutiny of photographs received, has given me new insight. His encouragement and interest has meant a great deal and his "Wows!" have shown me I was heading in the right direction; I adore him for it.

Mr. Bowerman has kept my eye on the project offering solid advice and increased my education about what all the Armed Guards did to function as a unit. He has encouraged me, laughed at my silly mistakes, not in an insulting manner, but in a way that made me all the more aware of my beginning awkwardness about a subject I had to learn from the beginning. He has willingly maintained my web site within his in addition to all the other responsibilities he created for himself, and because of my interest in learning, made me an honorary Armed Guard Wave and listed me "in the book."

This book could not have been written without the assistance of the men who served. Therefore, I wish to thank all those men who responded to my inquiries, sent me original photographs, told their stories, and to the relatives of the young men who could not speak for themselves as their bodies rest at the bottom of the seas where they died. Otherwise, this forgotten branch of the Navy would have remained forgotten and their stories never told.

Before my retirement, the attorneys and staff with whom I worked offered their support and encouragement, excited about obtaining this book upon publication, and expressing interest in my research. They told me of their own relatives who served in World War II. They are too numerous to mention; therefore, to one and all, I thank you.

The content of this book would not be so easily read had it not been for the expertise of Suzan J. Anderson. It was her eye to form and content, took this project home with her to read although she had enough work to keep her busy on her own weekends. Sue, I graciously thank you.

There are many others who should be acknowledged for special mention. You will find them in the pages of this book. Most of all, special kudos need to be shared with the men who were aboard the "Mac," their wives, widows, other relatives or whether the men were Armed Guards or Merchant Seamen, or young soldiers off to fight the war but never made it.

Much gratitude needs to be expressed for the watchful eye of Eileen M. Mineburg, my proofreader. Although quite busy herself, she found the time to work on this project. She gave me a wonderful compliment when she told me that history was not one of her favorite subjects in school, but there were times she became so involved in reading this story, she forgot to proofread and edit.

APPENDIX I

GOODBYE TO THE "MAC" AND MATES FOREVER; YOU MAY BE GONE BUT AS LONG AS ONE OF US LIVES, YOU'LL NOT BE FORGOTTEN.

NAME	DATE	TYPE SHIP	STATUS of MEN (KILLED)
SS[1] Admiral Y.S. Williams	Captured 12/25/41	Freighter	K /1 Imprisoned—20
M/V[2] Aeolus	Shelled 6/3/42	Fishing Trawler	No casualties
SS Afoundria	Torpedoed 5/5/42	Freighter	No casualties
SS African Star	Torpedoed 7/12/43	Freighter	Armed Guard K/1
SS Agwimonte	Torpedoed 5/28/43	Freighter	No casualties
SS Alamar	Bombed 5/27/42	Freighter	No casualties
SS Alaskan	Torpedoed & Shelled 11/28/42	Freighter	Crew—K/7 Armed Guard K/1
S/V3[3] Albert F. Paul	Shelled 3/13/42	4 Mast Schooner	Crew—K/8
SS Albert Gallatin	Torpedoed 1/2/44	Liberty Ship[4]	No casualties
SS Alcoa Cadet	Mined 6/21/42	Freighter	Crew—K/1
SS Alcoa Carrier	Torpedoed 5/25/42	Freighter	No casualties
SS Alcoa Guide	Shelled 8/13/44	Freighter	No casualties
SS Alcoa Leader	Deliberately sunk[5] 8/13/44	Freighter	No casualties
SS Alcoa Mariner	Torpedoed 9/28/42	Freighter	No casualties
SS Alcoa Partner	Torpedoed & Shelled 4/26/42	Freighter	Crew—K/10
SS Alcoa Pathfinder	Torpedoed 11/21/42	Freighter	Crew—K/5
SS Alcoa Pilgrim	Torpedoed 5/28/42	Freighter	Crew—K/31

[1] SS = Steam ship and designates a merchant ship as compared to U.S.S. which is designated as a U.S. Navy vessel and stands for United States Ship.
[2] M/V = Motorized vessel.
[3] S/V = Vessel run by steam.
[4] In 1941 President F. D. Roosevelt, referring to Patrick Henry's "Give me liberty or give me death" at the launching of the first Liberty Ship, the SS Patrick Henry, stated that these ships would bring liberty to Europe, and the name stuck, 'Liberty Ships'.
[5] Ships deliberately sunk or had already been scuttled and/or so badly damaged that repairs were futile were towed to assist in the invasion of Normandy. The Armed Guardsmen stayed on board on the main deck to fire their weapons for cover of the invading forces.

SS Alcoa Puritan	Torpedoed & Shelled 5/6/42	Freighter	No casualties
SS Alcoa Rambler	Torpedoed 12/14/42	Freighter	Crew—K/1
SS Alcoa Ranger[6] *	Torpedoed & Shelled 7/7/42	Freighter	No casualties
SS Alcoa Shipper	Torpedoed 5/30/42	Freighter	Crew—K/7
SS Alcoa Transport	Torpedoed 10/2/42	Freighter	Crew—K/6
SS Alexander Macomb	Torpedoed 7/3/42	Liberty Ship	Crew—K/4 Armed Guard—K/6
SS Alice F. Palmer	Torpedoed & Shelled 7/10/43	Liberty Ship	No casualties
SS Allan Jackson	Torpedoed 1/18/42	Tanker[7]	Crew—K/22
Barge Allegheny	Shelled 3/31/42	Barge	No casualties
SS Almeria Lykes	Torpedoed 8/13/42	Freighter	No casualties
SS American	Torpedoed 6/11/42	Freighter	Crew—K/4
SS American Leader	Torpedoed & Shelled 9/10/42	Freighter	Crew—K/10
SS Andrea F. Luckenbach	Torpedoed 3/10/43	Freighter	Crew—K/11 Armed Guard—K/11
SS Andrew George Curtin	Torpedoed 9/25/44	Liberty Ship	Crew—K/2 Armed Guard K/1
SS Andrew Jackson	Torpedoed 7/12/42	Freighter	Crew—K/3
SS Angelina	Torpedoed 10/17/42	Freighter	Crew—K/34 Armed Guard—K/13
SS Anne Hutchinson	Torpedoed & Shelled 10/26/42	Liberty Ship	Crew—K/3
SS Antinous	Torpedoed 9/23/42	Freighter	No casualties
SS Antoine Saugrain	Aerial Torpedoed 12/5/44	Liberty Ship	No casualties
SS Arcata	Shelled 7/14/42	Freighter	Crew—K/8
SS Ario	Torpedoed & Shelled 3/15/42	Tanker	Crew—K/8
SS Arkansan	Torpedoed 6/25/42	Freighter	Crew—K/4
SS Arlyn	Torpedoed 8/27/42	Freighter	Crew—K/12
SS Artemas Ward	Deliberately sunk 6/8/44	Liberty Ship	No casualties

[6] All the ships with an asterisk were a part of convoy PQ-17 in which most of the ships were from the United States, some Russian and British (35), were sunk by German U-boats, submarines, and aerial torpedo planes.

[7] A tanker carried oil, gasoline, benzene (volatile flammable petroleum), etc.

Ship	Event	Type	Casualties
SS Arthur Middleton	Torpedoed 1/1/43	Liberty Ship	Crew—K/11 Army—K/1 Armed Guard—K/3
SS Arthur Sewall	Torpedoed 12/29/44	Liberty Ship	Crew—K/2
SS Astral	Torpedoed 12/2/41	Tanker	Crew—K/37
M/S Atlantic Sun	Torpedoed 2/15/43	Tanker	Crew—K/46 Armed Guard—K/19
SS Atlas	Torpedoed 4/9/42	Tanker	Crew—K/2
SS Augustus Thomas[8]	Bombed 10/24/44	Liberty Ship	No casualties
M/S Australia	Torpedoed 3/16/42	Tanker	Crew—K/4
SS Azalea City	Torpedoed 2/20/42	Freighter	Crew—K/38
SS Balladier	Torpedoed 8/15/42	Freighter	Crew—K/12 Armed Guard—K/2
SS Barbara	Torpedoed 3/7/42	Freighter	Crew—K/19
Barge Barnegat	Shelled 3/31/42	Barge	No casualties
SS Beatrice	Shelled 5/24/42	Freighter	Crew—K/1
SS Bellingham *	Torpedoed 9/22/42	Freighter	No casualties
M/S Ben & Josephine	Shelled 6/3/42	Fishing Trawler	No casualties
SS Benjamin Brewster	Torpedoed 7/9/42	Tanker	Crew—K/24 Armed Guard—K/1
SS Benjamin Contee[9]	Aerial Torpedoed 8/16/43	Liberty Ship	Italian POWs—264 British Guards—26
SS Benjamin Harrison[10] *	Torpedoed 3/16/43	Liberty Ship	Crew—K/2 Armed Guard—K/1

[8] As unbelievable as it sounds, this Liberty Ship was carrying a cargo of ammunition and gasoline as well as 548 troops to the Philippines, was hit by a dive-bomber, set afire, and not one man was hurt!

[9] A very tragic incident of the war was in the Mediterranean. Traveling under a full, bright moon from Bone, Algeria to Oran she was carrying 1800 Italian POWs and 26 British guards. German bombers attacked with torpedoes, one of which blew a hole 50 feet wide and 21 feet deep between the #1 and #2 holds. Fortunately, two Italian-speaking men in the crew calmed down hundreds of shouting, screaming Italians who were filled with panic, broke out to the open deck, and rushed the lifeboats without knowing how to launch them. Panic finally subsided and the ship returned to Bone under her own power, but as noted above, there was loss of life. This ship later became a "mulberry" at Normandy even though she was attacked by JU-88s; she was still towed into position and scuttled.

[10] Of the 21 U.S. ships headed for Murmansk in convoy PQ-17, this ship was one of six new Libertys. The others were *Christopher Newport, William Hooper, John Witherspoon, Daniel Morgan,* and the *Samuel Chase.*

SS Bienville	Torpedoed 4/6/42	Freighter	Crew—K/24
SS Birmingham City	Torpedoed 1/9/43	Freighter	Crew—K/5 Armed Guard—K/5
SS Black Hawk	Torpedoed 12/29/44	Liberty Ship	Crew—K/1
SS Black Point[11]	Torpedoed 5/5/45	Collier	Crew—K/11 Armed Guard—K/1
SS Bloody Marsh	Torpedoed 7/2/43	Tanker	Crew—K/3
SS Broad Arrow	Torpedoed 1/9/43	Tanker	Crew—K/16 Armed Guard—K/7
SS Bushrod Washington[12]	Bombed 9/14/43	Liberty Ship	Crew—K/6 Armed Guard—K/1
SS Byron D. Benson	Torpedoed 4/4/42	Tanker	Crew—K/10
SS C. J. Barkdull	Torpedoed 1/10/43	Tanker	Crew—K/38 Armed Guard—K/20
SS Caddo	Torpedoed 11/23/42	Tanker	Crew—K/39 Armed Guard—K/14
SS California	Torpedoed & Shelled 8/13/42	Freighter	Crew—K/1
SS Camden	Torpedoed 10/4/42	Tanker	Crew—K/1
SS Canada Victory	Sunk by Kamikaze suicide plane 4/27/45	Freighter	Crew—K/1 Armed Guard—K/2
M/S Cape Decision	Torpedoed 1/27/43	Freighter	No casualties
SS Cape San Juan[13]	Torpedoed 11/11/43	Freighter	Army Troops—K/115

[11] This was the last ship sunk off the coast of Newport, Rhode Island. Because the war was over, U853 was hunted down and depth-charged by a large fleet of vessels and sank with the loss of her entire crew. It is believed that either the captain of the submarine did not know the war was over or decided to get in "one last kill" before sailing for home.

A collier is a coal-carrying ship.

[12] Just prior to being launched in Baltimore in April 1943, her first captain, John W. Wainwright, was the son of General Jonathan Wainwright of Bataan fame. John W. scratched his initials into the fresh paint remarking "That's for good luck." She arrived in Salerno with 7,000 drums of aviation gasoline, 75 tons of bombs, and 105-mm shells. After three days of continual attack, a 500-lb bomb started a gasoline fire in #4 hold. The entire forward section of the vessel was destroyed. Depending on which book one reads, the loss of life was four or seven.

[13] The *Cape San Juan* was carrying 1,429 soldiers, merchant seamen, and naval gunners. Four hundred eighty-three men were rescued. I presume the 115 killed as noted above to only the Army casualties. There is no mention as to what happened to the other 831 men.

SS Capillo	Bombed 12/8/41	Freighter	Crew—6—died in Japanese POW Camp
SS Cardonia	Torpedoed & Shelled 3/7/42	Freighter	Crew—K/1
SS Caribsea[14]	Torpedoed 3/11/42	Freighter	Crew—K/21
SS Caribstar	Torpedoed 10/4/42	Freighter	Crew—K/6
SS Carlton *	Torpedoed 7/5/42	Freighter	Crew—K/3
SS Carrabulle	Torpedoed & Shelled 5/26/42	Tankship[15]	Crew—K/22
SS Catahoula	Torpedoed 4/5/42	Tankship	Crew—K/10
M/S Challenger	Torpedoed 5/27/42	Freighter	Crew—K/5 Armed Guard—K/2 U.S. Military—K/1
M/S Chant	Bombed 6/15/42	Freighter	Crew—K/3
SS Charles C. Pickney	Torpedoed 1/27/43	Liberty Ship	Crew—K/36 Armed Guard—K/21 Army Security—K/2
SS Charles D. McIver[16]	Mined 3/23/45	Liberty Ship	No casualties
S.S. Charles Morgan[17]	Bombed 6/10/44	Liberty Ship	Crew—K/1 U.S. Army—K/7
SS Charles W. Elliott[18]	Mined 6/28/44	Liberty Ship	No casualties

[14] After the war Liberty ships made fortunes for many shipping magnates shrewd enough to buy them cheap when freight rates were high. They were renamed, sometimes many times over. This one had the names of *Holy Star* and *Symphony*. As one Greek master stated, "Still she goes after 22 years after the war, and still she goes."

[15] This ship's cargo consisted of gasses under pressure

[16] Returning from Antwerp, she hit a mine and sank in shallow water. Typical of those explosions caused by mines, men were thrown flat on deck, blasted typewriters loose from their desks, and three them against bulkheads. The explosion also ripped radiators from walls and tore doors off their hinges.

[17] The *Morgan* was hit by a bomb in the #5 hold just after unloading 500 troops and their equipment. She sank in 33 feet of water. After being declared a loss, a salvage party returned to retrieve valuable equipment.

[18] Depending on which book one reads, Elliott is spelled with one or both "l's" or "t's". The destructive force of the mine described by survivors which had just completed unloading its cargo states in part: "An explosion occurred under the after part of #3 hold, causing the vessel to rise up into the air and to shake violently. Two or three seconds later a second explosion occurred under the stern. Hull plates

SS Chatham	Torpedoed 8/27/42	Passenger Ship	Crew—K/7 U.S. Military—K/7
SS Chattanooga City	Torpedoed 2/22/43	Freighter	No casualties
SS Cherokee	Torpedoed 6/25/42	Passenger Ship	Crew—K/65 Armed Guard—K/1 U.S. Military—K/20
SS Chickasaw City	Torpedoed 10/7/42	Freighter	Crew—K/8 Armed Guard—K/1 U.S. Military—K/1
SS Chilore	Torpedoed 7/15/42	Bulk Carrier[19]	Crew—K/2
SS China Arrow	Torpedoed 2/5/42	Tanker	No casualties
SS Christopher Newport *	Torpedoed 7/4/42	Liberty Ship	Crew—K/3
SS Chung Cheng[20]	Torpedoed 2/5/44	Liberty Ship	Merchantmen—K/18 Armed Guard—K/1
SS Cities Service Empire	Torpedoed 2/22/42	Tanker	Crew—K/11 Armed Guard—K/3
SS Cities Service Missouri	Torpedoed 3/13/43	Tanker	Crew—K/2
SS Cities Service Toledo	Torpedoed 6/12/42	Tanker	Crew—K/11 Armed Guard—K/3
SS City of Alma	Torpedoed 6/2/43	Freighter	Crew—K/26 Navy—K/3
SS City of Atlanta[21]	Torpedoed 1/19/42	Freighter	Crew—K/43
SS City of Birmingham	Torpedoed 6/30/42	Passenger Ship	Crew—K/7 U.S. Military—K/2

cracked open. Hatch covers and beams out of #4 and #5 hatches were blown to a height of 300 feet causing the vessel to break just aft of #5 hatch. Fragments of steel and ballast were blown several hundred feet into the air. One hatch beam landed on the boat deck. Quarters of the amidships houses were wrecked with wash bowls knocked off the walls. Numbers 3, 4 and 5 holds were flooded. There were several injuries.

[19] This type of ship hauls bulk supplies, i.e., ore, coal as opposed to boxes, crates, vehicles, bombs, etc.

[20] The government of China operated this Liberty ship. She was bound from Chochin, India to Aden with 8,350 tons of ilmenite (heavy ore) when she was attacked by a German sub. She had a merchant crew of 29 Chinese and Armed Guardsmen of 27 Americans as well as 11 U.S. and 4 Chinese merchant marine officers. Because of her cargo, she sank quickly; therefore, not all of the lifeboats could be launched. Again, depending on which story one reads, 19 to 20 lives were lost.

[21] The *City of Atlanta* was sunk off the coast of Cape Hatteras with many lives lost.

SS City of Flint	Torpedoed 1/25/43	Freighter	Crew—K/3 Armed Guard—K/4
SS City of Joliet	Bombed & Aerial Torpedoed 5/28/42	Freighter	No casualties
M/S City of New York	Torpedoed 3/29/42	Passenger Ship	Crew—K/17 Armed Guard—K/2 U.S. Military—K/7
M/S City of Rayville	Mined 11/9/40	Freighter	Crew—K/1
SS Clare	Torpedoed 5/20/42	Freighter	No casualties
SS Clark Mills	Aerial torpedoed 3/9/44	Liberty Ship	No casualties
SS Coamo	Torpedoed 12/9/42	Passenger Ship	Crew—K/133
SS Coast Farmer	Torpedoed 7/20/43	Freighter	Crew—K/1
SS Coast Trader	Torpedoed 6/7/42	Freighter	Crew—K/1
SS Colin P. Kelly, Jr.	Mined 6/4/45	Liberty Ship	No casualties
SS Collamer	Torpedoed 3/5/42	Freighter	Crew—K/7
SS Collingsworth	Torpedoed 1/19/43	Freighter	Crew—K/8 Armed Guard—K/4
SS Coloradan	Torpedoed 10/9/42	Freighter	Crew—K/6
SS Commercial Trader	Torpedoed 9/16/42	Freighter	Crew—K/7 Armed Guard—K/3
SS Comol Rice	Torpedoed 4/4/42	Tanker	Crew—K/3
SS Connecticut	Torpedoed 4/23/42	Tanker	Crew—K/27 Armed Guard—K/11
SS Cornelia P. Spencer[22]	Torpedoed 9/21/43	Liberty Ship	Crew—K/2
SS Courageous[23]	Deliberately sunk 6/8/44	Freighter	No casualties
SS Cranford	Torpedoed 7/30/42	Freighter	Crew—K/9 Armed Guard—K/2
SS Cripple Creek	Torpedoed 8/13/42	Freighter	Crew—K/1
SS Cynthia Olson	Torpedoed 12/7/41	Steam Schooner	Crew—K/33 U.S. Army—K/2
SS Cyrus H. McCormick[24]	Torpedoed 4/18/45	Liberty Ship	Crew—K/4 Armed Guard—K/2

[22] One hundred fourteen Libertys were named after women of whom this was one. Ten were lost through enemy action.
[23] This ship was of World War I vintage.
[24] That last ship sunk in the battle for the Atlantic; the *McCormick* was 68 miles off the coast of France. She carried 8,400 tons of locomotives, cranes, trucks, and other heavy equipment. She sank in just a few minutes.

SS Dan Beard[25]	Torpedoed 12/10/44	Liberty Ship	Crew—K/17 Armed Guard—K12
SS Daniel Morgan[26] *	Bombed & Torpedoed **7/5/42	Liberty Ship	Crew—K-4
SS David H. Atwater	Shelled 4/2/42	Freighter	Crew—K/23
SS David McKelvey	Torpedoed 5/13/42	Tanker	Crew—K/16 Armed Guard—K/2
SS Deer Lodge	Torpedoed 2/17/43	Freighter	Crew—K/2
S Delfina	Torpedoed 6/5/42	Freighter	No casualties
SS Delisle	Mined 10/19/43	Freighter	No casualties
SS Delmundo	Torpedoed 8/13/42	Freighter	Crew—K/5 U.S. Military—K/2
SS Delplata	Torpedoed 2/20/42	Freighter	No casualties
SS Delvalle	Torpedoed 4/12/42	Freighter	Crew—K/2
SS Dixie Arrow	Torpedoed 3/26/42	Tanker	Crew—K/11
M/S Don Isidro	Bombed 2/19/42	Freighter	Crew—K/13 U.S. Army—K/1
M/S Dona Aurora	Torpedoed 12/25/42	Freighter	Crew—K/2 Armed Guard—K/1
SS Dorchester	Torpedoed 2/3/43	Passenger Ship	Crew—K/102 Armed Guard—K/11 U.S. Military—K/562
SS E. G. Seubert	Torpedoed 2/23/44	Tanker	Crew—K/3 Armed Guard—K/3
SS E. J. Sadler	Shelled 6/22/42	Tanker	No casualties

On one of her earlier trips from Charleston, South Carolina to Belfast, her log read: "Observing convoy regulations. Watch uneventful. Weather fine and clear."

[25] The "entertainment" equipment (kits) for many of the merchant ships contained boxing gloves, punching bag, medicine ball, Chinese checkers, chess, cribbage, checkers, and dominos as well as darts, playing cards, phonograph and records. All the ships received books with the purser acting as librarian. According to one book, the *Dan Beard* was either mined or torpedoed in October 1944 while bound from Barry, Wales to Belfast. In 40-knot winds, there occurred a tremendous vibration amidships, followed by the ship's back breaking just forward of the house. She broke in two within five minutes. One lifeboat was swamped by the heavy seas and capsized.

[26] The *Daniel Morgan* was heading for Nova Zembla when German JU88 bombers attacked. Nine sticks of bombs fell around her. Her 3-inch guns managed to down two of the attackers but so many near misses ruptured a number of hull plates causing her to take on water fast. The crew abandoned ship and a submarine torpedoed her and she sank to the bottom. A Russian tanker picked up the survivors.

SS E. M. Clark	Torpedoed 3/18/42	Tanker	Crew—K/1
M/S East Indian	Torpedoed 11/3/42	Freighter	Crew—K/33 Armed Guard—K/14 U.S. Military K/10
SS Eastern Sword	Torpedoed 5/4/42	Freighter	Crew—K/16
SS Ebb	Shelled 7/28/42	Fishing Trawler	Crew—K/5
SS Edgar Allen Poe	Torpedoed 11/8/42	Liberty Ship	Crew—K/2
SS Edith	Torpedoed 6/7/42	Freighter	Crew—K/2
SS Edmund F. Dickens	Mined 5/2/45	Liberty Ship	No casualties
SS Edward B. Dudley	Torpedoed 4/11/43	Liberty Ship	Crew—K/42 Armed Guard—K/27
SS Edward Bates[27]	Aerial Torpedoed 2/1/44	Liberty Ship	Crew—K/1
SS Edward Luckenbach	Mined 7/2/42	Freighter	Crew—K/1
SS Effingham	Torpedoed 3/30/42	Freighter	Crew—K/12
SS Eldena	Torpedoed 7/8/43	Freighter	No casualties
SS Elias Howe[28]	Torpedoed 9/24/43	Liberty Ship	Crew—K/2
SS Elihu B. Washburne	Torpedoed 7/3/43	Liberty Ship	No casualties
SS Elihu Yale[29]	Bombed 2/15/44	Liberty Ship	Crew—K/3 Armed Guard—K/2
SS Elizabeth	Shelled & Torpedoed 5/20/42	Freighter	Crew—K/6
SS Elizabeth Kellogg	Torpedoed 11/23/43	Tanker	Crew—K/8 Armed Guard—K/2
SS Emidio[30]	Shelled & Torpedoed 12/20/41	Tanker	Crew—K/5

[27] This ship took part in the Salerno action. When she was torpedoed, she went down so far by the head that fish could have swum across the foredeck; however, she stayed afloat long enough to be beached on the coast of North Africa and then abandoned.

[28] Liberty ships were named after inventors as well. The gentleman's name who had this ship honored, invented the sewing machine. Without such a machine, tarpaulins could not have been made.

[29] A glide bomber got the *Yale* while she was loading artillery shells into a LCT at the time. Both ships were a total loss.

[30] Some 18 miles off the coast of Crescent City, California, the tanker *Emidio* was torpedoed by a Japanese sub. She had the "distinct" honor of being the first ship sunk in American coastal waters in World War II.

SS Esparta	Torpedoed 4/9/42	Freighter	Crew—K/1
SS Esso Baton Rouge	Torpedoed 2/23/43	Tanker	Crew—K/3 Armed Guard—K/1
SS Esso Boston	Torpedoed & Shelled 4/12/42	Tanker	No casualties
SS Esso Gettysburg	Torpedoed 6/10/43	Tanker	Crew—K/37 Armed Guard—K/20
SS Esso Harrisburg	Torpedoed 7/6/44	Tanker	Crew—K/4 Armed Guard—K/4
SS Esso Houston	Torpedoed 5/12/42	Tanker	Armed Guard—K/1
SS Esso Williamsburg	Torpedoed 9/22/42	Tanker	Crew—K/42 Armed Guard—K/18
SS Eugene V. R. Thayer	Shelled 4/9/42	Tanker	Crew—K/11
SS Examelia	Torpedoed 10/9/42	Freighter	Crew—K/8 Armed Guard—K/3
SS Excello	Torpedoed 11/13/42	Freighter	Crew—K/1 Armed Guard—K/1
SS Executive	Torpedoed 3/5/43	Freighter	Crew—K/8 Armed Guard—K/1
PSS Exford	Deliberately sunk 8/16/44	Freighter	No casualties
SS Examoor	Shelled 4/6/42	Freighter	No casualties
SS Exmouth	Mined 7/31/44	Freighter	No casualties
SS Expositor[31]	Torpedoed 2/23/43	Freighter	Crew—K/6 Armed Guard—K/3
SS Express	Torpedoed 6/30/42	Freighter	Crew—K/11 Armed Guard—K/2
SS Ezra Weston[32]	Torpedoed 8/8/44	Liberty Ship	No casualties
SS F. W. Abrams	Mined 6/11/42	Tanker	No casualties
SS Fairfield City *	Bombed 7/5/42	Freighter	Crew—K/8 Armed Guard—K/9
SS Fairport	Torpedoed 7/16/42	Freighter	No casualties
SS Federal	Shelled 4/30/42	Tanker	Crew—K/5
SS FitzJohn Porter	Torpedoed 3/1/43	Liberty Ship	Armed Guard—K/1
SS Flora MacDonald	Torpedoed 5/30/43	Liberty Ship	Crew—K/7

[31] One of the first ships to be so protected by Navy guns and gunners, she sailed for Murmansk early in 1942 with an armed guard crew of four seamen and a signalman. Her gunners blew the conning tower off a submarine.

[32] She was "seen to rise out of the water" after a mine explosion and sunk within minutes. All hands were rescued. Noted above, it states she was torpedoed although the last information I have is the aforementioned.

SS Florence D.	Bombed 2/19/42	Freighter	Crew—K/3 Armed Guard—K/1
SS Florence Luckenbach	Torpedoed 1/29/42	Freighter	No casualties
SS Foam	Shelled 5/17/42	Fishing Trawler	Crew—K/1
SS Fort Lee	Torpedoed 11/2/44	Tanker	Crew—K/16 Armed Guard—K/9
SS Frances Salman	Torpedoed 1/18/42	Freighter	Crew—K/28
SS Francis Asbury[33]	Mined 12/3/44	Liberty Ship	Crew—K/10 Armed Guard—K/7
SS Francis E. Powell	Torpedoed 1/27/42	Tanker	Crew—K/4
SS Francis W. Pettygrove	Aerial torpedoed 8/13/43	Liberty Ship	No casualties
SS Franklin K. Lane	Torpedoed 6/8/42	Tanker	Crew—K/4
SS Frederick Douglas[34]	Torpedoed 9/20/43	Liberty Ship	No casualties
M/S Galveston	Deliberately sank 6/8/44	Freighter	No casualties
SS George Calvert	Torpedoed 5/20/42	Liberty Ship	Armed Guard—K/3
SS George Cleeve[35]	Torpedoed 2/22/44	Liberty Ship	Crew—K/1
SS George Clymer	Torpedoed 6/7/42	Liberty Ship	Crew—K/1
SS George Hawley[36]	Torpedoed 1/21/45	Liberty Ship	Crew—K/2
SS George S. Wasson	Mined 1/31/44	Liberty Ship	No casualties
SS George Thacher[37]	Torpedoed 11/1/42	Liberty Ship	Crew—K/5 Armed Guard—K/5 U.S. Army—K/8

[33] One of the youngest captains in the merchant marines had command of this ship. She hit a mine off Ostend exploding under the engine room. The explosion broke the ship's back and so violently shaking her that her machinery was blown out of the engine spaces.

[34] The *Douglas* was the lead ship in the port (the left side of the ship as one faces forward) column in convoy ON202 as she made her way from England to New York. A torpedo exploded in #5 hold and she began to settle by the stern. All crewmen were rescued.

[35] She refused to sink! The *Cleeve* was torpedoed in convoy GUS21. She had to be towed to the nearest port and was a complete loss.

[36] Two of the engine room watches were killed en route from Cherbourg to Cardiff, Wales, but the rest were rescued. The *Hawley* was towed to port.

[37] En route from Charleston, South Carolina to Freetown and Takoradi, West Africa, and despite two escorts of Free French frigates, the *Thacher* was sunk by a U-boat. Her cargo consisted of trucks, ambulances, road-building equipment, and gasoline in drums. Two torpedoes had hit her, forward and aft, setting the ship on fire after the drums of gasoline exploded. These heavily loaded ships went down quickly.

SS George W. Childs[38] *	Deliberately sank 6/8/44	Liberty Ship	No casualties
M/S Gertrude	Time bombed 7/16/42	Fishing Vessel	No casualties
M/S Green Island	Torpedoed 5/6/42	Freighter	No casualties
SS Greylock	Torpedoed 2/3/43	Freighter	No casualties
SS Gulfamerica	Torpedoed & Shelled 4/10/42	Tanker	Crew—K/17 Armed Guard—K/2
SS Gulfoil	Torpedoed 5/16/42	Tanker	Crew—K/17 Armed Guard—K/4
SS Gulfpenn	Torpedoed 5/13/42	Tanker	Crew—K/13
SS Gulfstate	Torpedoed 4/3/43	Tanker	Crew—K/30 Armed Guard—K/6
SS Gulftrade[39]	Torpedoed 3/10/42	Tanker	Crew—K/18
SS Gurney E. Newlin	Torpedoed 10/27/42	Tanker	Crew—K/3
SS Gus W. Darwell	Aerial torpedoed 11/23/44	Liberty Ship	No casualties
SS H. D. Collier	Torpedoed & Shelled 3/13/44	Tanker	Crew—K/33 Armed Guard—K/12
SS H. G. Blasdel[40]	Torpedoed 6/29/44	Liberty Ship	U.S. Army—K/76
SS H. M. Storey	Torpedoed 5/18/43	Tanker	Crew—K/2
SS Hagan	Torpedoed 6/11/42	Tanker	Crew—K/6
SS Hahira	Torpedoed 11/3/42	Tanker	Crew—K/2 Armed Guard—K/1
SS Halo	Torpedoed 5/20/42	Tanker	Crew—K/39
SS Halsey	Torpedoed 5/6/42	Tanker	No casualties
SS Hampton Roads	Torpedoed & Shelled 6/1/42	Freighter	Crew—K/5
SS Harrison Gray Otis[41]	Mined 8/4/43	Liberty Ship	Crew—K/2

[38] Depending on which book one reads, the middle initial is sometimes an "M". The *Childs* was also used in the "Mulberry field" at Normandy.
[39] This ship went to the bottom 20 miles off Southampton, Long Island.
[40] Although torpedoed in a 20-ship convoy en route from Southampton, England to Utah Beach, she managed to return to England and declared a total loss. At the time she carried 509 men including 436 American troops. There were many casualties but most of the men were taken off safely.
[41] Although a total loss after two explosions just forward of the engine room rupturing the bulkhead and flooded the engine spaces. What was an interesting but strange aspect of sea war in the Mediterranean, were the successful efforts of

SS Harry Luckenbach	Torpedoed 3/17/43	Freighter	Crew—K/54 Armed Guard—K/26
SS Harvey W. Scott	Torpedoed 3/3/43	Liberty Ship	No casualties
SS Hastings	Torpedoed 2/23/43	Freighter	Crew—K/9
SS Heffron	Mined 7/5/42	Freighter	Crew—K/1
SS Henry B. Plant	Torpedoed 2/6/45	Liberty Ship	Crew—K/9 Armed Guard—K/7
SS Henry Bacon[42]	Aerial torpedoed 2/23/45	Liberty Ship	Crew—K/15 Armed Guard—K/7

Italian frogmen to sink or damage merchant ships by attaching mines to the hulls of the ships, especially in the harbor of Gibraltar where vessels waited for convoys to be formed.

The deck watch aboard the *Otis* pulled out a man who appeared to be exhausted and near drowning. When picked up out of the water, he was found to be an Italian and turned over to the British who discovered he had attached a mine to her hull.

[42] During the last voyage of the *Bacon* in a 34-ship convoy and on which there were 35 Norwegian refugees—men, women, and children—who had fled Russia when the Nazis invaded and were being sent to England. During a violent storm with turbulent seas, the ships had to scatter. The *Bacon* was not one of the ships rounded up and lagged approximately 50 miles behind because of steering engine problems. Once the problems were fixed, the ship attempted to catch up with the rest of the convoy but was attacked by planes and U-boats.

Men fell out of their bunks, grabbed helmets, lifejackets, and extra clothing for protection against the wintry winds. The steward summoned his cooks and messmen to get out the bandages, splints, and anesthetics including covering the wardroom tables with blankets in the event of casualties.

A torpedo finally hit the #3 hold on the starboard side, forward. A 50-foot column of water shot up above the bulwarks (the ship's side above the deck) causing her to shudder. A second torpedo hit and the order to abandon ship was given. She carried four lifeboats and a number of rafts but there was small hope of survival in those heavy seas. One engineer heroically gave his position in the lifeboat to a young naval gunner of about 17. The lifeboats drifted off into the mist and watched the *Bacon* settle slowly beneath the sea, with her ensign snapping to and fro in the wind.

Soon forgotten in Murmansk were the heroic deeds of ships and men who braved the hazards of the convoy routes to carry aid to them in World War II. There is not a single testimonial there to the merchantmen and their naval comrades who died to keep supplies going to the Russian front. The Murmansk museum contains many World War II relics but no remembrance whatsoever of those gallant ships and brave men, many of whom were just boys.

SS Henry Knox	Torpedoed 6/19/43	Liberty Ship	Crew—K/13 Armed Guard—K/13
SS Henry Miller	Torpedoed 1/3/45	Liberty Ship	No casualties
SS Henry R. Mallory	Torpedoed 2/2/43	Passenger Ship	Crew—K/49 Armed Guard—K/15 Passengers—K/208
SS Heredia	Torpedoed 5/19/42	Freighter	Crew—K/29 Armed Guard—K/5 U.S. Military—K/1
SS Hobart Baker	Bombed 12/29/44	Liberty Ship	Crew—K/1
SS Hobbs Victory	Sunk by Kamikaze suicide plane 4/6/45	Freighter	Crew—K/11 Armed Guard—K/1
SS Honolulan	Torpedoed 7/22/42	Freighter	No casualties
SS Honomu *	Torpedoed 7/5/42	Freighter	Crew—K/12 British Gunner—K/1
SS Hoosier *	Bombed 7/10/42	Freighter	No casualties
SS Horace Binney[43]	Mined 5/8/45	Liberty Ship	No casualties
SS Horace Bushnell	Torpedoed 3/20/45	Liberty Ship	Crew—K/5
SS Horace Gray	Torpedoed 2/14/45	Liberty Ship	No casualties
SS Hybert	Mined 7/5/42	Freighter	No casualties
SS Illinoian[44]	Deliberately sank 7/28/44	Freighter	No casualties
SS Illinois	Torpedoed 6/1/42	Freighter	Crew—K/31
SS India Arrow	Torpedoed & Shelled 2/4/42	Tanker	Crew—K/26
SS Irenee Dupont	Torpedoed 3/17/43	Freighter	Crew—K/7 Armed Guard—K/5 U.S. Military—K/1
SS Isaac Shelby	Mined 1/6/45	Liberty Ship	No casualties
SS Isabela	Torpedoed & Shelled 5/19/42	Freighter	Crew—K/3
M/S J. A. Moffett, Jr.	Torpedoed & Shelled 7/7/42	Tanker	Crew—K/1
SS J. N. Pew	Torpedoed 2/21/42	Tanker	Crew—K/33
SS Jack	Torpedoed 5/27/42	Freighter	Crew—K/29 Armed Guard—K/3 U.S. Army—K/7

[43] The *Binney* was the last Liberty ship to be put out of service in the European Theater.

[44] Also of World War II vintage, the *Illinoian* became a part of the "Mulberry field" in Normandy.

SS Jack Carnes	Shelled & Torpedoed 8/30/42	Tanker	Crew—K/17 Armed Guard—K/11
SS Jacksonville	Torpedoed 8/30/44	Tanker	Crew—K/48 Armed Guard—K/28
SS James A. Farrell[45]	Torpedoed 6/29/44	Liberty Ship	U.S. Army—K/4
SS James B. Stephens	Torpedoed 3/8/43 3/8/43	Liberty Ship	Armed Guard—K/1
SS James Eagan Layne[46]	Torpedoed 3/21/45	Liberty Ship	No casualties
SS James Guthrie[47]	Mined 3/21/45	Liberty Ship	No casualties
SS James H. Breasted[48]	Bombed 12/26/44	Liberty Ship	No casualties
SS James Iredell[49]	Bombed 10/23/43; Scuttled 6/7/44	Liberty Ship	No casualties
SS James McKay	Torpedoed 12/7/42	Freighter	Crew—K/46 Armed Guard—K/25
SS James Oglethorpe[50]	Torpedoed 3/16/43	Liberty Ship	Crew—K/31 Armed Guard—K/11 U.S. Military—K/2
SS James Robertson	Torpedoed 7/7/43	Liberty Ship	Armed Guard—K/1
SS James Russell Lowell[51]	Torpedoed 10/15/43	Liberty Ship	No casualties

[45] The *Farrell*, hit by a torpedo, was towed to Spithead and written off as a total loss. The injuries and casualties occurred when heavy, steel hatch beams fell into the troop quarters.

[46] Torpedoed en route from Barry, Wales to Ghent, she was beached after being towed to Whitesand Bay. She was considered a total loss.

[47] Hitting a mine off the coast of Naples, the *Guthrie* was saved by being towed into port and beached.

[48] Prior to being hit by an aerial bomber, the *Breasted* managed to unload 600 Army troops without a single injury to passengers or crew.

[49] Commencing on D-Day, the blockships a.k.a. "Mulberries", arrived at the beachheads scheduled at various times. The *Iredell*, a veteran of the Mediterranean campaign, was one of the first to be scuttled.

[50] When the *Oglethorpe* went down, her cargo consisted of a load of planes, tractors, and trucks. Many of her crew and Armed Guard detachment also went down with her.

[51] This happened time and time again during the course of the war; the *Lowell* was torpedoed off the coast of Bizerte, abandoned, reboarded, and towed successfully to Algiers.

SS James Sprunt	Torpedoed 10/15/43	Liberty Ship	Crew—K/43 Armed Guard—K/28
SS James W. Denver[52] *	Torpedoed 4/11/43	Liberty Ship	Crew—K/2
SS James W. Marshall[53]	Bombed 9/15/43	Liberty Ship	Crew—K/13 Armed Guard—K/17 U.S. Army—Unkn.
SS Jean Nicolet[54]	Torpedoed & Shelled 7/2/44	Liberty Ship	Crew—K/30 Navy—K/19 U.S. Military—26
SS Jeremiah Van Rennselaer[55]	Torpedoed 2/2/43	Liberty Ship	Crew—K/35 Armed Guard—K/11
SS Jeremiah Wadsworth	Torpedoed 11/27/42	Liberty Ship	No casualties

[52] See excerpts from diary at the end of this section.

[53] Arriving in Salerno on 11 September, the *Marshall* was hit almost immediately and set afire. The fire was extinguished and unloading continued. Two days later she was hit by another bomb killing many crew and Army cargo handlers. A landing craft had been loaded with ammunition and was burning when a cadet showed courage and presence of mind by cutting the craft loose and flooding the after magazine. She was used later as a "mulberry" at Normandy.

[54] Sunk by a Japanese sub in the Indian Ocean homeward bound from the Arabian Sea, many of the crew were shot or drowned. Many of the casualties were returning after spending two or more years in the Persian Gulf. One of the missing men was Francis J. O'Gara who had been a sports writer for the Philadelphia Inquirer. A new Liberty was named for O'Gara. After spending 15 months in a Japanese prison camp, he arrived home. He was the only man to see his own Liberty ship and was later presented the builder's plaque from "his" ship. After the war, this ship joined the U.S. Navy as the *Outpost* as a radar picket ship.

The survivors in lifeboats were ordered to the Japanese submarine. They were prodded with bayonets; ordered to kneel and hands were tied behind their backs with wire lines and strips of clothing. A messboy who did not kneel fast enough to please the guard shot him in the back and his body thrown overboard. A nightlong orgy of torture and murder had begun. All the above listed as having been killed, were killed by the Japanese.

[55] Depending on which book one reads, the last name is spelled with two "n's" or two "s's". She was hit by three torpedoes and set on fire while en route from New York to England. Two of the lifeboats capsized and 46 of the merchant crew were lost. Please note above figures disagree with this figure, unless the number also includes the Armed Guard lost. She continued to burn and had to be sunk by gunfire from an escort vessel.

SS John A. Johnson[56]	Torpedoed 10/30/44	Liberty Ship	Crew—K/4 Armed Guard—5 U.S. Army—K/1
SS John A. Poor	Torpedoed 3/19/44	Liberty Ship	Crew—K/25 Armed Guard—K/9
SS John A. Treutlen	Mined or Torpedoed 6/29/44	Liberty Ship	No casualties
SS John Adams[57]	Torpedoed 5/5/42	Liberty Ship	Armed Guard—K/5
SS John Barry	Torpedoed 8/28/44	Liberty Ship	Crew—K/2
SS John Bascom[58]	Bombed 12/2/43	Liberty Ship	Crew—K/4 Armed Guard—K/10 **
SS John Bell	Torpedoed 8/26/43	Liberty Ship	Crew—K/1

[56] The Japanese killed survivors by being shot or by drowning, as one will shortly determine. The *John A. Johnson* left San Francisco for Honolulu with a cargo of food, explosives, and a deckload of trucks. This area of the Pacific was not considered especially hazardous and she was running alone. Lookouts were posted and the gun crew readies for any eventuality. No one saw the submarine or torpedo that struck the #3 hold. Making a heavy roll at the time, the explosion at the turn of the bilge (the rounded, lower part of a ship's hold) was fatal. As the last man left the ship, she broke in two.

The raider turned on the lifeboats after finishing off the two sections of the *Johnson*. With the intent of ramming the lifeboat, the men jumped into the water and swam out of the way. Several Japanese fired on the survivors with pistols and machine guns. Climbing back into the lifeboat, they had to jump back into the water when the sub made another attempt at ramming. Finally, after the third time, the sub sank the raft. Three men were killed by machine gun fire and the sub finally disappeared into the darkness.

[57] The *John Adams* was the first Liberty ship sunk in the Pacific. Her cargo was 2,000 tons of gasoline. She was torpedoed during the night near New Caledonia. A survivor stated that the lights went out and things, which weren't bolted down, fell and scattered all over the place. A crew of 45 abandoned ship.

The following day a Greek ship discovered the *Adams* still on the surface. A boarding party was sent aboard with the hopes of towing her into port. The amidships deckhouse was found to be gutted by fire and the ship's cat was alive on the bow. There was a tremendous explosion in #3 hold and the boarding party left quickly. The ship sunk shortly afterward.

[58] The bombing of this ship occurred in Bari, Italy. It is commonly known as "The Second Pearl Harbor." Any ships destroyed in this raid by German planes are marked with a double asterisk. You will read more about the raid on Bari in the body of this book.

SS John Burke[59]	Sunk by Kamikaze suicide plane 12/28/44	Liberty Ship	Crew—K/40 Armed Guard—K/28
SS John Carter Rose	Torpedoed 10/8/42	Liberty Ship	Crew—K/5 Armed Guard—K/3
SS John D. Gill	Torpedoed 3/12/42	Tanker	Crew—K/19 Armed Guard—K/4
SS John Draytom	Torpedoed & Shelled 4/21/43	Liberty Ship	Crew—K/21 Armed Guard—K/5
SS John H. Couch[60]	Aerial torpedoed 10/11/43	Liberty Ship	Crew—K/l Armed Guard—K/1
SS John Hancock	Torpedoed 8/18/42	Liberty Ship	No casualties
SS John Harvey	Bombed 12/2/43	Liberty Ship	Crew—36 Armed Guard—38 ** U.S. Army—10
SS John L. Motley	Bombed 12/2/43	Liberty Ship	Crew—39 Armed Guard—24 **
SS John Penn[61]	Aerial torpedoed 9/13/42	Liberty Ship	Crew—K/3

[59] Children in school took part in a national scrap-metal salvage (which I remember) campaign and invited to suggest names for some of the Liberty ships. John Burke, governor of North Dakota, was one who received this honor.

During the winters of 1943 and 1945, among the worst on record in Alaskan waters, it was not uncommon for ships to report winds up to 75 to 100 knots and seas from 40 to 50 feet high. The *Burke* had made this trip successfully nine times. On her tenth trip, the paragraph below explains it all.

In a convoy that left Leyte for Mindoro, the *Burke* suffered a tremendous loss. After being hit by a dive-bomber, the ammunition-laden ship disappeared in a blast so devastating that when the smoke cleared away, there wasn't even a handful of floating debris to mark where she and her 68 crewmen had been.

[60] Selling off serviceable ships after the war, the U.S. Maritime Administration offered for sale the wrecks of hundreds of ships. Some of the ships were hulks deep in the sea whereas others were cargo-laden vessels in a relatively few feet of water below the surface. The *John H. Couch* was one of these ships lying off the coast of Guadalcanal.

[61] *John Penn* was one of eight American ships in convoy PQ18. The convoy had begun with 20 ships and arrived with seven. The convoy suffered a steep price in ships and cargo but it also caused a heavy toll from the enemy. By this time there were urgent demands upon the Germans for more aircraft elsewhere. Further massive air attacks was discouraged against the heavily protected Murmansk convoys.

SS John R. Park[62]	Torpedoed 3/21/45	Liberty Ship	No casualties
SS John R. Williams	Mined 6/24/42	Tug	Crew—K/14
SS John Randolph[63]	Mined 7/5/42	Liberty Ship	Crew—K/5
SS John Sevier	Torpedoed 4/6/43	Liberty Ship	No casualties
SS John Winthrop	Torpedoed & Disappeared 9/24/42	Liberty Ship	Crew—K/39 Armed Guard—K/15
SS John Witherspoon *	Torpedoed 7/6/42	Liberty Ship	Crew—K/1
SS Jonas Lie	Torpedoed 1/9/45	Liberty Ship	Crew—K/2
SS Jonathan Sturges	Torpedoed by subs 2/23/43	Liberty Ship	Crew—K/29 Armed Guard—K/21
SS Jose Navarro	Torpedoed 12/26/43	Liberty Ship	No casualties
SS Joseph Carrigan	Mined 9/10/45	Liberty Ship	No casualties
M/S Justine Foss	Captured by Japanese 12/23/41	Tug	Crew—2; murdered by Japanese
SS Joseph M. Cudahy	Torpedoed 5/4/42	Tanker	Crew—K/27
SS Joseph Wheeler[64]	Bombed 12/2/43	Liberty Ship	Crew—26 Armed Guard—15 **
SS Julia Ward Howe[65]	Torpedoed 1/27/43	Liberty Ship	Crew—K/2 Armed Guard—K/1 U.S. Army—K/1
SS Kahuku	Torpedoed & Shelled 6/15/42	Freighter	Crew—K/6 Armed Guard—K/3 Passengers—K/9
SS Kaimoku	Torpedoed 8/8/42	Freighter	Crew—K/2

[62] She was torpedoed approximately nine miles off Lizard Head but sank several hours later. There were no casualties.

[63] She was one of the first Liberty ships to make the run to Murmansk early in 1942 and only one of two to make the convoy run in convoy PQ16.

[64] Again, depending upon which book one reads, this one states that 44 men out of her crew of 56 were killed when she blew up.

[65] This ship was headed for North Africa with a cargo of 60 medium tanks. She straggled from the convoy southwest of the Azores. A U-boat fired two torpedoes, missing with one but the second one broke the *Howe* in two. She was gone to the bottom in five minutes. The submarine surfaced, questioned the survivors in the lifeboats and gave them the course to steer to the Azores. The survivors were surprised at the joviality of the U-boat's crew and in good English, their executive officer told them they were the 30th ship they had sunk. Survivors in the lifeboats were rescued and taken to Ponta Delgada, Azores **which is the same port the *McAndrew* was taken after their collision with the *Bearn*.**

SS Kentuckian	Deliberately sunk 8/12/44	Freighter	No casualties
SS Kentucky	Torpedoed 9/18/42	Freighter	No casualties
SS Keshena	Mined 7/19/42	Tug	Crew—K/2
SS Keystone[66]	Torpedoed 3/13/43	Freighter	Crew—K/1 Armed Guard—K/1
SS Knoxville City	Torpedoed 6/1/42	Freighter	Crew—K/2
SS Krofresi	Deliberately sunk 7/14/44	Freighter	No casualties
SS L. J. Drake	Torpedoed 6/5/42	Tanker	Crew—K/35 Armed Guard—K/6
SS Lahaina	Shelled 12/11/42	Freighter	Crew—K/4
M/S Lake Osweya	Torpedoed 2/20/42	Freighter	Crew—K/30
SS Lammot Dupont	Torpedoed 4/23/42	Freighter	Crew—K/18 Armed Guard—K/1
SS Larry Doheny	Torpedoed 10/5/42	Tanker	Crew—K/2 Armed Guard—K/4
SS LaSalle[67]	Torpedoed 11/7/42	Freighter	Crew—K/39 Armed Guard—K/13
SS Lebore	Torpedoed 6/14/42	Bulk Carrier	Crew—K/1
SS Lee S. Overman	Mined 11/11/44	Liberty Ship	No casualties
SS Lehigh	Torpedoed 10/19/41	Freighter	No casualties
SS Lemuel Burrows	Torpedoed 3/14/42	Collier	Crew—K/20
SS Lena Luckenbach	Deliberately sunk 8/4/44	Freighter	No casualties
SS Leslie	Torpedoed 4/12/42	Freighter	Crew—K/4

[66] A ship's log of another reads:

March 12. 1600 hours. *SS Keystone* dropped out of convoy.

2117 hours. Bright white light on port side of convoy. Two 45 degree turns to starboard. Two rounds fired from large gun from ship on starboard side of convoy. Three depth charges dropped. More gun fire. Two emergency turns to port.

2118 hours. General alarm sounded.

2315 hours. About 15 depth charges dropped in 15 minutes.

March 13. Received message. *SS Keystone* torpedoed.

[67] Becoming one of the mystery ships of World War II, the ammunition-laden American steamer was one of those routed across the South Atlantic and around the Cape of Good Hope. She never arrived at her destination. It is thought she was probably a victim of a submarine that also failed to return as no clue to the sub's fate was obtained from their records after the war.

SS Lewis L. Dyche[68]	Sunk by Kamikaze suicide plane 1/4/45	Liberty Ship	Crew—K/41 Armed Guard—K/30
SS Liberator	Torpedoed 3/19/42	Freighter	Crew—K/5
SS Liberty	Torpedoed 1/11/42	Freighter	No casualties
SS Lihue	Torpedoed 2/23/42	Freighter	No casualties
SS Logan Victory	Sunk by Kamikaze suicide plane 4/6/45	Freighter	Crew—K/12 Armed Guard—K/3
SS Losmar	Torpedoed 9/24/42	Freighter	Crew—K/24 Armed Guard—K/3
SS Louise Lykes	Torpedoed 1/9/43	Freighter	Crew—K/50 Armed Guard—K/24 U.S. Army—K/10
M/S Louisiana	Torpedoed 8/17/42	Tanker	Crew—K/42 Armed Guard—K/8
SS Lydia M. Child	Torpedoed 4/27/43	Liberty Ship	No casualties
SS McDowell	Torpedoed 12/16/43	Tanker	Crew—K/3
SS McKeesport	Torpedoed 4/29/43	Freighter	Crew—K/1
SS M. F. Elliott	Torpedoed 6/3/42	Tanker	Crew—K/10
SS Mae	Torpedoed & Shelled 9/17/42	Freighter	Crew—K/1
SS Maiden Creek II	Torpedoed 3/17/44	Freighter	Crew—K/6 Armed Guard—K/5
SS Major General Henry Gibbins	Torpedoed 6/23/42	US Army Transport	No casualties
SS Major Wheeler	Torpedoed 2/6/42	Freighter	Crew—K/35
SS Malama	Bombed 1/1/42	Freighter	Crew—K/33[69] Air Corps—K/5
SS Malantic	Torpedoed 3/9/43	Freighter	Crew—K/19 Armed Guard—K/5 Military—K/1
SS Malchace	Torpedoed 4/9/42	Freighter	Crew—K/1
SS Maltran	Torpedoed 7/5/43	Freighter	No casualties
SS Manatawny	Bombed 12/31/41	Tanker	No casualties
SS Manini	Torpedoed 12/17/41	Freighter	Crew—K/3
SS Manuela	Torpedoed 6/24/42	Freighter	Crew—K/2

[68] The *Dyche* was sunk off Magrin Bay. She was loaded with ammunition; she and her crew were completely disintegrated.

[69] All surviving crewmembers were taken to a Japanese POW camp. Two died and one was taken to a mental hospital. Repatriated in October 1945, the fate of the hospitalized engineer was never mentioned.

SS Marcus Whitman[70]	Torpedoed & Shelled 11/8/42	Liberty Ship	No casualties
SS Margaret	Torpedoed 4/14/42	Freighter	Crew—K/29
SS Mariana	Torpedoed 3/5/42	Freighter	Crew—K/35
SS Marore	Torpedoed 2/26/42	Bulk Carrier	No casualties
SS Mary Luckenbach	Torpedo bombers 9/14/42	Freighter	All crew and 16 Armed Guard—K
SS Matthew Luckenbach	Torpedoed 3/19/43	Freighter	No casualties
SS Mauna Loa	Bombed 2/19/42	Freighter	Crew—K/1
SS Meigs	Bombed 2/19/42	Freighter	Crew—K/1
SS Melville E. Stone	Torpedoed 11/24/43	Liberty Ship	Crew—K/12 Armed Guard—K/3 U.S. Military—K/1
M/S Melvin H. Baker	Torpedoed 6/6/42	Freighter	No casualties
SS Menominee	Shelled 3/31/42	Tug	Crew—K/16
M/S Mercury Sun	Torpedoed 5/18/42	Tanker	Crew—K/6
SS Meriwether Lewis[71]	Torpedoed 3/2/43	Liberty Ship	Crew—K/44 Armed Guard—K/28
SS Merrimack	Torpedoed 6/9/42	Freighter	Crew—K/35 Armed Guard—K/8
SS Metapan	Mined 10/1/43	Refrigerator Ship	No casualties
SS Meton	Torpedoed 11/5/42	Tanker	Crew—K/1
SS Meyer London	Torpedoed 4/16/44	Liberty Ship	No casualties
SS Michigan[72]	Torpedoed 4/30/43	Freighter	No casualties
SS Millinocket	Torpedoed 6/17/42	Freighter	Crew—K/8 Armed Guard—K/3
SS Minotaur	Torpedoed 6/17/42	Freighter	Crew—K/6

[70] A torpedo blew off her rudder and propeller on 9 November as she was en route from Cape Town to Dutch Guinea. Everyone considered himself or herself lucky. The crew abandoned ship. A second torpedo hit the engine room but still she did not sink. A submarine surfaced and fired 20 shells into the ship before the *Whitman* finally went down. Four lifeboats reached the African coast in a few days. Please note the difference in dates from the chart and this paragraph.

[71] Her cargo consisted of ammunition and automobile tires. She disappeared from the HX227 convoy, presumed torpedoed and sunk. A convoy escort searched for 48 hours attempting to locate survivors but all they found was a 30-mile long line of floating tires.

[72] In the early convoys ships were too lightly armed to put up much of a fight against air attacks and submarines. They fought valiantly with what they had. The *Michigan* shot down two planes with her meager armament.

SS Mobiloil	Torpedoed & Shelled 4/29/42	Tanker	No casualties
SS Molly Pitcher[73]	Torpedoed 3/17/43	Liberty Ship	Crew—K/2 Armed Guard—K/2
SS Montanan	Torpedoed 6/3/43	Freighter	Crew—K/5 Armed Guard—K/2
SS Montebello	Torpedoed & Shelled 12/23/41	Tanker	No casualties
SS Mormacsul	Bombed 5/27/42	Freighter	Crew—K/3
SS Munger T. Ball	Torpedoed & machine-gunned 5/4/42	Tanker	Crew—K/30
SS Muskogee	Torpedoed 3/22/42	Tanker	Crew—K/34
SS Naeco	Torpedoed 3/23/42	Tanker	Crew—K/24
SS Nashaba	Mined 2/26/45	Freighter	Crew—K/1 Pilot—K/1
SS Nathaniel Greene[74]	Torpedoed 2/24/43	Liberty Ship	Crew—K/4
SS Nathaniel Hawthorne	Torpedoed 11/7/42	Liberty Ship	Crew—K/30 Armed Guard—K/7 U.S. Military—K/1
SS New Jersey	Torpedoed & Shelled 5/28/42	Tanker	No casualties
SS Nicarao	Torpedoed 5/15/42	Freighter	Crew—K/8
M/S Nickeliner	Torpedoed 5/13/43	Tanker	No casualties
SS Norlandia	Torpedoed 7/3/42	Freighter	Crew—K/9
SS Norlantic	Shelled & Torpedoed 5/13/42	Freighter	Crew—K/7
SS Norlavore	Torpedoed 2/24/42	Freighter	Crew—K/28
SS Norlindo[75]	Torpedoed 5/4/42	Freighter	Crew—K/5

[73] Usually it took more than one torpedo to sink a Liberty. Either the submarine or an escort ship had to sink the hulk by gunfire. She was en route from New York to Casablanca in convoy and torpedoed by a U-boat. She finally had to be sent to the bottom by gunfire from another of our ships.

[74] Having left Mostagonem, Algeria to join a passing convoy, German bombers attacked and although three torpedoes hit she did not sink. The ship was beached at Salmanda, a total loss.

[75] The crew of these types of ships were typical of sailors who knew no other home than their ship. They were hardworking, conscientious, and hard drinkers in port. They made good shipmates, did their jobs well and expected the same of others. It is an eternal tribute to the quality of these men: rough, tough, and unpolished. Their ships never lacked crews or missed a sailing date even though many of them had no guns or armed escorts for protection.

SS Norvana	Torpedoed 1/22/42	Freighter	Crew—K/29
SS Oakmar	Shelled 3/20/42	Freighter	Crew—K/6
SS Ogontz	Torpedoed 5/19/4	Freighter	Crew—K/17 Armed Guard—K/2
SS Ohioan	Torpedoed 5/8/42	Freighter	Crew—K/17
SS Oklahoma	Torpedoed 4/8/42	Tanker	Crew—K/19
SS Oklahoma	Torpedoed 3/28/45	Tanker	Crew—K/36 Armed Guard—K/14
SS Olga	Torpedoed 3/12/42	Freighter	Crew—K/1
SS Oliver Ellsworth	Torpedoed 9/13/42	Liberty Ship	No casualties
SS Olopana *	Torpedoed & Shelled 7/7/42	Freighter	Crew—K/5 Armed Guard—K/1
SS Oneida	Torpedoed 7/13/42	Freighter	Crew—K/6
SS Onondaga	Torpedoed 7/23/42	Freighter	Crew—K/18 U.S. Military—K/1
SS Oregon	Shelled 2/28/42	Tanker	Crew—6—murdered by Japanese with machine guns
SS Oregonian	Aerial torpedoed 9/13/42	Freighter	Crew—K/22 Armed Guard—K/7
SS Otho	Torpedoed 4/3/42	Freighter	Crew—K/23 Armed Guard—K/5 U.S. Military—K/3
SS Pan Atlantic *	Bombed 7/6/42	Freighter	Crew—K/18 Armed Guard—K/7
SS Pankraft *	Bombed 7/5/42	Freighter	Crew—K/2
SS Pan Massachusetts	Torpedoed 2/19/42	Tanker	Crew—K/20
SS Pan New York	Torpedoed 10/29/42	Tanker	Crew—K/26 Armed Guard—K/16
SS Pan Pennsylvania	Torpedoed 4/16/44	Tanker	Crew—K/15 Armed Guard—K/10
SS Papoose	Torpedoed 3/18/42	Tanker	Crew—K/2
SS Parismina	Torpedoed 11/18/42	Freighter	Crew—K/15 Armed Guard—K/2 U.S. Military—K/3
SS Pat Harrison[76]	Mined 5/18/43	Liberty Ship	Crew—K/2

[76] In another frogman attack at Gibraltar, a mine exploded beneath the engine room with enough force to throw men out of their bunks. Although it further states there were no fatalities, this does not agree with what is in the chart. The ship was beached as a complete loss.

SS Patrick J. Hurley	Shelled 9/12/42	Tanker	Crew—K/13 Armed Guard—K/4
SS Paul Hamilton[77]	Aerial torpedoed 4/20/44	Liberty Ship	Crew—K/47 Armed Guard—K/29 Army Air Force—K/504
SS Paul Luckenbach	Torpedoed 9/22/42	Freighter	No casualties
SS Penelope Barker	Torpedoed 1/25/44	Liberty Ship	Crew—K/10 Armed Guard—K/5 Royal Navy Doctor—K/1
SS Pennmar	Torpedoed 9/23/42	Freighter	Crew—K/2
SS Pennsylvania	Deliberately sunk 8/4/44	Freighter	No casualties
SS Peter Kerr *	Bombed 7/5/42	Freighter	No casualties
SS Peter Sylvester[78]	Torpedoed 2/6/45	Liberty Ship	Crew—K/1 Armed Guard—K/7 U.S. Army—K/24
SS Peter Skene Ogden[79]	Torpedoed 2/22/44	Liberty Ship	No casualties
SS Phoebe Hearst[80]	Torpedoed 4/30/43	Liberty Ship	No casualties
SS Pierce Butler[81]	Torpedoed 11/21/42	Liberty Ship	No casualties
SS Pipestone County	Torpedoed 4/21/42	Freighter	No casualties

[77] The *Hamilton* produced the largest casualty list in all of World War II to become the most costly Liberty ship disaster. She was making her fifth voyage as a part of a huge convoy when German bombers attacked her. In addition to her high explosive cargo and bombs, she carried a large number of troops. After the torpedo hit, a violent explosion threw debris and dense black smoke high into the air. When the smoke cleared, there was no sign of the ship. According to this story, not one of the 498 men survived. The number in the chart is 585 men who were casualties.

[78] Depending on which book one reads, this ship's name is spelled with an "I" or a "y"—Sylvester or Silvester. Her story is more thoroughly covered in this book and a separate book will be written.

[79] The *Ogden* is another ship that refused to sink after being torpedoed. Her captain and ten volunteers sailed her to the nearest port and beached her.

[80] Again, depending on which book one reads, the name of this ship could have been the *Phoebe A. Hurst*.

[81] This ship was headed toward Suez from Durban with cargo of 9,787 tons of military material when two torpedoes went into her. She sank within 30 minutes. The crew spent some hours in the lifeboats before being picked up and returned to Durban.

The Ship That Never Was

SS Plow City	Torpedoed 5/21/42	Freighter	Crew—K/1
SS Polybius	Torpedoed 6/27/42	Freighter	Crew—K/10
SS Portmar	Bombed 2/19/42	Freighter	Crew—K/1 U.S. Army—K/1
SS Potlatch	Torpedoed 6/27/42	Freighter	Crew—K/8
SS President Coolidge	Mined 10/26/42	Passenger Ship	Crew—K/1 U.S. Army—K/4
SS President Harrison	Captured by Japanese 1/7/41	Passenger Ship	Crew—K/3 164 of crew sent to Japanese POW camps[82]
SS Prusa	Torpedoed 12/19/41	Freighter	Crew—K/10
SS Puerto Rican[83]	Torpedoed 3/9/43	Freighter	Crew—K/39 Armed Guard—K/25
SS Quaker City	Torpedoed 5/18/42	Freighter	Crew—K/11
SS R. M. Parker, Jr.	Torpedoed & Shelled 8/13/42	Tanker	No casualties
SS R. P. Resor	Torpedoed 2/28/42	Tanker	Crew—K/40 Armed Guard—K/8
SS R. W. Gallagher	Torpedoed 7/13/42	Freighter	Crew—K/9 Armed Guard—K/1
SS Raphael Semmes	Torpedoed 6/8/42	Freighter	Crew—K/19
SS Rawleigh Warner	Torpedoed 6/23/42	Tanker	Crew—K/33
SS Republic	Torpedoed 2/21/42	Tanker	Crew—K/5
SS Reuben Tipton	Torpedoed 10/23/42	Freighter	Crew—K/3
SS Richard Bland	Torpedoed 3/10/43	Liberty Ship	Crew—K/19 Armed Guard—K/15

[82] This occurred before the Armed Guards were being assigned on merchant ships. The *Harrison* was attempting to get to China to evacuate Marines. They were captured and the Master intentionally ran his ship aground to prevent use by the Japanese. Three members of the crew in a lifeboat were pulled into the ship propellers and killed. Twelve of the crew died while in captivity; the Master was sent to a Japanese jail for grounding the ship.

[83] Sending a SOS, the American freighter had been torpedoed and sinking fast. There were not any survivors found by escort ships although an extensive oil patch, one empty and waterlogged lifeboat was found. It was later learned that she had been separated from the convoy during a storm and was 25 miles astern (behind) when she went down. Only one lifeboat could be lowered as the davits and ropes were iced over and could not be released. It capsized throwing its occupants into the sea. Eight men swam to a small raft that was found two days later but by then, only one man was alive.

SS Richard Caswell	Torpedoed 7/16/43	Liberty Ship	Crew—K/9
SS Richard D. Spaight[84]	Torpedoed & Shelled 3/10/43	Liberty Ship	Crew—K/1
SS Richard Henderson	Torpedoed 8/26/43	Liberty Ship	No casualties
SS Richard Hovey[85]	Torpedoed 3/9/44	Liberty Ship	Crew—K/3 Armed Guard—K/1 Master and 3 crew taken prisoner
SS Richard Montgomery	Bombed 8/20/44	Liberty Ship	No casualties
SS Richard Olney[86]	Torpedoed 9/22/43	Liberty Ship	Crew—K/2
SS Roanoke	Torpedoed 1/11/45	Refrigerator Ship	Crew—K/2 Armed Guard—K/2
SS Robert Bacon	Torpedoed 7/13/43	Liberty Ship	Crew—K/3 Armed Guard—K/2
SS Robert E. Hopkins	Torpedoed 2/7/43	Tanker	Crew—K/14 Armed Guard—K/1
SS Robert E. Lee	Torpedoed 7/30/42	Passenger Ship	Crew—K/10 U.S. Military—K/15
SS Robert H. Colley	Torpedoed 10/4/42	Tanker	Crew—K/20 Armed Guard—K/8
SS Robert Gray	Torpedoed 4/23/43	Liberty Ship	Crew—K/39 Armed Guard—K/23
SS Robert L. Vann[87]	Mined 3/1/45	Liberty Ship	No casualties

[84] Many strange experiences were met by crewmembers of Liberty ships to the far corners of the world. The most unique had a touch of the Arabian Nights about it for there was a magic carpet ride for one man. The ship was in the Mozambique Channel between Madagascar and Africa. This man was relaxing on a mattress he had placed on top of a forward hatch. A torpedo hit the ship right beneath him. The man and his mattress were hurled over the ship and into the sea. The mattress landed with him still laying on it and the man wasn't hurt.

[85] Homeward bound from India, a sub attacked the *Hovey*. After the crew abandoned ship, the Japanese pursued the accustomed practice of shooting at the survivors and running down the lifeboats. Aim was either bad or their heart was no longer in their work in this sadistic endeavor.

[86] Escorts by British corvettes and armed trawlers, one of three ships in a convoy, she was torpedoed. The engine was knocked off its foundation and the engine room flooded; however, she stayed afloat and was towed to Bizerte.

[87] The *Robert L. Vann* was named for one of the nation's pioneer Negro newspaper publishers.

SS Robert Rowan	Bombed 7/11/43	Liberty Ship	No casualties
SS Robin Goodfellow	Torpedoed 7/25/44	Freighter	Crew—K/41 Armed Guard—K/19
SS Robin Gray	Deliberately sunk 8/18/44	Freighter	No casualties
SS Robin Hood	Torpedoed & Shelled 4/15/42	Freighter	Crew—K/14
SS Robin Moor	Torpedoed & Shelled 5/21/41	Freighter	No casualties
SS Rochester	Torpedoed & Shelled 1/30/42	Tanker	Crew—K/4
SS Roger B. Taney[88]	Torpedoed 2/7/43	Liberty Ship	Crew—K/3

This ship was in a single line convoy en route from Antwerp to the Thames (England). It broke in two and sank after hitting a mine just off Ostend. Several men were injured but sustained no casualties.

[88] The *Taney* underwent the longest open-boat trip of World War II that began in the South Atlantic while being hunted down by a U-boat. The first torpedo was a white streak that missed by 20+ feet. The crew went immediately to general quarters. The submarine surfaced when it was dark and began to chase them that continued for an hour but the *Taney* could not outrun the sub. A torpedo hit the starboard side in the engine room killing the third assistant engineer, the oilier, and the fireman on watch.

One of the survivors looked over the side and saw flames. The oil in their fuel tanks was ablaze. The guns were being fired but it was impossible to see a target. The explosion knocked the two lifeboats on the starboard side overboard.

During 42 days in two lifeboats the men talked about food but their biggest worry was water. With no rain falling for 30 days, the water beakers (a container with a beak-like lip for pouring) were empty. Finally, a rainsquall came up and the men had the opportunity to spread the sail and catch their drinking water. They knew they were getting close to land when they saw birds. A dolphin was speared, the blood drank and the meat cooked in a bucket. They finally saw lights glowing in the distance with them being brighter the following night. A Brazilian passenger ship spotted the survivors, changed course and picked them up.

Although the men were weak from being in the lifeboat for so long, and in such cramped positions, each man was able to climb up Jacob's ladder and reach the deck unaided. The captain had brought his men safely through their ordeal. They had sailed more than 2,600 miles in which they suffered through long days, cold nights, and every kind of weather from flat calm to half gales to a terrifically violent tropical storm where winds reached close to hurricane force.

SS Rosario	Torpedoed 2/21/43	Freighter	Crew—K/30 Armed Guard—K/3
SS Royal T. Frank	Torpedoed 1/28/42	Army Transport	Crew—K/7 U.S. Army—K/14
SS Ruth	Torpedoed 6/29/42	Freighter	Crew—K/31
SS Ruth Alexander	Bombed 1/31/41	Cargo/Passenger Ship	Crew—K/1 Crew members taken prisoners—17; 2 died in captivity
SS Ruth Lykes	Torpedoed & Shelled 5/16/42	Freighter	Crew—K/6
SS Sagadahoc	Torpedoed 12/3/41	Freighter	Crew—K/1
SS Sahale[89]	Deliberately sunk 8/24/44	Freighter	No casualties
SS Sam Houston	Torpedoed & Shelled 6/28/42	Liberty Ship	Crew—K/8
SS Samuel Gompers	Torpedoed 1/30/43	Liberty Ship	Crew—K/3 Armed Guard—K/1
SS Samuel Heintzelman	Torpedoed & Disappeared 7/1/43	Liberty Ship	Crew—K/42 Armed Guard—K/19
SS Samuel Huntington[90]	Bombed 1/9/44	Liberty Ship	Crew—K/5
SS Samuel J. Tilden	Bombed 12/2/43	Liberty Ship	Crew—K/10 American Military—K/14 British Military—K/3**
SS Samuel Jordan Kirkwood	Torpedoed 5/6/43	Liberty Ship	No casualties
SS Samuel Q. Brown	Torpedoed 5/23/42	Tanker	Crew—K/3 Armed Guard—K/4
SS San Jacinto	Torpedoed & Shelled 4/1/42	Passenger Ship	Crew—K/5 U.S. Military—K/9
SS Santa Catalina	Torpedoed 4/24/43	Freighter	No casualties

[89] The *Sahale* was one of the "Hog Islanders" (as well as others) was also used as a "mulberry." These ships were called "Hog Islanders" as they were built during World War I at Hog Island, Pennsylvania. These were pre-fabricated ships as the different parts were built elsewhere all over the eastern half of the United States and put together at the shipyard.

[90] Loaded with gasoline, bombs, and TNT a glide bomb hit the engine room killing four men although the chart above states 5 were killed so it depends on which book one reads. If the bomb had hit a hold, the ship would have disintegrated into nothing!

SS Santa Elena	Aerial torpedoed 11/6/43	Passenger Ship	Crew—K/4
SS Santa Elisa	Torpedoed 8/13/42	Freighter	No casualties
SS Santa Rita	Torpedoed & Shelled 7/9/42	Freighter	Crew—K/3 Master taken prisoner
SS Santore	Mined 6/17/42	Collier	Crew—K/3
M/S Sawokla	Shelled & Torpedoed 11/29/42	Freighter	Crew—K/16 Armed Guard—K/4[91]
SS Scottsburg	Torpedoed 6/14/4	Freighter	Crew—K/5 Armed Guard—K/1
SS Seakay	Torpedoed 3/18/44	Tanker	Armed Guard—K/1
SS Sea Thrush	Torpedoed 6/28/42	Freighter	No casualties
SS Seattle Spirit	Torpedoed 6/18/42	Freighter	Crew—K/4
SS Sebastian Cermeno	Torpedoed 6/7/43	Liberty Ship	Crew—K/5
SS Selma City	Bombed 4/6/42	Freighter	No casualties
SS Sicilien	Torpedoed 6/7/42	Freighter	Crew—K/5 U.S. Army—K/19
SS Silver Sword *	Torpedoed 9/20/42	Freighter	Crew—K/1
SS Sixaola	Torpedoed 6/12/42	Cargo/Passenger Ship	Crew—K/29
SS Solon Turman	Torpedoed 6/13/42	Freighter	Crew—K/1
SS Soreldoc	Torpedoed 2/28/45	Freighter	Crew—K/15
SS Staghound	Torpedoed 3/3/43	Freighter	No casualties
SS Stanvac Calcutta	Shelled & Torpedoed 6/6/42	Tanker	Crew—K/14
SS Star of Oregon	Torpedoed & Shelled 8/30/42	Liberty Ship	Repatriated Seaman 1
S/V Star of Scotland	Shelled 11/13/42	6 Masted Schooner	Crew—K/1
SS Starr King[92]	Torpedoed 2/10/43	Freighter	No casualties
SS Steel Age	Torpedoed 3/6/42	Freighter	Crew—K/33 One crew member taken prisoner

[91] Additionally, 30 crewmembers and 9-Armed Guard were taken prisoner.
[92] The *Starr King* was en route to New Caledonia from Sydney when a periscope was sighted but disappeared as the guns were manned. Being relieved from battle stations, the gunners relaxed, as did the rest of the crew. Early the following morning either the same sub or another one fired four torpedoes, two of which hit its mark. Another ship tried to tow her into port but she gradually settled and went down in the mid-afternoon.

SS Steel Maker	Torpedoed 4/19/42	Freighter	Crew—K/2
SS Steel Navigator	Torpedoed 10/19/42	Freighter	Crew—K/26 Armed Guard—K/10
SS Steel Scientist	Torpedoed 10/11/42	Freighter	Crew—K/1
SS Steel Seafarer	Bombed 9/5/41	Freighter	No casualties
SS Steel Traveler	Mined 12/18/44	Freighter	Crew—K/2
SS Steel Voyager	Torpedoed 9/23/43	Freighter	No casualties
SS Steel Worker	Mined 6/3/42	Freighter	No casualties
SS Stella Lykes	Torpedoed & Shelled 7/27/42	Freighter	Crew—K/1 Master and Chief Engineer to POW camp in Germany
SS Stephen Hopkins[93]	Shelled 9/27/42	Liberty Ship	Crew—K/31 Armed Guard—K/9

[93] The survivors' battle against enormous odds ranks as one of the truly great epics of the sea. She came upon two ships as they came out of the mist—the German *Steir* and the *Tannenfels*. In particular, the *Steir* carried six 5.9-inch guns (enough for a destroyer) and two torpedo tubes. Both German ships had machine guns and both used incendiaries, shrapnel and contact fuses. The *Hopkins* had one 4-inch gun on her stern, two 37-mm guns on the bow, four 50 caliber and two 30 caliber machine guns.

Merchant sailors and Armed Guard gunners manned their stations hurriedly. A brand-spanking new ensign, larger than the usual, had never been flown before and was raised. The two strange ships ran up German flags and opened fire. A shell hit amidships killing two crewmembers. Despite a serious stomach wound, the Ensign took charge of the gun and returned fire. The next shot made a solid hit on the *Steir* causing the sailors to yell and cheer.

Opening up with small arm fire from the German ships, hot lead chattered and pinged against gun tubs and deckhouses. In the engine room, boiler fires sputtered, electric lights shattered, and the emergency lamps were switched on. When a shot hit amidships, glasses broke and hot water dripped on to the deck. Insulation was knocked from the steam lines and asbestos looked like snow covering the floor plates.

The men in the engine room never knew what happened when a 5.9 salvo smashed through the thin hull plates filling the engine room with live steam and cordite fumes. The *Hopkins*' 37-mm guns got some telling hits on the *Steir*. The bow guns kept firing until the gun tub was filled with empty cartridges, the platform was a mass of twisted metal from enemy hits, and every man there was killed or wounded.

SS Sumner I. Kimball	Torpedoed 1/16/44	Freighter	Crew—K/39 Armed Guard—K/24
M/S Sunoil	Torpedoed 4/4/43	Tanker	Crew—K/43 Armed Guard—K/16
SS Susana	Torpedoed 10/12/42	Freighter	Crew—K/28 Armed Guard—K/10
SS Suwied	Torpedoed 6/7/42	Freighter	Crew—K/6
SS Swiftscout	Torpedoed 4/187/45	Tanker	Crew—K/1
SS Swiftsure	Torpedoed 10/8/42	Tanker	No casualties but 16 crew lost on the SS Zaandam returning to the United States
SS Syros[94]	Torpedoed 5/26/42	Freighter	Crew—K/11
SS T. C. McCobb	Torpedoed & Shelled 3/3/42	Tanker	Crew—K/4
SS Tachira	Torpedoed 7/12/42	Freighter	Crew—K/4 Armed Guard—K/1
SS Tamaulipas	Torpedoed 4/10/42	Tanker	Crew—K/2
SS Texan	Torpedoed & Shelled 3/11/42	Freighter	Crew—K/10
SS Theodore Dwight Weld[95]	Torpedoed 9/20/43	Liberty Ship	Crew—K/20 Armed Guard—K/13
SS Thomas Donaldson	Torpedoed 3/20/45	Liberty Ship	Crew—K/4

This is not all the story but to make it come to an end, the *Hopkins* sank 20 minutes after the battle was begun. After the crew got into the lifeboats and were pulling away just as their ship went down blazing from stem to stern but the new Ensign still flying in the breeze. There were 19 men in the lifeboat, at least five seriously wounded, which was all of the 60 Armed Guard and merchant sailors left. The German ships, obscured by mist and rain, the lifeboat sailed away under a good wind. Some time later there was a thunderous explosion and they knew the *Steir* finally blew up and sank.

[94] This ship, carrying tons of ammunition, disintegrated in one terrific blast after being torpedoed.

[95] As a part of the convoy ON202 making its way from England to New York, a torpedo struck this ship, exploded the boilers, blew lifeboats overboard, and broke the ship in two. Survivors jumped; the good swimmers found rafts to cling to and the stern section of the ship sank shortly thereafter. From the floating bow section 38 men were rescued. They were choking and half-blinded by fuel oil from the ruptured tanks. A rescue ship went back to check the bow section again and there was one more man waving from the hulk. He was saved.

SS Thomas McKean[96]	Torpedoed & Shelled 6/29/42	Liberty Ship	Crew—K/1 Armed Guard—K/4 Master lost on SS Onondaga returning him to United States
SS Thomas Masaryk[97]	Torpedoed 4/16/44	Liberty Ship	No casualties
SS Thomas Ruffin	Torpedoed 3/9/43	Liberty Ship	Crew—K/4 Armed Guard—K/2
SS Thomas Scott	Torpedoed 2/17/45	Liberty Ship	No casualties
SS Thomas Sinnickson	Torpedoed 7/7/43	Liberty Ship	No casualties
SS Tiger	Torpedoed 4/1/42	Tanker	Crew—K/1
SS Tillie Lykes	Torpedoed 6/18/42	Freighter	Crew—K/28
SS Timothy Pickering[98]	Bombed 7/14/43	Liberty Ship	Crew—K/22 Armed Guard—K/8 U.S. Army—K/100

[96] Again, depending on which story one reads, the spelling could be either McKean or McKeen. As one of the first Liberty ships sunk by a U-boat, she was sailing alone from New York to the Persian Gulf. Her cargo was planes, tanks, machinery, and ammunition. Some 1200 miles east of Jacksonville, Florida, a torpedo set her on fire. The U-boat surfaced and put 57 more shells into her before the vessel sank. Survivors abandoned ship and arrived safely at several Caribbean ports.

[97] This ship caught fire after being torpedoed off Algiers. Purposely she was sunk in 28 feet of water to put out the fire and for salvage operations later. A ship and her crew went aboard with British soldiers and sailors assisting. Millions of dollars were saved in the salvage of P39 and P47 fighter planes including trucks, tires, canned goods, weapons, and other material.

Salvage with makeshift equipment called for a lot of ingenuity under the most difficult conditions including long hours of labor. To make matters worse, hundreds of tons of rotten egg powder and flour created a terrible stench which had to be tolerated 16 hours a day, seven days a week until all the useable cargo was removed.

[98] The *Timothy Pickering* never received her traditional baptism with champagne nor the traditional words of the sponsor, "I christen thee". At the time the christening was to take place, the steel anchor plate broke and she slid down the ways ahead of schedule, injuring some of the workers.

She vanished in a mushroom-shaped cloud of smoke and fire towering hundreds of feet into the air. Of all the men aboard the ship, only 23 survived when they were blown overboard in the explosion. This occurred during the invasion of Sicily.

SS Tivives	Aerial torpedoed 10/21/43	Freighter	Crew—K/1
SS Topa Topa	Torpedoed 8/29/42	Freighter	Crew—K/18 Armed Guard—K/7
SS Touchet	Torpedoed 12/3/43	Tanker	Armed Guard—K/10
SS Tuscaloosa City	Torpedoed 5/4/42	Freighter	No casualties
SS Velma Lykes	Torpedoed 6/4/42	Freighter	Crew—K/15
SS Venore	Torpedoed & Shelled 1/23/42	Collier	Crew—K/17
SS Victory Sword	Deliberately sunk 6/18/44	Freighter	No casualties
SS Vincent	Torpedoed 12/12/41	Freighter	Crew of 37 put in Japanese POW camp; two died in captivity.
SS Virginia	Torpedoed 5/12/42	Tanker	Crew—K/26
SS Virginia Sinclair	Torpedoed 3/10/43	Tanker	Crew—K/7
SS Virginia Dare[99]	Mined 3/6/44	Liberty Ship	No casualties
SS W. D. Anderson	Torpedoed 2/22/42	Tanker	Crew—K/35
SS W. E. Hutton	Torpedoed 3/18/42	Tanker	Crew—K/13
SS W. L. Steed	Torpedoed & Shelled 2/2/42	Tanker	Crew—K/34
SS Wacosta	Aerial torpedoed 9/14/42	Freighter	No casualties
SS Wade Hampton[100]	Torpedoed 2/28/43	Liberty Ship	Crew—K/4 Armed Guard—K/5

[99] This ship struck a mine in the Bay of Tunis. The forward part of the ship was severed just a few feet ahead of the deckhouse and engine room. The rest of the vessel was towed to port and salvaged.

[100] March 1943 was one of the worst months of the war with 120 merchant ships being sunk in the Atlantic, mostly by U-boats. Of this total, 82 went down in the North Atlantic taking with them 470,000 tons of shipping, vast amounts of food, and war material, not including hundreds of merchant seamen.

The *Hampton* had fallen behind in heavy weather. A U-boat blew off her stern. A British ship picked up survivors, but two men were not seen in the darkness and drifted off into the night on a small raft. One of the men died of exposure. The other was determined to live even though he was water-soaked and half-frozen by wind and spray. Continuous movement of his arms and legs, and rubbing his feet when they became numb, talking, singing, and shouting to keep himself awake; his determination was rewarded. Three days later a British ship spotted him, picked him up, wrapped him in warm blankets, and given a shot of hot rum.

SS Walter Camp	Torpedoed 1/25/44	Liberty Ship	No casualties
SS Walter Q. Gresham[101]	Torpedoed 3/19/43	Liberty Ship	Crew—K/22 Armed Guard—K/5
SS Warrier	Torpedoed 7/1/42	Freighter	Crew—K/3 Armed Guard—K/4
SS Washington *	Bombed 7/5/42	Freighter	No casualties but most suffered from exposure and frozen limbs.
SS Washingtonian	Torpedoed 4/7/42	Freighter	No casualties
S/V Wawaloam	Shelled 8/6/42	3 Masted Schooner	No casualties
SS West Celina	Torpedoed 8/19/42	Freighter	Convoy Commodore lost
SS West Cheswald	Deliberately sunk 6/11/44	Freighter	No casualties
SS West Chetac	Torpedoed 9/24/42	Freighter	Crew—K/22 Armed Guard—K/9
SS West Grama	Deliberately sunk 6/8/44	Freighter	No casualties
SS West Hardaway	Torpedoed 6/15/42	Freighter	No casualties
M/S West Honaker	Deliberately sunk 6/8/44	Freighter	No casualties
SS West Humhaw	Torpedoed 11/8/42	Freighter	No casualties
SS West Imboden	Torpedoed & Shelled 4/20/42	Freighter	No casualties
SS West Ira	Torpedoed 6/20/42	Freighter	Crew—K/1
SS West Irmo	Torpedoed 4/3/42	Freighter	African Stevedores—K/10
SS West Ivis	Torpedoed 1/26/42	Freighter	Crew—K/35
SS West Kebar	Torpedoed 10/29/42	Freighter	Crew—K/3

[101] Unfortunately, there is more than one instance where a captain loses his head and forgets to order "stop engines" or give commands to abandon ship that only causes confusion and loss of life. In a Naval report, the captain of the *Gresham* was highly praised by his men for his coolness, ability, assistance, and general good conduct. The men all agreed that he was directly responsible for the orderliness in abandoning ship. Her cargo consisted of 9,000 tons of powdered milk, sugar, and other supplies. She took a torpedo in #5 hold which blew off the propeller, leaving her out of control. An unnamed Armed Guard sailor swam from the overcrowded raft to an empty raft and helped to transfer ten men to it, thereby saving 20 men who might have otherwise been lost. Two of the lifeboats had capsized in the heavy seas.

SS West Lashaway	Torpedoed 8/30/42	Freighter	Crew—K/25 Armed Guard—K/9 U.S. Military—K/4
SS West Madaket	Torpedoed 5/5/43	Freighter	No casualties
SS West Maximus	Torpedoed 5/4/43	Freighter	Crew—K/5 Armed Guard—K/1
SS West Nilus	Deliberately sunk 7/7/44	Freighter	No casualties
SS West Nohno	Deliberately sunk 6/11/44	Freighter	No casualties
SS West Notus	Shelled 6/1/42	Freighter	Crew—K/4
SS West Portal	Torpedoed 2/5/43	Freighter	Crew—K/40 Armed Guard—K/12
SS West Zeda	Torpedoed 2/22/42	Freighter	No casualties
M/S Wichita	Torpedoed 9/19/42	Freighter	Crew—K/40 Armed Guard—K/10
SS William A. McKenney	Torpedoed & Shelled 10/5/42	Freighter	Crew—K/1
SS William B. Allison	Aerial torpedoed 5/25/45	Freighter	Crew—K/3 Officers—K/3 Stevedore—K/1
SS William B. Woods[102]	Torpedoed 3/10/44	Liberty Ship	Armed Guard—K/1 U.S. Army—K/51
SS William C. Gorgas[103]	Torpedoed 3/10/43	Liberty Ship	Crew—K/34 Armed Guard—K/21
SS William Clark	Torpedoed 11/4/42	Liberty Ship	Crew—K/18 Armed Guard—K/13
SS William D. Burnham	Torpedoed 11/23/44	Liberty Ship	Crew—K/10 Armed Guard—K/8 All killed when second torpedo hit lifeboat.
SS William Dawes	Torpedoed 7/22/42	Liberty Ship	Armed Guard—K/4 U.S. Army—K/1
SS William Eustis	Torpedoed 3/17/43	Liberty Ship	No casualties

[102] There is quite a serious difference here regarding how many men died. As you can see by the table, 7 were killed whereas in one of the books I read, more than a hundred men died. She was carrying American troops and ammunition when she was torpedoed and blew up. A British ship rescued survivors.

[103] The *Gorgas* carried 900 tons of TNT. A submarine put torpedoes into her. Amazingly, both torpedoes missed the TNT, but the engine room watch was killed. One book says absolutely nothing about the other members of the crew and Armed Guard being killed.

SS William F. Humphrey	Shelled & Torpedoed 7/16/42	Tanker	Crew—K/4 Armed Guard—K/3 Crew of 26 taken to Japanese POW Camp where 3 died and 2-Armed Guard taken to Japanese POW camp.
SS William Gaston	Torpedoed 7/24/44	Liberty Ship	No casualties
SS William Hooper *	Aerial & Submarine Torpedoed 7/4/42	Liberty Ship	Crew—K/3
SS William J. Salman	Torpedoed 5/18/42	Freighter	Crew—K/6
SS William K. Vanderbilt	Torpedoed 5/16/43	Liberty Ship	Crew—K/1
SS William King	Torpedoed 6/6/43	Liberty Ship	Crew—K/6 Master sent to Japanese POW camp and later killed in sinking of SS Junyo Maru while still a POW.
SS William L. Marcy[104]	Torpedoed 8/7/44	Liberty Ship	British Army—K/1
SS William P. Frye[105]	Torpedoed 3/29/43	Liberty Ship	Crew—K/35 Armed Guard—K/22
SS William S. Ladd	Sunk by Kamikaze suicide plane 12/10/44	Liberty Ship	No casualties
SS William S. Rosecrans	Mined 1/6/44	Liberty Ship	No casualties
SS William S. Thayer	Torpedoed 4/30/44	Liberty Ship	Crew—K/23 Armed Guard—K/7 U.S. Military—K/13
SS William W. Gerhard	Torpedoed 9/21/43	Liberty Ship	Armed Guard—K/2
M/S Wilcox	Deliberately sunk 6/8/44	Freighter	No casualties

[104] The *Marcy* was docked six miles off Juno Beach. She was empty and awaiting a convoy when a torpedo hit her. She was towed to England and beached.

[105] Only seven men survived when the *Frye* was torpedoed. Seas were tumultuous and heavy. She outmaneuvered the U-boat for one day with evasive action, but the next night two hit her and she sank in such a short time the crew was able to launch only one lifeboat.

SS William Boyce Thompson	Torpedoed 7/7/43	Tanker	Crew—K/5
SS William Rockefeller	Torpedoed 6/28/42	Tanker	No casualties
SS Yaka[106]	Torpedoed 11/18/42	Tanker	No casualties
SS Yorkmar	Torpedoed 10/9/43	Freighter	Crew—K/11 Armed Guard—/2
M/S Zaandam	Torpedoed 11/2/42	Freighter	45 survivors from ships that had been sunk.

---

[106] Getting to Murmansk was one thing, staying alive and in one piece after arrival was another. The *Yaka* went through 156 air raids while off-loading her cargo. Whether she sustained serious effects from the raids is not mentioned.

APPENDIX II

LOG OF THE UNKNOWN SHIP
(Probably written by First Mate)

April 11	Ship hit at 5 p.m. Second explosion 9:40 p.m. Rough and large, choppy sea. Wind northeasterly all night.
April 12	Lost sea anchor 11 a.m. Rig up new one and put over side 12:05. Mounting [*rising*] sea. Sea anchor out all night. Men living on one cracker, two ounces water.
April 13	6:00 a.m. Hoist sails. 6:30 a.m. Take sails down. Sea too rough. Put sea anchor out again. Boys feeling fair. Still living on two crackers, four ounces water. Found out had no flares. Cans empty. No chocolate in food containers. Drifting southwesterly. Out 48 hours.
April 14	5:30 a.m. Hoist sail, heading south. Wind NNE. Medium sea and swell. Men living on two crackers, four ounces water. Sun came out for first time today. 9:45 a.m., chop sail. Sea too large. Put out sea anchor. Wind force 6. Lost sea anchor at 6:53 p.m. Had to rig up another from two oars. 9:45 p.m. cleared up a little. Hoisted sail. Head south. Wind during night. All men have wet clothes now four days.
April 15	Day started clear. Sea moderate with westerly winds. Force 3. 7 a.m. set sail heading south by east. North wind. Sun out again and feels good. 11:30 p.m. wind died down. Everything calm, put out oars. 3 p.m. wind sprung up from northwest. Force 3. Put up sail and made good time. Raining. Everything wet.
April 16	Friday. Raining. All calm. Try to catch water. No luck. Went to three ounces of water, two crackers and pemmican (*concentrated food of beef, dried suet, dried fruit, etc.*) also one malt milk tablet. 12 noon approximately 600 miles from coast. Try fishing. No luck. Fish all around. Won't bite. Air stirring a little. 5 p.m. Breeze freshing to NNE. Making a little time. Sun out. Maybe we'll dry out. Everyone's clothes damp. Getting on everyone's nerves. All snapping at one another. Set regular watches. Five men to watch. 5:30 a.m. Men talking of food and water and what they like to have. Also talking of religion. Rain during night. Try to catch water. No luck.

April 17	Saturday. Eight miles south of yesterday's position. Calm sea. Air stirring slightly. Might have to row. Back to two ounces of water. Haven't seen a thing in six days now. 10 p.m. started to row. Men got extra two ounces of water. 11 p.m. wind freshing to northwesterly. Quit rowing. Getting small sea. Up speed. Continued sailing all night on easterly course.
April 18	Palm Sunday. Clear NWly breeze. Continued sailing easterly course. Men got four ounces of water but not eating much. 12 N. Still sailing easterly course. Small following sea. Making good time. 3 p.m. gave men extra two ounces water. Wind change to westerly. Have not seen a thing yet. Men feeling pretty good. Doing a little singing. Now and then a man is a little seasick. Have not eaten since in boat. Given extra two ounces of water. First ass't. and lieutenant pretty sick. Given extra water. Deck cadet feet swelling. Can't get in shoes. Clothing starting to dry out a little now, but with night everything wet and cold again. 11 p.m. continued on easterly course. 4 a.m. rain squalls. Still heading easterly. Wind westerly. Following small sea.
April 19	Monday. Fresh westerly breeze. Force 3. Large following sea. Occasional squalls. Men growling now and then. Sea getting worse. Shipping water. 8 p.m. took in sail. Wind change to northerly. Can only make leeway. 12 midnight. Cold and damp. Full moon. Jib (*triangular sail secured forward of mast*) up only makes leeway (*drifting from course*). Saw few birds today. Men got 4 ounces water. Must have 450 miles to go.
April 20	Tuesday. Bob has birthday. 27 years old today. Gave men six ounces of water. 6 p.m. moderate northerly sea and swell. Put up main sail. Can't seem to get clothes dry and makes men cold and snappy. Can't get civil answer anymore. 8 p.m. small northerly sea and swell heading easterly. Second assistant pretty sick. Made 75 miles today.
April 21	Wednesday. Clear and calm. Wind mod. northerly. Heading southeasterly. Making fair time. App. 400 miles

to go. 6 p.m. Clear, full moon. Occasional rain squalls. Making fair time.

April 22 Thursday. 6 a.m. clear and bright. NW wind and mod. sea. Quite a sharp current southerly. Men singing a little and hoping to be picked up soon. 12 midnight. Wind NE and mod. [*moderate*] sea. Cold damp. Overcast.

April 23 Friday. Overcast. Beam sea. Fresh NE breeze. Not making any time. Men pray now before breakfast and after supper. Not a thing sighted as yet. Still have hope. Body starting to ache. Damp clothing. Can't keep them dry.

April 24 Saturday. Overcast and cloudy. Cold NE winds. Heading south. Tide to west. Large, rough, choppy, quarter seas. Shipping (*ocean coming into lifeboat over the edges*) sea occasionally. Must bale frequently. Everybody's nerves on edge. Still living on six ounces of water, crackers and pemmican. Now and then men will talk of home and what they would like to be doing or different food and wine. Worse part is you can't lay out straight. Always cramped up. No wonder we ache.

April 25 Easter Sunday. First time and hope it is the last I ever spend Easter in a lifeboat. Not sure of your position or anything. Day started clear. Put up sail. Wind from east, force 3. Large swell. Shipping water occasionally. Heading south. 12 noon. Men got treat. Half can of pemmican, ten ounces of water. Nothing in sight. Still have hope.

April 26 Monday. Heading south. Drift to west. Large mountain sea and swells. 7 a.m. lower sail. Shipping too much water. Drifting to west. 12 noon wind much same. Hoist sail, head south again. Can't seem to get any easting (*direction*) at all. Dear God, how we pray for a ship to pick us up or for the sight of land. Men starting to lose hope now. Second assistant talking out of his head regularly now. Cut down on rations. Have enough to last 11 days reduced ration. Cold and damp. Can't seem to get warm. Most of men joints swelling. Rough beam sea all night. Force 3.

April 27	Tuesday. High mountainous beam sea. Wind northeasterly. Force 4. Shipping water. Temperature 72 degrees. Everything damp. 12 noon. Cut down on rations again. Can't see anything. Must make food and water last. Try fishing. Nothing bites. Have no bait. Let's hope we see something soon. Men's feet swelling at joints and every word a complaint. Hoping to hit mainland or Cape Verde Islands. Strong westerly winds and sea. Small swell. Making fair time. Heading SE.
April 28	Wednesday. Daybreak clear. Nothing in sight. Hurley thought saw submarine but did not surface. Wind NE. Force 2. Small swell. Heading SE. Must have app. [*approximately*]150 miles to mainland. Taking one box crackers, two cans pemmican, eight ounces water for 11 men now. Making mash. Let's hope what we have left lasts till picked up.
April 29	Thursday. Daybreak clear. Had prayer and breakfast. Small sea. Easterly swell. Wind NE heading SE. Made app. 50 miles yesterday. Men starting to break. Sure wish I was in my ap't [*apartment*] with my wife and baby. Hope I can keep up my courage and stop thinking of home too much. Made fair time last night.
April 30	Friday. Daybreak clear. Plenty of hope left yet. Cut down to one can of pemmican, one box of crackers, eight ounces of water. Expect to see land sometime this week yet. Wind from E. Heading SE. small sea and swell. 12 noon. Took sight for latitude. Everything looks all right. About 75 miles to go if calculations right. Bound to hit coast this week. Wind change NEly. Second assistant very low. Small sea and swell.
May 1	Saturday. Second assistant passed away during night. Gave burial at sea this morning 7:20 a.m. Men feel bad. 12 noon. Went in swimming for a bath. Water felt good. Wind force 3. Making good time.
May 2	Sunday. Daybreak cloudy. Wind force 2. Small sea and swell. Force 1, making little headway. 11:25 a.m. sighted plane. Sent out smoke bomb. Think we were seen. Sure felt good after 21 days to see something. Will know

within 24 hours whether we were or not. If not, expect to see land tomorrow if calculations right. Wind from E. Making little headway.

May 3   Monday. Daybreak clear and calm. Drift SW. Losing quite a bit of distance covered. Small sea and swell. Sight seven whales at 10:05 a.m. Close enough we could have hit them with a stone. Sighted raft at noon. Boarded it to look for food and water. No luck. Found some marine growth so ate that. No sign of life yet. Looks like plane did not see us yesterday.

May 4   Tuesday. (position 21 degrees 55 minutes north. 17 degrees, ten minutes west). Sighted smoke on horizon, but too far away to signal. Makes one feel low to see help so near yet so far. Daybreak clear. Wind strong NE. Heading SEly. Sighted fishing vessel 10 p.m. Sent up flare. They sighted us and picked us up. We were 30 miles from African coast. Fed us and wined us in style. Now heading for Lisbon. Will be there in five days. Treat us like gentlemen. Gave us clothes and washed ours. Fed us again. Gave up their bunks so we may sleep. They keep feeding us every time we open our eyes. They really are wonderful people. They just can't seem to do enough for us.

May 5   Wednesday. Aboard the *Albufeira*. Daybreak clear. Making ten knots. Had fish for breakfast and soup and wine. Then a nap. Feel like a million. Now supper. Cabbage and beef noodle soup, beef and potatoes. Abeam Canary Islands now. Only three days to Lisbon. Had spot of tea before going to sleep. These men give you their bunks and sleep on deck. Too bad there is nothing we can do in return.

May 7   Friday. Breakfast coffee and sea biscuit. Had bath. Dinner fried fish and potatoes, bread and wine. Supper fish chowder and rice, baked fish, wine and bread. Tea before retiring. Eat, sleep.

May 8   Saturday. 4 p.m. Casablanca abeam. 8 p.m. today ends clear.

May 9   Sunday. Passed Cabo de Sae Vincente.

May 10   Monday. **Passed pilot boat at mouth of Tagus River and proceeded up river to Lisbon where we disembarked at the pier about 5 a.m. amid many officials, police and a large crowd. After clearance with local officials proceeded at once to the British Hospital.**

Italics were done by the author.

APPENDIX III

Declassified Department of the Navy Records
This is part of the SS Expositor's Ship's Log to Russia
SS Expositor[107]
Murmansk, USSR
May 6, 1942

From:	Commanding Officer, Armed Guard Unit, SS Expositor
To:	The Chief of Naval Operations.
VIA:	The Naval Attaché, Murmansk, USSR
Subject:	Outbound Voyage of the SS EXPOSITOR, with Naval Armed Guard Unit: report of.
Reference:	General Instructions for Commanding Officers of Naval Armed Guards on Merchant Ships.
Enclosure:	Copy of reference, part IV, (b) 38 (d).

1. At 0900 March 4, 1942, the SS EXPOSITOR with the U.S. Naval Armed Guard Unit aboard got underway from Pier 98, Philadelphia, PA. The EXPOSITOR steamed from Philadelphia to New York via Ready Isle where 5,000 cases of T.N.T. were taken aboard. From New York the EXPOSITOR proceeded to Narragansett Bay and underwent calibration tests for the degaussing system. As a result the vessel was recommended for deperming. After completing the calibration tests, the EXPOSITOR proceeded to Halifax, N.S., arriving there at 1730 March 10, 1942. At 1144 March 15, the EXPOSITOR proceeded out of Halifax in convoy bound for the Clyde

---

[107] Taken from **The Pointer**, May through August 2004, courtesy of Charles A. Lloyd, Chairman & Secretary-Treasurer of the United States Navy Armed Guard, World War II Veterans.

Anchorage off Goureck, Scotland. At 0230 March 27, the EXPOSITOR came to anchor in Loch Long, Gourock, Scotland. On April 1, the EXPOSITOR proceeded out of the Clyde River in convoy with the SS LANCASTER, SS ALCOA RAMBLER and the SS PAUL LUCKENBACH bound for Loch Ewe, Scotland. The Captain of the EXPOSITOR was named Commodore of the convoy. At 1600 the same day, a message was received from the British Admiralty ordering the return of the convoy to Gourock, Scotland. At 2300 April 1, the EXPOSITOR again came to anchor in Gourock, Scotland. There it was made known that the convoy had been recalled for more armament as the D.E.M.S. Office decided they were not sufficiently armed. April 2 work was begun to install two 20mm Oerlikon machine guns and one twin mount Hotchkiss machine gun on the EXPOSITOR. On the afternoon of April 6 the above armament was completely installed and ammunition, spare parts and cleaning gear were all stowed. April 7, the EXPOSITOR proceeded under way in convoy bound for Oban, Scotland, in accordance with orders issued by the British Admiralty. April 8, at 0900 the EXPOSITOR came to anchor in the Lynn of Lorn, just off Lismore Island. April 10, Commodore Anchor of the Royal Naval Reserve, came aboard the EXPOSITOR as Commodore of the convoy. At 1700 the same day the convoy steamed out of the Lynn of Lorn bound for Reykjavik, Iceland. April 15, at 1818 the convoy arrived just off Reykjavik harbor and was ordered to proceed to Hvalfjordur Bay, and the Commodore transferred to the SS BOTHAVEN, a British merchant ship. April 26, at 0800 the EXPOSITOR departed Hvalfjorjur Bay in convoy bound for the port of Murmansk, USSR. On May 6, the EXPOSITOR with the convoy, came to anchor in the port of Murmansk, USSR.

2. The reports of engagements and incidents out of the routine are listed as follows:

a) March 5—at 1000 the wreckage of a motor whale boat was sighted two points on the starboard bow approximately 150 yards from the ship.

b) March 17—about 0200 several depth charges were dropped by the escorts and gun fire heard. No signal was made to indicate what had happened.

c) March 22—about 0115 a submarine was sighted two points on the port quarter. The after lookout at the gun reported to the bridge and rang the gunner's alarm. As the gun crew manned the guns the submarine disappeared and was not sighted again. Fire was not opened nor did any other action take place.

d) March 25—at 0900 the air attack signal was hoisted by the Commodore. No action took place and at 1115 the signal was hauled down.

e) April 1—eight floating mines were encountered during the day's steaming, most of which the destroyers attempted to sink by gun fire.

f) April 15—six more floating mines were encountered and the same procedure carried out as above.

g) April 27—after leaving Reykjavik, Iceland, floating mines were encountered along the route to the USSR.

h) April 30—at 2145 an aircraft was sighted and definitely identified as hostile. The commence firing signal was hoisted and firing immediately began. The plane did not attempt to bomb the convoy but circled just inside firing range while scouting. As the gun fire increased in volume, the plane was driven off with no apparent damage. When last sighted, it was flying over the horizon.

i) May 1—two unidentified planes were sighted at about 1531. The planes made no attempt to fly over the convoy, but circled far out of firing range above the horizon. The planes continued to circle until about 2020. Then one of the planes attempted to attack from the starboard wing of the convoy toward the port wing. As the anti-aircraft fire began to find the range the plane abandoned this attack, and climbed high into the clouds. Emerging over the center of the convoy, he was again met by a terrific anti-aircraft barrage, which forced him back into the clouds. After a few minutes, he was sighted diving directly at the port wing of the convoy. Then as fire was again directed at him, he was hit and crashed into the ocean. The remaining plane made no attempt to attack the convoy, but flew far over the horizon.

j) May 2—about 1206 between the snow flurries that continued all day and night, a single plane was again observed circling the convoy out of firing range. This procedure was maintained until about 2124 when the plane disappeared from sight. At approximately the same time, however, the Commodore hoisted a signal to expect an attack. At 2256 three planes were sighted on the starboard wing of the convoy and fire was immediately opened. The planes continued their approach in formation toward the convoy. The plane on the left of their formation as seen from the convoy attempted to attack the port wing of the convoy.

Just before passing over the center of the line of leading ships, he was shot down in flames.

At the same time, the leading plane and the plane on the right of their formation as seen from the convoy, dived and successfully torpedoed the S.S. BOTHAVEN, which was the Commodore's ship, and the S.S. JUTLAND, another British ship. At about the same time that the first attacking plane crashed in flames, the midship section of the S.S. CAPE CORSO, British merchantman, blew skyward in an hundred and fifty foot flame. In less than thirty seconds the ship sunk in a flaming mass with no apparent survivors. This ship is believed to have been torpedoed by a submarine. After the BOTHAVEN was torpedoed, she went down by the bow until her foredeck was awash. However, three boat loads of survivors were rescued. Just a few minutes after the JUTLAND was sunk, the after lookout on this ship sighted the exposed part of a submarine's conning tower in the center of the convoy and just a few yards off our starboard quarter. In fact, she was so close aboard that neither the four-inch gun mounted on the stern nor the machine gun mounted on the poop deck were able to be brought to bear on it. Evidently realizing that we had sighted her, the submarine changed course and came across to the port quarter. When she was about twenty five yards away from the ship, fire was opened with the four-inch gun. The second shot struck her squarely on the conning tower. As the shell exploded, the top of the conning tower was blown off. As she appeared to sink, the water boiled up in a great froth of air and bubbles. After observing the spot where she sank, we saw an oil slick forming with occasional bubbles rising to the surface. At this point one of the gunners reported a torpedo track crossing our bow from port to starboard. The ship immediately backed at full speed and the torpedo missed us by a few feet. During the time we were engaging the submarine, one of the

British corvettes was attacked and sunk by one of the two remaining planes. After successfully sinking the corvette, the two planes were driven off.

k) at 2325 an air attack signal was hoisted. Two torpedo bombers appeared, one at each wing of the convoy, and proceeded to attack. The plane on the starboard side of the convoy attempted to dive and attack a ship on that side. Fortunately the ship was not hit, and the plane was driven off. The plane on the port side of the convoy dived to attack a corvette astern of the convoy. The corvette suffered no damage from this attack, and this plane also was driven off by heavy anti-aircraft fire. Unfortunately, both planes escaped without being damaged.

3. The following route was used in departing United States and entering foreign waters:

(a) From Cape Cod Lightship steering northeasterly courses and north courses to Halifax Lightship, then to pilot station and through regular channel to Bedford Basin just off Halifax.

(b) Departed Bedford Basin and proceeded through regular channel to open sea where convoy rendezvous was established. The convoy proceeded south of Cape Sable Island and by Mercator courses to the North Channel. From there up through the Firth of Clyde to Loch Long where the convoy anchored.

(c) Departed Loch Long, steamed through Firth of Clyde and entered North Channel, at which point convoy headed north and proceeded along the west coast of Scotland. The convoy was recalled before reaching Mull of Cantyre. After proceeding back to the North Channel, the same courses were followed for entering Loch Long as described above.

MEMORANDUM FOR FILE

April 2, 1943

SUBJECT: Summary of Statements by Survivors of SS EXPOSITOR, American Freighter, 4959 G.T., owners American Export Line

1. The "EXPOSITOR" was torpedoed without warning at 2132 GCT on February 23, 1943 at approximately 46 degrees N., 36 degrees W., while enroute from Belfast, N.I. to New York, N.Y. with 1500 tons of slag ballast in #2 and #4 holds and 450 tons of water ballast in #3 deep tank. The ship settled by the stern but did not sink. At 2400 GCT, the same day, she was sunk by depth charges from an escort vessel which blew off the stern.

2. The ship was on a South Westerly course in 2400 fathoms, in the process of a turn ordered by the Convoy Commodore, speed 9 knots, showing no lights, radio silent, five lookouts—two on bridge, two aft, one on boat deck and sixteen members of the gun crew standing alert. The weather was overcast with fair visibility, sea choppy, westerly wind, force 5, no moonlight, the whole convoy in sight.

3. About 2125 GCT an explosion was seen on a ship directly astern and general quarters was sounded. At 2131 GCT the first explosion caused by the boiler blowing up occurred, sending steam across #3 hatch, the boat deck and the bridge. All lighting circuits went out immediately. The ship took a decided list to starboard and then righted, settling by the stern. Distress signal could not be sent due to radio damage. No counter offensive was offered. Confidentials secured overboard in a weighted metal containers.

4. At 2140 ship was ordered abandoned in orderly fashion in the one lifeboat not smashed, and 3 liferafts. The survivors were picked up in about 2 hours by the HMCS TRÏLLIUM and landed in St. Johns. All of the crew saved except 7. Two seriously injured men died later; one on the corvette and the other at St. Johns.

5.   The sub was not sighted.

6.   Armed Guard officer stated that if any of his crew had been in their quarters they would have been lost. The quarters were on the waterline, directly over the fire room and were extremely difficult to get out of under any circumstances.

Comments on this convoy appear generally uniform.

(a) Masters should furnish proof their ship will be able to maintain convoy speed to eliminate stragglers.

(b) Commodore's ship should be motor ship rather than coal burner since the former is better able to maintain a steady course. Commodore of ON-166 varied speed quite frequently without signalling, making station keeping difficult.

(c) British radio stations picked up the SSS calls and rebroadcast them, giving the position of the attack. This was felt to be poor practice as it gave away the position of the convoy.
After each attack, many vessels fired a number of snowflakes, lighting up the whole area surrounding the convoy.

(d) Torpedo tracks were very definitely not seen. In several instances the informant was watching certain ships just before they were torpedoed but nothing was seen prior to the torpedo explosion. Survivors of one ship stated that the approach and resulting explosion of the first torpedo differed from anything they had seen or heard before.

BIBLIOGRAPHY

Ambrose, Stephen E., *Americans at War*, University Press of Mississippi, 1997

Ambrose, Stephen E., *Citizen Soldiers*, Simon & Schuster, 1997

Ambrose, Stephen E., *Band of Brothers*, Simon & Schuster, 1992

Ambrose, Stephen E., *The Wild Blue*, Simon & Schuster, 2001

Armed Guard Training Film, 1943

The Army Weekly, *Yank*, April 27, May 4, May 11, May 18, July 27, Sept. 7, Sept. 14, Sept. 28, Nov. 23, Nov. 30, 1945, by the men . . . for the men in the service

Bekker, Cajus, *Hitler's Naval War*, Zebra Books, Kensington Publishing Corp., 1974

Bowerman, Thomas R., *Fireclay*, Artex Publishing, 1996

Brokaw, Tom, *The Greatest Generation*, Random House, Inc., 1998

Bunker, John Gorley, *Liberty Ships—The Ugly Ducklings of World War II*, Naval Institute Press, 1972

Carse, Robert, *A Cold Corner of Hell—The Story of the Murmansk Convoys—1941-1945*, Doubleday & Company, Inc., 1969

Costello, John and Hughes, Terry, *The Battle of the Atlantic*, The Dial Press/James Wade, 1997

Cutler, Thomas J., The Battle of Leyte Gulf—23-26 October 1944, Harper Collins, 1994

Dorris, USNR, Lt. Donald Hugh and Others, *A Log of the Vincennes*, The Standard Printing Company, 1947

Farrington, Karen, *WWII Ground, Sea & Air Battles*, Abbeydale Press, 1995

Gannon, Michael, *Black May... The Epic Story of the Allied Defeat of the German U-Boats in May 1943,* HarperCollins, 1998

Glerchief, Justin F., *Unsung Sailors—The Naval Armed Guard in World War II,* Institute Naval Press, 1990

Greene, Bob, *Our Finest Hour—The Triumphant Spirit of America's World War II Generation,* Life, 2001

Harris, Robert, *Enigma,* Ballantine Books, 1995

Higgins, Jack, *Storm Warning,* Holt, Rinehart & Winston, 1976

Hough, Richard, *The Longest Battle—The War at Sea, 1939-45,* Hough Writing Ltd., 1986

Irving, David, *The Destruction of Convoy PQ-17,* St. Martin's Press, 1968

Jordan, Killian, Editor, *Our Finest Hour—The Triumphant Spirit of the World War II Generation,* Time, Inc., 2001

Junger, Sebastian, *The Perfect Storm—A True Story of Men Against the Sea,* Harper Paperbacks, 1998

Kahn, David, *Seizing the Enigma—The Race to Buck the German U-Boat Rule,* Barnes & Noble, Inc., 1991

Lloyd, Charles A., *The Pointer—Armed Guard Quarterly Newsletter,* Charles A. Lloyd, 1982 to present

Lott, Arnold S., LCDR, U.S. Navy (Ret.), *The* Bluejackets' Manual, *19th Ed.,* United States Naval Institute, 1973

Author Unknown, *USS Sitkoh Bay CVE 86,* Publisher Unknown, 1945

McGee, William L., *Bluejacket Odyssey,* Glencannon Press, 1997

Newark, Tim, *Turning the Tide of War—50 Battles that Changed the Course of Modern History,* Hamlyn, Great Britain, 2001

Sanders, Jacquin, *A Night Before Christmas*, Putnam's & Sons, 1963

Sontag, Sherry and Drew, Christopher, *Blind Man's Bluff—The Untold Story of American Submarine Espionage*, Harper Paperbacks, 1999

SS Lane Victory, Cargo ship tour docked at Berth 94, Los Angeles Harbor, San Pedro, California, I took several people from work on this tour 1998.

Stanton, Doug, *In Harm's Way—The Sinking of the USS Indianapolis and the Extraordinary Story of its Survivors*, Henry Holt & Co., 2001

Stillwell, Paul, Editor, *Assault on Normandy—First Person Accounts from the Sea Services*, Naval Institute Press, 1994

Sulzberger, C. L., *The American Heritage Picture History of World War II*, American Heritage Publishing Co., Inc., 1966

Taylor, A. Marjorie, *The Language of World War II*, The H. W. Wilson, Co., 1948

U.S. Armed Forces, *The Stars and Stripes—Daily Newspaper of the U.S. Armed Forces in the European Theater of Operation*, November 13, 1944 through March 11, 1945

Wendy, Lloyd, *Gunners Get Glory*, Bobb-Merrill Co., 1943

Zumwalt, Jr., Elmo R., *On Watch—A Memoir*, The New York Times Book Co., 1976